Thank you so very much for your support of K-LOVE. May God continue to bless you with and through many more miracles in and your life.

Never stop Dreaming!

Best + Blue skies,

Jeff

WHERE
BREAKTHROUGH
HAPPENS

Discover How the Power of
CLARITY, PURPOSE, & MOMENTUM
Will Set You Free to Reach Your Dreams

JEFF RASOR

BLUE
SKY
ink

A Publishing Division of Blue Sky Ventures, LLC

COPYRIGHT

Published in the United States of America by Blue Sky Ink, a publishing division of Blue Sky Ventures, LLC.

Author: Jeff Rasor

Cover Design & Interior Graphics: Matt Coffman

ISBN 978-1-7327058-0-7 (hardback)

Additional formats may be available through the publisher:

ISBN 978-1-7327058-1-4 (paperback)

ISBN 978-1-7327058-2-1 (ebook)

ISBN 978-1-7327058-3-8 (audiobook)

Library of Congress Control Number: 2019901373

Printed in the United States of America

2019 – First Edition

10 9 8 7 6 5 4 3 2 1

For those who have been told:

you cannot, you will not, and you are not enough.

May this book begin to reverse and redeem every lie
that has ever been whispered, uttered,
spoken, or shouted over your life.

CONTENTS

Blue Sky… A Manifesto…

When I dream, I dream of *Blue Sky…*

I dream of cutting through the wind, the weather, the clouds, and finding the pure thin air where only the most courageous soar.

I dream of taking people there—to see from a greater perspective, to soar above the clouds, and to look beyond what has been and what is, in order to see what may lie ahead.

Individuals, couples, leaders, and visionaries can make the ascent. Teams and organizations can too.

Blue Sky…

It is the atmosphere of fellow dreamers—dreamers who want to see their every effort account for greatness, who want to shake off their limitations and resolve to become all they are destined to become.

The horizon is not without its changing winds, storms, and uncertainties, but those who are daring enough to embrace their purpose and pursue their potential—despite any circumstance, environment, or obstacle they face—are rewarded for their perseverance.

I invite you to join a community of dreamers—a community that examines what was and what is, with the purpose of truly discovering the possibility of what can be.

I invite you… to look up into the bright, *Blue Sky* and begin to soar with me.

Jeff Rasor
   - Manifesto originally crafted January 2011

INTRODUCTION — INVITATION TO AN ADVENTURE

You have probably taken a number of journeys before—some of them, you expected adventure yet got none. Some journeys, you expected no adventure and found it—or perhaps, it found you.

Any journey embarked upon can have a certain level of adventure. And, most of us have a predefined desired level of adventure. Yet, rarely do the journeys go exactly as planned, which can leave us at the end of the road with all sorts of memories—good and bad, rich and painful.

Because of this, new adventures can feel intimidating, scary, and filled with uncertainty. Yet, those same feelings and emotions are simply shadows of the excitement, adrenaline, and expectation of what the adventure may hold. That excitement and expectation often comes to us both in terms of the joy of the journey itself and as the fruit of the growth and discoveries that happen as a result of taking the journey.

These experiences are what turn good journeys into great adventures, and great adventures into legendary stories.

Up until now, I imagine your life has been a journey filled with these same realities. There have been times when you expected adventure and instead found the people or the experiences left you without the excitement and depth you longed for.

At other times, you were looking for a season of smooth sailing, only to find that life swept you into a painful twist and turn you would never have asked for or even wished upon your worst enemy.

It can be tiring, frustrating, and even debilitating. When things don't go as planned, even the most ardent adventure seekers can find life clouded by doubt, fear, and to a large extent, apathy.

If asked, you may not define your life by these three terms, but when you look inside yourself, past the exterior shell of "I'm doing great, thank you," you can probably feel some level of cloudiness. Doubt, fear, and apathy are tainting your reality, obscuring your vision, snuffing out your desire, suppressing your purpose, and stifling your dreams.

Earlier in the journey, you had dreams, desires, ambitions, hopes, vision, and maybe even purpose. You had a certain expectation of life, of *your life*, that you could live in those dreams, that you could discover and live to your fullest potential. But now, those ideas seem like pipe-dreams at best, futile efforts, and maybe even not worth giving another thought.

I have been there, my friend. Many times. Some of those times on the outside, I was "doing just great, thanks for asking" because to others, my life looked admirable, my journey desirable, and my surroundings valuable. At other times in my life, finances were bleak, the prognosis of doctors dark, and the future daunting to say the least.

No matter if the circumstances were good or poor, it was often all the same internally, really. On the inside, significant amounts of doubt and fear were swirling around my heart and mind, especially when looking inside at the areas of dreams, desires, ambitions, hopes, vision, and purpose.

The doubt and fear then *unknowingly* led to a paralyzing level of apathy. At times, not an outward apathy, mind you. My career was advancing, family growing, health improving—all seemingly great exterior signs of a successful leader. At other times, discouragement, depression, and despair could be observed only by those closest to me.

In both cases, internal apathy was clouding my ability to tap into my genuine dreams, desires, ambitions, hopes, vision, and purpose. Said another way, the fear, doubt, and resulting apathy were severely limiting my potential, if not completely keeping my potential stifled, out of reach, and locked up.

My assertion is that if you are honest with yourself, you have found yourself in this same place—a fair measure of external success and still your potential feels stifled, or even nonexistent. Maybe externally things are "just great," and people are looking at your life with envy. And yet, you know there is so much more for you. A potential you have yet to discover or even begin to tap into.

Or maybe externally, your life isn't that great at all. Maybe you are in the midst of overwhelming difficulty, and people view your life with pity. Most likely, the internal reality of your life is mirroring that external reality. You are feeling a certain amount of self-pity and find your inner world filled with doubt, fear, and apathy to the point where the idea of tapping into your potential is hardly even on the radar.

Again, I have been there too. For me, the feeling that my potential is locked up, and even out of reach, has not been a one-time experience. In fact, it's something I have experienced numerous times.

In those times, no matter how great or how poor the circumstances of my life were going, I found myself at the intersection of stuck and lost. The intersection of stuck and lost is a long way away from living my fullest potential, which is to say a long way from freedom, let alone reaching my dreams. The tendency in these times is to intuitively begin to settle and think "that is just how life works" or worse, "that is just how *my* life works."

My friend, is that where you find yourself today? Somewhere near the intersection of stuck and lost, feeling your potential and your dreams are out of reach or out of sight, quite possibly restrained by fear, doubt, and the resulting apathy?

If those thoughts resonate inside you heart and mind at all, please do not despair. *Why*, you ask? Well, I have found you. Or, you have found me.

Either way you look at it, at least you aren't stuck, lost, *and* alone (go ahead and chuckle a sigh of relief, or maybe just roll your eyes). All kidding aside, much like a "find my friend" app on a smartphone guided by coincidence, a sovereign hand, or even God, our GPS coordinates have aligned, and we have found each other. And that makes a *huge* difference. Here's why:

There is strength in numbers, and two of us is 100% more than one of you. You are already better off than you were just a few minutes ago. And what's more, I know the way from the corner of stuck and lost to the intersection of found and free. I have moved from doubt, fear, and apathy into confidence, courage, and conviction—all the necessary fuel for being set free, for reaching dreams, and for soaring into your Blue Sky Potential.

What's more important, and most likely even more encouraging to you, is that I have helped many others who found themselves leashed to this same intersection. I tend to be attracted to the corner of stuck and lost. But, I tend to stay there only temporarily, as it is my joy and privilege to find others at that intersection and invite them into a journey toward unleashing their potential, a journey that has set them free to reach their dreams.

Through a variety of means, methods, and leadership roles, I have guided thousands of people from the intersection of stuck and lost to found and free, pointing them toward their potential.

I have become an expert guide of sorts—not necessarily in the great outdoors, but definitely in the great indoors—that is, the interior world of the heart and mind, spirit and soul, where all the elements for reaching your potential exist.

It has become my lifetime pursuit to guide others to freedom so that they can reach their dreams. The very prospect of helping someone like you discover and reach your potential is what keeps me up at night dreaming on your behalf and is what excitedly wakes me up in the morning ready to seize the day to make it happen.

Again, I am so glad we have found each other. However we ended up here together, I want to invite you into a journey of discovering and pursing your potential—this time with a guide, one who has done it before and has given his life to helping others in that pursuit too.

By the way, while we are getting ready to embark, would you consider inviting another friend or two to grab a copy of this book and join us on this journey? As I said before, *two of us* is already better than *one of you*, but three or four of us together is *even better*.

Consider this anonymous proverb that applies directly to this journey, "if you want to go fast, go alone, but if you want to go far, go together." Our journey is too important to go fast, but so vital, we will need to go far—as far as necessary to set you free to reach your dreams.

Therefore, let's not go alone, but let's go the distance with the support of a few others together. For all you know, they may need it just as much as you. Maybe they just need your invitation, not unlike the one I have offered to you.

This journey I am inviting you to join (along with a few of your friends) can and will become a great adventure—an adventure in being set free, finding hope, and reaching your dreams. Of course, it will have some ups and downs, twists and turns, but it will be rich, rewarding, and fruitful along the way.

By the end, the journey we go on together and the great adventure that ensues will result in your life becoming one of those legendary stories—a life that others honor and esteem, a life that leaves its mark on history based on the purpose for which you were made.

The first step in this journey is to finish reading this book and then to consider becoming a member of the growing online community. From there, you will have plenty of opportunity to engage more deeply with online courses and coaching programs or business workshops and retreats. However, let's not worry about that for now. Our focus is this first step, and just because it is only the first step in the journey does not make it any less important.

In fact, completing the first step of reading this book is the most important leg of the journey. This book sets the foundation for freedom—a type of freedom that is required so you can reach your dreams and soar into the blue sky of your potential.

Without that freedom, you will likely remain tethered to the corner of stuck and lost, never truly breaking free from what holds you back, and never truly discovering, pursuing, and reaching your fullest potential.

The concepts and strategies in this book are so foundational to your future success that I have even created a 28-day reading plan to help you make consistent forward progress. Included in that reading plan is a series of weekly reflective exercises so you can harness the power of the truths in this book as deeply as possible.

The first reflective exercise is just a few pages away, so please download the free 28-day reading plan and weekly reflective exercises at:

www.wherebreakthroughhappens.com/readingplan

Now, as you choose to continue on this first leg, let me set some clear expectations. This book is *not* the answer to your every problem. I'm not going to guarantee your success as long as you follow my "7 steps of success" or "5 keys to health." The truth is this: you would not want me to guarantee that pursuing your potential is that prescriptive *or* that easy. That would be a cheap view of your potential and a cheap view of your life.

And, to be candid, you've most likely already purchased those products, followed those fad diets, and ordered those gadgets. That book and its guaranteed "7 steps of success" is gathering dust on your shelf. You can quote fad-based recipes as well as the "experts" who wrote them. And, that gadget (or two or three of them) is in a random storage box in your basement, shed, or garage. All of that stuff is laying around, and you are still at the intersection of stuck and lost, not all that much closer to freedom, or to your dreams, or to your potential.

Instead of making cheap claims and inflated promises, this book is simply (and profoundly) intended to do four things: 1) guide you to discover where breakthrough happens, 2) demonstrate the power of clarity, purpose, and momentum, 3) provide you with a flight plan to help you reach your dreams, and 4) inspire you to begin to soar toward your Blue Sky Potential.

To experience that freedom and start soaring, you must understand the nature of potential, the three simple truths of transformational breakthrough, and the perseverance required to be set free to fully pursue and reach your dreams.

In doing that for you, I'm not solving every one of your problems, but instead, I'm showing you the way to freedom and providing a flight plan around, above, in spite of, or even right through those very same problems.

I won't promise success, fortune, or fame, but I will give you my word that if you can begin to understand and apply the principles in this book, as well as engage more deeply in the online community and coaching programs, you will no longer reside at the corner of stuck and lost. You will be well on your path to discovering and living more fully in the blue sky of your potential. This book does not guarantee success, but it does have the *power to change your life*.

And when it does…

Just maybe, you will discover that your transformation into the best version of yourself is the greatest definition of success you could ever know.

Wow, right? The best version of yourself… now, that is going to be quite a success. As I said before, I invite you to join me on a journey toward your potential, to find freedom in the great adventure that will ensue, and to consider *your* life as a legendary story, and one worthy of pursuing your dreams.

I imagine there are a whole bunch of thoughts and feelings swirling around in your head and heart. So, take a few moments, write them down, or type them up. If you journal, put those thoughts and feelings there. If not, well, consider this the first exercise in reflection, so find a place and at least a few minutes to get it all down. Remember, I have included a series of free reflective exercises along with that 28-day reading plan. The journaling prompts for this first exercise will definitely help you, especially if journaling feels foreign, new, or uncomfortable.

So, pause right now and write your thoughts and feelings down. Download and answer the questions in the reflective exercises. Yes, now, as in *right now*. Yes, even before you finish these last few paragraphs. Here's why I want you to do this. When you get to your dreams, you will want to be able to reflect back on this moment and remember how far you have come. Go ahead, I'll wait…

Now, like with any great adventure, it's a good idea to let people know where you a headed. I recommend that you take few of those thoughts and feelings and post them on social media, and maybe even a picture of this book. Or, better yet, a selfie of you and the book, along with those thoughts and feelings.

Tag me on Facebook, or tag @wherebreakthroughhappens and @jeffrasor on Instagram, and I will be sure to respond. We're taking this journey *together* after all, and I would truly love to meet you!

Okay, great job reflecting (and posting)! You are now ready to move ahead. Where are we again? Oh, that's right…

You and I (and hopefully a few of your friends) are standing here at the intersection of stuck and lost. What are we waiting for? Let's leave this corner behind. Nothing good happens around here anyway. Together, let's begin to unleash your Blue Sky Potential.

We are going to cover a lot of ground together, and it will set the foundation for all that is ahead of you. You will be inspired. You will be strengthened. And at the end of this adventure, you will most likely never be the same. Together, let's discover freedom, hope, transformation, and *where breakthrough happens*.

Let's go!

Best & Blue Skies,

Jeff Rasor

PART 1

GRAVITY: LEASHED TO THE GROUND

CHAPTER 1

IMPOSSIBILITY — REACHING FOR THE SKY

---

*"It is kind of fun
to do the impossible."*

- WALT DISNEY

NOT MUCH LONGER THAN A CENTURY AGO, TWO BROTHERS FINALLY tasted their first moments of success by reaching the sky, after having spent years studying and experimenting how to do the impossible—powered, piloted flight.

On December 17, 1903, Orville and Wilbur Wright were the first in history to experience pilot-controlled, heavier-than-air, machine-powered flight. After winning a coin toss, Orville was first and managed to pilot the craft for 12 seconds, covering 120 feet of distance in the face of 27 mph blistering cold costal winds.

Next was Wilbur's turn, then again Orville's, and then again, Wilbur's, extending the time, distance, and experience that each had at the controls. That fourth and final flight of the day, piloted by Wilbur, extended the groundbreaking, record-breaking day by flying the machine for 59 seconds, covering a distance of 852 feet or nearly 3 football fields long.[1]

Walt Disney, who envisioned a "magic kingdom," spoke of the fun that is experienced in doing the impossible. For the Wright Brothers, *fun* was probably an understatement; it must have felt *magical…*

Years of study, experimentation, engineering, building, prototyping, met with frustrating attempts, broken parts, and broken dreams had finally paid off. The potential for powered and controlled flight had finally been realized.

At that very moment, a barrier that had never been broken had released its grip on potential and surrendered its control over history. No longer was it impossible for humankind to power flight. No longer were there the same limitations that had eternally stumped the human race. No longer would the past have the ability to define the future. No longer was the idea and reality of soaring into the blue sky out of reach.

As surely as that day happened for the Wright Brothers, *the same is possible for you*. No longer will your past have the ability to define your future. No longer will the idea of soaring into blue sky be out of your reach. No longer will the same limitations that have stumped you up to this point have control over your life. Oh, it is coming, my friend… genuine breakthrough is coming.

ORIGINS OF FLIGHT

Those familiar with the history of flight would point out that humans had already been "flying" for nearly 121 years to that very day, when the age of the hot air balloon was launched. On December 14, 1782, another set of brothers, Joseph-Michel and Jacques-Étienne Montgolfier, launched their first test flight of a globe-shaped balloon, made of taffeta cloth, a lightweight, quality fabric of woven silk.[2] Creating more lift than expected with a fire of wool and hay, the unmanned balloon rose so quickly they lost control of it, only able to watch it drift away until it ultimately came crashing down more than a mile away, destroying the balloon in the process.

It wasn't until June of the following year that the Montgolfier Brothers made a *successful* unmanned balloon flight before a small gathering of dignitaries in southern France. From there, word quickly made it to Paris, and just three months later, a test flight with a sheep, a duck, and a rooster in an attached basket was launched as a demonstration in Versailles before King Louis XVI, Queen Marie Antoinette, and a crowd.[3] The animals were used as "crash test dummies" of sorts, given the unknown risks and impact air travel could pose to humans.

After the approval of King Louis, along with other scientists, the Montgolfier Brothers began to send humans in the air, thereby giving the brothers credit for truly inventing manmade "flight." From that moment, a new era of hot-air-powered balloons, steerable balloons (airships), parachutes, and later, gliders began to awe and inspire scientists, inventors, engineers, risk-takers, and passersby alike.

The Montgolfier Brothers had seemingly solved "flight" more than one hundred years prior to the Wright Brothers history-making day, and the technology was quickly advancing. Yet so few of us know their names, let alone any of the names of those scientists, engineers, inventors, and risk-takers that advanced the science of flight prior to the Wright Brothers.

Why is it then that the Wright Brothers are accepted in culture, in history, and in all of our minds, as the pioneers of flight? Why is it not the Montgolfier Brothers or any of the others that advanced the technology of balloons and gliders?

In my opinion, here's why—all of those early solutions to "flight" were *passive* in nature. Don't let that concept of passivity drift by; it will come up again later. A hot air balloon or even a powered airship leverages the physics of lighter-than-air gasses to elevate the balloon into the air, but then are mostly subject to the dynamics of the wind and the environment. As beautiful as a ride in a hot air balloon can be, it is more of a passive experience of *rising* than it is an active experience of *flying* or *soaring*.

As for the other winged flying contraptions, they all had to do with falling from the sky and allowing the physics of wing aerodynamics to take over as they "soared" downward, never generating enough lift to truly elevate and reach into the blue sky. Yes, airships and gliders could be steered and, therefore, to some extent, be flown. But, they were limited at best. For years, inventors had been working on a new concept—the powered, piloted flight—yet the Wright Brothers were the first to make the impossible possible.

OVERCOMING GRAVITY

What exactly was different about what Orville and Wilbur Wright accomplished, allowing them to be largely credited with inventing the airplane and pioneering humankind's ability to truly fly? It is all based in the specifics of the type of machine they built and the control they had over it.

First, their flying machine, known today as an airplane, was heavier than air. The Wright Brothers didn't use the principles of air density simply to rise, as the Montgolfier Brothers had. Left to itself, powered or not, the Wright Brothers' flying machine would always be on the ground, subject to the laws of gravity. Because it was heavier than air, it had the physical reality of being stuck on the ground, leashed by gravity.

Second, their airplane was self-powered, meaning it had a working engine. The momentum that was generated to provide forward movement, or thrust, came from onboard, not from simply rising into the sky based on the pull of heated air (balloon) or falling through the sky based on the pull of gravity (glider).

Third, their airplane was the first powered machine that incorporated the ability for the pilot to fully control the flight, and this made the biggest difference of all. In fact, the Wright Brothers created a mechanism that would allow the pilot to control the flying machine three-dimensionally, now known in aviation as a *three-axis flight control system* which allowed for the aircraft to rotate in three dimensions—pitch, roll, and yaw.

This breakthrough alone is attributed solely to the work of the

Wright Brothers and is specifically why they are credited with the ingenuity of inventing the first airplane.

Combining these three elements set the Wright Brothers' first flights above all other flights in history. Their flights were not *passive*, as described before. Their flights were *powered and piloted*—the power was directed and under control with intention, purpose, and direction. Because of this, history esteems them as the true inventors, manufacturers, and pilots of the first successful airplane flight in history.

It was the ability to direct and pilot the flying machine that truly set the Wright Brothers apart, and as a result, they are credited as the pioneers of aviation. Their inventing and engineering of the systems that allowed for three-axis control is what enabled the pilot to steer the aircraft effectively and to maintain its equilibrium in the air.

Truly revolutionary in their era, it continues to be the single invention that aviation is still built upon today. What was impossible became possible—not based on conventional thinking, but because the Wright Brothers saw the impossibility of flight from such a different perspective.

Most inventors were following the conventional thought of their day and were focused on building more powerful engines. However, the Wright Brothers had an extreme conviction around the idea that the ability to control the airplane was what would actually unleash the truth of flight.

As such, they focused the large majority of their effort and research in this area. They believed the solution to the "flying problem" was not in higher powered engines. Instead, they believed the solution to flight was giving the pilot the ability to control, direct, and maneuver the airplane once it was in air.

In fact, nearly three years *after* that legendary day on the outer bank beaches four miles south of Kitty Hawk, North Carolina, they were awarded their first patent—not for a powered flying machine, mind you. Instead their patent specifically included their invention of the mechanical control system that allowed the pilot to manipulate the winged surfaces, giving the pilot the ability to steer and direct the airplane into the blue sky.[4] They inherently knew that no matter how much power was added, if an aircraft could not be maneuvered and directed by the pilot, it was still effectively leashed to the ground.

During their early research, before they proved the ability to fly, can you imagine the mocking they received from other inventors—those creating powerful engines? Imagine the inventor bully that may have swung by their bicycle shop, now turned airplane lab, "Hey, Wright Brothers! You've got it all *wrong*. You must be the *Wrong Brothers*. Your engines are so wimpy, you'll never get off the ground. Look at you, wasting all that time on levers and pulleys for the wings and rudder. Your ideas will never fly with that way of thinking. Look at how much time you're *wasting* in the lab. See you later, losers!" revving his high-powered engine as he zoomed off down the road. (I know, muscle cars hadn't been invented yet, either, but you get the picture.)

Yet, the Wright Brothers had known better and risked as much. In their bicycle shop, they had discovered that much of the truth inherent in the riding of a bicycle was not in the force or thrust that the rider could provide. No, it wasn't about the power behind the bicycle. Instead, it was in the ability for that rider to control the balance and intended direction of the bicycle once power was added to the equation.

With this conviction deeply imbedded in their hearts, they spent countless days working to discover the science and to create the systems that would provide a flying machine balance and give the pilot the ability to control the intended direction.

CAN YOU SENSE WHERE I AM HEADED WITH THIS? I KNOW THERE have been plenty of times in my life where I have spent inordinate amounts of time trying to power up, strengthen, self-motivate, goal set, commit, become more productive, etc. By and large, most of those efforts to add horsepower to my life have resulted in very little success.

At times, they made absolutely no impact on my potential, let alone brought me the freedom needed to reach the blue sky of my dreams. At other times, the additional horsepower simply drove me faster into the proverbial concrete wall. Not only that, but those efforts also took up a lot of time and, at times, a lot of money.

When my life never truly took flight like I knew it could, and to a certain extent knew it *should*, these experiences of adding power but remaining stuck caused me to think something was wrong with me. They tended to cause more doubt than confidence, either causing me to try harder next time, or worse, leaving me fearful to keep trying.

When I was trying to build a more powerful engine, I should have been working on engineering my life in a way that provided balance and a system that gave me the ability to pilot and steer the trajectory of the flight of my life. I was the one wasting time building horsepower, when I should have been studying and fine tuning the systems to set me free and unleash my potential.

I don't have to say it, do I? *You* have been there too. Working so hard to get stronger, smarter, fitter, faster, further, etc. And where has it gotten you? Maybe it got you stronger, smarter, fitter, faster, further, but as we discussed in the Introduction, you are still somewhere near the corner of stuck and lost, aren't you?

There are a lot of people working on helping you become more powerful, find more super-charged energy, achieve more goals, strive for more with a side hustle, reach more success, and make more money. "More, more, more," is their claim. Good for them, and good for you if those things have helped. They aren't all bad. I have done those same things, and as much as some were a waste of time and money, some of them actually had a lasting impact on my life. And, I'm sure I will subscribe to some of them again.

But, "more, more, more" is not what I want to see manifest in your life, at least not as the specific objective. Here's why: I have worked with so many people who have that type of success—the success of more, better, bigger, fitter, faster, and further. And yet, with rare exception, it hasn't helped them get off the ground toward their potential, nor has it set them free, nor has it helped them achieve their true dreams—not in any way, shape, or form.

In fact, for many of them, *the success of more* has had the opposite effect; it has caused them to move further away from the true and noble potential of their lives. From running multi-million-dollar companies, to producing multiple gold albums on the wall, you may be surprised that most people I have worked with who have accomplished the *more* in life are just as empty, lack just as much fulfillment, and are just as leashed to the corner of stuck and lost as anyone else.

Don't get me wrong, there are plenty of people with *less* in life, who are just as far from their true and noble potential. So, I'm not at all saying that material or financial success in life is inherently bad, nor something we should not work for. All I am saying is that even that type of success, without a genuine sense of meaning, purpose, and fulfillment in life, is likely to feel completely empty.

My objective is to help you discover and live the life of your dreams. If that leads to a humble existence, but a life that is rewarding and is soaring in blue skies, I honor that. And, if the life of your dreams leads to what the world calls success, I honor that too, as long as you don't lose yourself in the success.

So, again, I don't necessarily want to help you build a higher-powered engine. If it is already impossible to get off the ground and soar toward your potential, going faster in that wrong direction isn't going to help any.

More importantly to me, and I believe more importantly to you, I want you to be set free from what holds you back, and I want you to be able to pilot your life toward your dreams and into your fullest potential. In other words, I want to place in your hands a type of three-axis control system that will allow you to pilot your life toward and into the blue skies.

I want you to have a balance, an equilibrium, and the ability to determine and pursue your desired direction, to control the pitch, roll, and yaw, if you will. I do not want you to *passively* hope to rise, or *passively* glide downward, and nor do I want to power you full speed into a proverbial concrete wall. Instead, I want to give you the tools and the flight plan to pilot your life with intentionality, in a way that allows you to soar and to reach your dreams.

When you truly understand the nature of your potential, and the power behind the truths that will set you free, you will truly be piloting your life upward. From there, you can always add more power. But, until you have a better handle on how to pilot yourself through transformation and into breakthrough, all the power in the world is only going to accelerate you while still on the ground. It won't launch you toward the blue sky of your potential, and as a result, soaring toward your dreams will remain nearly impossible.

ONE OF MY QUESTIONS ABOUT THE HISTORY OF FLIGHT IS THIS: WHY did it take so long to achieve this breakthrough? Why did it take until the 20th century for the human race to finally figure this out? I mean, the discovery of gravity and so many other scientific principles during the Renaissance, or the civil engineering marvels of the Roman Empire two full millennia ago, or the great Pyramids upwards of 2,700 years BC—all substantive accomplishments of the impossible in their time. But, why not powered flight? Why not sooner?

Here's my belief. *It wasn't time yet.* You see, in a historical sense, the four forces of flight that related to aerodynamics had just recently begun to be figured out. The principles of aerodynamics and forces of lift had only recently begun to be solved.[5] Small, but powerful engines were just coming onto the scene. And, the mechanical engineering to build a control system was emerging in the heart and mind of two brothers who were willing to approach the "flying problem" from a new perspective.

We are going to talk about perspective later, but I'll say this for now: *perspective* changes everything, especially perspective that challenges the conventional wisdom of more, more, more. Without the right perspective, your potential is likely to remain leashed to the ground.

Based on a fresh perspective, and their understanding of what made a bicycle "pilotable," the Wright Brothers approached flying with a new clarity no one else had come to. *It was now time.* It was time for all the elements of breakthrough in the pursuit of flight to come together. It was Orville and Wilbur's time. What was impossible before was about to be possible. What was only a figment of the imagination and a dream was about to be reality. Flight was impossible, and at the right time, it became entirely possible.

This is as true for your life as it was for flight.

As much as we all would like to pursue life on *our* terms and on *our* timing, the truth is that timing isn't always in our hands. Yet, let me encourage you with this… the timing for your life to begin to soar has come. It is just on the horizon. Stay on this journey with me and we will get there together.

We are going to talk about timing more later, too. This is part of the journey—to realize we can imagine things before they are possible. These things are called *dreams.*

We must dream about the possibility of the impossible before we can ever take flight and pilot our lives toward the blue sky. We are going to need to address those dreams, and rediscover them as a form of potential greatness in your life. We are going to rekindle your heart, and it all starts with your dreams.

CHAPTER 2

AWAKEN — REKINDLING A DESIRE TO DREAM

"I like the dreams of the future
better than the history of the past."

- THOMAS JEFFERSON

AS A YOUNG BOY, I WAS QUIET, SHY, AND CAUTIOUS. NORMALLY, WITH that description, you may begin to get the mental picture of an anti-social, socially awkward kid, maybe even subpar, or perhaps even a less-than-average hermit. Those things, I was not.

I had many friends in school and sports, had a high aptitude for studies, athletics, and music, and was well-liked by teachers and classmates. I genuinely enjoyed being with friends—whether jumping bikes at the local dirt jumps, building skateboard ramps with the neighbor kids, or playing a pickup game of football in the schoolyard.

Yet, I was just as happy alone as I was with others. Being alone gave me room to feel free to be another version of myself. For some, being alone feels like a prison. For me, being alone allows me to explore my feelings, to look inward, and to discover the expanse of what is inside—less of a prison, more of a sweeping freedom to let my heart, mind, spirit, and soul dream without limitation.

Just as it is now, it was when I was a child. If I was with friends, life was great. If I was alone, life was great. So, even at a young age, I recognized the two worlds of my life—the exterior world of friends, community, and action, and the interior world of my heart, mind, and dreams.

As a quiet, shy, and cautious kid, however, I did not like attention. That shy side of me did not enjoy the pressure of meeting new people, nor did I enjoy being the center of attention—of any kind. Whether it was raising my hand in class with the right answer, getting congratulated in front of my teammates by a coach, or even being the point of conversation between my parents and their friends—attention made me squirm, if not feel downright nauseous. Forget stage performances, speeches, and presentations. Those were out of the question, unless I could hide in the third row of the choir risers—blending in as just one of the many.

I simply did not want to be celebrated, focused on, pointed out, or called upon, let alone stand in the spotlight. I preferred to fly under the radar, achieving success quietly, without the notice of others. I became a master at being able to regularly score high in my grades, but not high enough to get noticed.

I could land the second or third highest grade with pinpoint accuracy, missing a question or two (not on purpose, but because it didn't bother me to miss a question or two). By avoiding a score of 100%, I was still be able to identify and empathize with the complaints of lower scorers about how hard or unfair any given question might have been. For me, 97% was perfect because 100% drew too much attention. And, when I did get acknowledged, I was a master at deflecting praise.

This skill to fly under the radar, motivated by a desire to not draw attention to myself, was transferrable to other settings too. I also become a master at avoiding trouble. The upside of this is that getting in trouble rarely happened. However, when it did, even in the smallest of ways, it was painful. The attention was always more painful than any punishment or consequence. In fact, the drawing of attention via getting in trouble was painful enough that rarely were additional consequences needed.

From my earliest memories, even the slightest level of attention drawn over a misstep would cause me to reorient my whole life around the instruction or rebuke, or at least reorient my life around never getting in that kind of trouble a second time. In fact, I learned at an early age it was far less costly to me if I could learn from the mistakes of others.

If I saw someone else get in trouble, I would reorient my life around avoiding the mistake I saw *them* make. And, when I did do something wrong myself, it took only one small mistake for me to learn how to not go down the same path again. The avoidance of attention was paramount.

This ability to quickly learn and adapt by observation first and experience second is a rich gift and has been and continues to be a huge personal strength of mine. Regularly and consistently, I have been able to avoid so many of the mistakes others make in life. I'm far from perfect, and I have my own laundry list of devastating screwups, but by and large, I have avoided a fair share of difficulty as a result of my strength to observe, learn, and adapt.

Beyond simply avoiding mistakes, by quickly learning and adapting to success of others has often caused me to advance beyond my peers. It has not necessarily been because of greater talent or aptitude, but simply by applying positive learning more quickly than others can.

Yet, like all of our greatest strengths, those same strengths can be our greatest weaknesses, and for me, the weakness comes with a dark side. The dark side is something I have learned to overcome, but it's something that at times wrecked my childhood. When I did something wrong and got in trouble, the attention that came caused an overinflated sense of shame. Not only was I in trouble (I hated messing up), but now it was being pointed out in front of others—even if it wasn't, I felt like it was.

That attention, in this case negative attention, was like a magnifying glass amplifying the heat of the mistake, melting me like an ant under the glare of a school kid's magnifying glass on a hot summer day. The self-shame was so great, I learned to fling myself to the opposite side of the spectrum of behavior, rarely ever going back near the treacherous waters of the mistake again. Unfortunately, in first grade, this reality played out with nearly devastating internal consequences.

DREAMS—FOUND & LOST

To this day, I can remember the experience vividly. I was minding my own business in the first-grade classroom, listening well to Mrs. Eklund, most likely quieter and better behaved than almost everyone else in class. But, I was near a window, and what was on the other side of that window had not only caught my eye and my attention, it also caught my soul.

Blue sky.

Yes, that's it. Blue sky. For the first time, I appreciated just how blue the sky could truly be. I don't know where you grew up, but in the skies above suburban Denver, Colorado, there is a whole lot of glorious, unadulterated blue sky.

The urban legend that Colorado natives like myself love to quote as if it is scientific fact is that Colorado enjoys 300+ days of sunshine every year. I have read articles that prove the myth, and I have read articles that disprove the myth. Either way, it doesn't really matter.

What matters is that the blue sky in Colorado is rich, deep, and abundant. And, on this blue-sky day, the glory of the expanse captured my heart for the very first time. It wasn't just that it was blue, so much as what the blue was representing to me. While I wouldn't have had the words for it then, there was something both metaphorical and mystical in the unending blue sky.

There was a transcendent depth to the blue sky that stirred something inside of me. Something I really couldn't explain, but I could *feel* in my core. You know that feeling too. Maybe your mind is sweeping your memories and landing on a few moments where something captured your heart, spirit, and soul, and you couldn't answer why. Maybe you still can't answer why… that's okay, we will look into that on the journey together.

Maybe it was a beautiful mountain landscape, a wave crashing, an eagle soaring. Maybe it was a huge downtown cityscape, a nurse administering care, a fireman attending to someone in need, a fancy car, a dress at a fashion show, or a baby in your arms for the very first time. It could be anything that has at one time or another captured your heart in a transcendent way. What captured mine was *blue sky*.

Well, that morning in first grade, I was so captivated, I fell behind on my work as I continued to stare out the window—at what I now know as unlimited possibility that blue sky represents to me. For what felt like a glorious eternity, I could not move my gaze away from the window and the seemingly unending expansion of blue sky beyond it.

It didn't take all that long for my first-grade teacher to notice either. While I'm sure Mrs. Eklund handled the situation well, the consequences of me not paying attention in class were significant for this shy, quiet, attention loathing kid. Not only did it cause me to be called out in class, to my own public humiliation, but it also caused me to stay in from lunch and therefore to miss out on recess in order to catch up and complete my work.

Nearly 35 years later, my mom ran into Mrs. Eklund while holiday shopping in our hometown, and one of the first things Mrs. Eklund recounted to my mom was how remorseful she felt for having kept me in from recess. She added how she wished she hadn't had to, because I was such a great student and always had such a great attitude in class. I'm not making this stuff up. She remembered the experience as much as I did, three and a half decades later.

Of all the thousands of students that went through her class-room, she still remembered the pain of having to give me such a small discipline and its impact on me. Her memory to my mom was that this scenario of me staring out the window at blue sky played out 2 – 3 times before I fully got a handle on it. Whether it was once or a few times, it doesn't matter. The impact was deep.

It may not sound like much to you, but for me, it was devastating. I got in trouble in class. My peers saw it happen. I missed out on recess. My absence on the playground would be obvious, and my friends would *know* I did something wrong. I had drawn attention to myself while daydreaming. And the vow in my heart followed... I *must never* let that happen again. I *should not dream*, well at least in the context of a learning environment. School is for paying attention, not for dreaming, so I internalized.

I stopped looking out that window. I stopped allowing my heart to long for whatever it was that wooed me in the blue sky. My self-corrective nature told me that looking out the window, especially getting captivated by the blue sky, was off limits, dangerous, and would only cause me to get in more trouble. So... I stopped dreaming. I told myself that dreaming was bad. Because it causes you to be corrected in front of your friends and miss out on playground basketball.

You may be rolling your eyes at this point, thinking, *Seriously? That's trouble? Not believable.* Well, that's how the mind of this normally never-in-trouble kid worked. Such was the logic of a quiet, shy, never-wanting-to-draw-attention-to-himself six-year-old. And this time, it worked to my severe disadvantage. I completely stopped dreaming.

LET'S PAUSE FOR A MOMENT. THERE IS SOMETHING I DON'T WANT *you* to miss here. I know you have been a dreamer before too. And, maybe those dreams were not the blue sky specifically, but of your own personal version of blue sky—some other thing, experience, or idea that captured your heart and soul, as we discussed before.

If even faintly in a distant place of memory, you can remember dreaming... If you work at it, even now you can see the flickering image of your past dreams that just never formalized. It's hard to make out exactly, but there were dreams in there, way back when, in the distant past. You too have your own blue sky, or at least you had it at one time.

I am going to whisper something to your soul, and it is likely going to bring a bit of freedom and maybe a bit of trepidation. Listen…

Your dreams… they are still in there, and they are still alive.

Let that sink in for a few moments…

Your dreams are waiting for you to reawaken them. They are waiting for you to rekindle them. They are waiting for you to rediscover them. They are waiting for you to restore them and then unleash them as you pursue your own version of blue sky.

Maybe those dreams feel long gone, left behind, or left for dead. That's okay… for now. Yet, I assure you that no matter how small the remnant of dreams is in your heart and soul, a dream can be reawakened, rekindled, rediscovered, and restored. But, not always to its original condition.

Usually, better.

In my experience of more than 20 years of leadership, giving myself to the effort of helping people, couples, teams, and organizations experience transformation and breakthrough, I have discovered something powerful. I have found that a restored dream, genuinely lived out well, manifests into a better version than the original dream could have ever provided. Yes, *better*. We will talk more about that in the next chapter, so for now, just let your heart reawaken and begin to rekindle your dreams. It still has the potential (there's that word again) to be restored to a better condition than it ever was before.

However, I'm not talking about the types of dreams that are truthfully more like wishes. For example, a few years ago, I crossed over into my 40s, and any dream, or wish, of becoming the future quarterback of the Denver Broncos is not going to come into reality. Even though the post-Peyton Manning era has not been so good to us, I have no business dreaming (or wishing) about playing QB for my beloved Orange and Blue.

Truth is that I have never played organized football, let alone quarterback, and any dream-wish of playing professional football is well past its last ember. Probably because it never had a spark in the first place. So... no problem. Now past 40, it is probably a wish in reverse, as I watch my own teenage son enjoy the hard work and joy of training physically and mentally to become an elite quarterback.

The types of dreams I'm talking about—the types that can be reawakened, rekindled, rediscovered and restored—are very different. The types of dreams I'm talking about are the types of dreams that go deep, at the level of the soul, planted there as seeds even before your own awareness of them—like a gift from someone or something outside yourself.

At this point, it doesn't matter if you refer to the gift-giver as I do - a loving God who majestically created the universe, you, and your dreams. Instead, you may see the gift-giver more impersonally, such as the universe itself, or maybe you don't identify with a reality that is outside yourself.

If so, I encourage you to consider how this can limit your view of the world, not to mention limit your view of yourself, and therefore provide only a small glimpse into the beauty of what it is to dream. The truth is you have been given a gift - that gift is your life, which also contains the seeds of great dreams.

True dreams are planted inside our hearts from outside ourselves. Therefore, reawakening and pursuing those dreams will also take us outside ourselves.

So, as you search inside, begin to look for those dreams that are transcendent, otherworldly, and bigger than yourself.

THE DREAM THAT SEEMED TO FIND ME AS I WAS FINDING IT, AND THE dream that was somewhere at the level of the soul, even at six years old, was somewhere in that beautiful blue sky. Blue sky was on my heart, and then because of the painful, attention-drawing experience in first grade, I stopped dreaming. It felt like the dream died, or worse, I killed it. Because my dreams got me in trouble.

As an aside, I didn't know it was dead. Sadly, I didn't even know it had been born. I didn't even remember this experience until I was in my early 30s, working through a LifePlan process with a mentor and doing some deep introspective work on the story of my life and key turning points. As I reflected on that day in first grade, I realized that, in fact, way back in that elementary classroom, a dream had been birthed.

I also realized that the dream didn't die but instead went dormant, until it woke up again somewhere around the age of 10 to 12. Unfortunately, when the dream came back in front of me, it was missed and squandered, probably because I had forgotten about the dream in the first place. But, let's not get too far ahead—I will save that story for the next section.

To provide a bit of hope, I will share this—the dream *has now been* reawakened, rekindled, rediscovered, and restored. Albeit decades later in the journey, it has been restored nonetheless, and it is so much *better* than I could have imagined.

For now, it may be hard for you to imagine those dreams in your memory ever seeing the light of day again. My guess is that you have had a painful experience that put a stop to your dreaming. That something was most likely far more painful than my missing a first-grade recess, the negative attention, and the related self-induced shame I felt. Yet, I share that story as a way of exposing how even the subtlest of pains in our past can stop us from dreaming.

My assumption is that once your dreaming stopped, so too did a freedom in life, and so too did a vibrancy of life. No longer did you look toward dreams and toward the future with quite as much hope. No longer did you find joy in what could be; no longer did imagining how to do the impossible seem so romantic or even helpful.

A strength was lost. A beauty was stolen.

There is power and beauty in dreaming, and there is a loss of power and beauty when dreams are lost—when they are taken from us, or when we lose sight of them, or when we bury them like I did.

No matter how large or small, my guess is that something has happened to you, or a series of things have happened to you. Maybe someone has failed you greatly, or maybe you have failed yourself in some way, or maybe life has just been consistently hard for a little or a long while. As a result, you have stopped dreaming. And even stopped desiring to dream.

It is time for a mini-breakthrough. Let me stir something up inside of you, something that maybe has not been stirred in a long time.

It's time to dream again, my friend.

Because unleashing and soaring into the blue sky of your potential requires a dream or, at the very least, a willingness to dream again. Those dreams were not placed there by accident, and no matter how long ago you lost them, you are going to need to rekindle them. You are going to need to dream, or at the very least, be willing to dream again. Those dreams you had and still have are little indicators of *your* purpose and of the potential that is stored up within you. We will get to that soon enough, but first, let's look at another way that we lose a handle on our dreams.

DREAMS—MISSED & SQUANDERED

At six years old, I had already stopped dreaming. Or, at least, I don't remember dreaming again. That is, until my parents took me to my first airshow. I don't remember my exact age, probably somewhere between 10 and 12 years old, but I do remember the feelings and the experience. Overwhelming. Emotional. Beautiful. Powerful. Elegant. Significant. Blue Skies. Dreams Awakened. Dreams Rekindled.

That year, the Rocky Mountain Air Show, often held at the regional airport near our home between Denver and Boulder, featured the Navy's expert fighter pilot demonstration team, known as the Blue Angels. Mind you, this was right around the time period, when I was 10, that Tom Cruise starred in the famed movie *Top Gun*, based on a cocky pilot who was sent to the Naval Fighting Weapons School to train and refine his elite fighter pilot skills. The timing in my life as an adolescent boy could not have been better. What I saw in the movie in terms of power, agility, and air superiority was outmatched by 100 times in experiencing the Blue Angels in person.

The three-dimensional backdrop to their show was an unlimited canopy of Colorado's blue sky. The whole experience, from the maneuvers, to the stunts, to the teamwork, to the precision, to the command of their every move, inch by inch, at times at speeds of nearly 700 mph was and still is beyond description. It is truly something that must be experienced to be appreciated. Out of nowhere, staring upward with awe, I was once again dreaming about blue sky.

This time, it was more than simply gazing out a physical window. I felt as if I was gazing into a metaphorical window—a window into my future. This time, my heart and soul were not captured simply by the blue sky but instead by the canvas the blue sky played as a backdrop to these unbelievably beautiful and powerful airplanes.

At that moment, the dream of becoming one of the nation's best fighter pilots—to become a Blue Angel—birthed in my heart. And, as far as I could tell, the dream of serving our nation, and thereby serving its people, and doing so in the unlimited blue skies, was a dream worth living for.

From there, I began to orient my world around the dream. For Christmas, I asked for a 12-month Blue Angel monthly wall calendar. As each month passed, I would cut out the amazing photograph, have my mom laminate it, and I would staple it to my childhood bedroom wall or ceiling. The next year, the same airshow hosted the Air Force's elite flying team, the Thunderbirds. We attended the show again, and the Thunderbirds were every bit as profound, powerful, and inspirational.

The dream continued to grow, and that Christmas, I received a Thunderbird calendar, filling my walls with those pictures as well. Every night when I went to bed, and every morning when I woke up, I was inspired by the imagery and power of the world's best pilots soaring in the majesty of blue sky. It was not just when I was

10–12 years old. These homemade posters filled the walls and ceiling on my half of the bedroom I shared with my younger brother throughout middle school, high school, and even as I went away to college.

Speaking of college, it wasn't much longer after those first couple of airshows that I realized the Air Force Academy was only 90 minutes down the highway, in Colorado Springs, Colorado. In early middle school, I began to dream of attending the Academy after high school graduation. My Dad and Mom even took me down there on occasion for some of the public tours, to walk the grounds, and imagine what it might be like to attend.

We watched the cadets scurry between one class and another and could easily identify the freshman. Freshmen are required to walk in a focused, chin tucked, eyes not roaming manner, following each other distinctly on the right and left turns of a narrow path through the commons. Anyone walking outside of this pattern was clearly an upperclassman. Anyone walking on the lines was clearly a freshman, trying at all costs to avoid messing up and being called out.

But something happened along the way from middle school to high school to college. Or, maybe more accurately, *nothing* happened along the way. I didn't move toward my dream. I mean, I did the best I could in school, took advanced placement courses, graduated near the top of my class, and after high school, I found myself going to a great university; however, I was *not* at the Air Force Academy. Still to this day, I can't really explain how I missed the opportunity.

During those years, no one in my life (including myself) took the initiative to research what it would take to be accepted by the Air Force Academy. I probably had the grades, or could have worked harder to get them, but no one (including myself) figured out the huge amount of effort it takes to apply, let alone be accepted. In addition to phenomenal grades, it takes hundreds of hours of community service and intentionally developed leadership skills spread over a multitude of opportunities to name just a few.

Beyond that, it requires the candidate to begin the application process during the junior year of high school, much earlier than most students those days were thinking about a post-high-school reality. The application process itself isn't easy either, and it begins with acquiring a letter of nomination from a member of the United States Congress—all these things I learned about *long after* I needed to know them.

Somewhere between my dreams being rediscovered at that airshow and my attendance at a university that was *not* the Air Force Academy, you might think I had lost sight of the blue sky. Well, truth is that I went to many more airshows throughout high school, and I saw the posters on my wall every morning and night.

I took a Principles of Aviation course as an elective in my first year of high school. Later in high school, my high school sweet-heart's parents (now my in-laws) even bought me an introductory piloting lesson in a small Cessna for my birthday. I hadn't lost sight of the blue sky dream in my heart in any way at all. It was always in sight. But, it was only that. It was in sight, but it was a *passive* dream.

Or, maybe more accurately…

I have discovered I was a passive dreamer.

Remember in Chapter 1, when I told you to hang onto the idea of passive air flight? Not all that unlike the early flights of the first hot air balloons by the Montgolfier Brothers, or even some of the flying hang-gliders in the early days, the flying machine of my life wasn't powered, steered, piloted, or anything like that. I was passively living life, the whole time with my dream in sight, and yet, the dream was slowly and passively drifting away.

As a result, I wasn't *soaring*, let alone *flying*. I wasn't even *rising*. As discussed, the Wright Brothers are credited with inventing flying because their machine was powered, steered, and piloted with intention and with purpose. I wasn't powering, steering, or piloting my life toward the dream in any way whatsoever.

As a result, I had missed and squandered a genuine dream in my life—to become a fighter pilot. Worse yet, I missed out on my dream without even having attempted to do something about it. It is one thing to attempt to pursue a dream and fall short, but the sense of failure when not even trying is mystifyingly painful.

We have discussed how the pain in life, whether small and subtle, or large and destructive, can cause you to stop dreaming. But, what about the pain in life of a missed or squandered dream? What about the pain we experience when we realize we let an opportunity slip through our hands and pass us by only to wonder how we could allow such a thing to happen—to miss and squander a dream?

This pain is known as the pain of *regret*.

Sometimes the pain of regret is the most painful of all. And, I'm not talking about regret for a mistake: that is remorse. I am talking about genuine deep, shame-inducing regret. Regret is the pain of not trying something, not taking a risk, not pursuing a dream, and giving ourselves to something bigger than ourselves, even if it is a risk to ourselves.

We can learn to get over the remorse for making a mistake but regret for missing an opportunity can corrode the heart of a dreamer for a lifetime. At times that pain of regret slowly and relentlessly corrodes our soul, like unending annoying drips of toxic water. At other times, we are drenched with overwhelming buckets of toxic regret.

I want to ask this... So, now what? What can we learn from all this? Let's pause again. Through this experience, years of reflection, and decades of studying this process in the lives of clients, employees, and communities I have led and served, I have learned a major lesson. It is a lesson that everyone who has a dream, or is even rekindling a dream, needs to hear and hold onto.

There is a significant difference between
having a dream and pursuing a dream.

No mic drop needed. You already know this. And yet, you still needed to hear it. Let that sink in for a moment. If it hurts, that's ok. That is not the pain of remorse, or regret. Instead, it is the pain of a fresh perspective, like a glass of cold water tossed in your face, and one that can wake you up and lead to motivation. So, wake up. Stop simply *having* a dream and instead, start *pursuing* your dream.

Anyone can have a dream.
Only the courageous chose to pursue a dream.

This goes back to the *passive* vs. *piloted* conversation. Maybe you are stuck in some sort of passivity. Many of your dreams lay dormant, seemingly lost to history because you have simply left them there. You were either ignorant of the steps it would take to pursue the dream, or you didn't feel you had the means, the time, the permission, the talent, the you name it, to truly pursue the dream. As a result, in the rearview mirror of your life, there may be a dream or a series of dreams that were missed and/or squandered.

Maybe the pain that killed your dream and the passivity that has caused your dreams to lay dormant have led to the self-induced shame of regret. Maybe regret has taken over and corroded your dreams as regret often does, keeping you from even daring to imagine what a dream could look like again.

Corroded dreams just do not seem as interesting to dream about after all. And if they are still interesting, they feel too dirty, used, and tired to be worth rekindling. Or, maybe you feel too dirty, used, and tired to make it worth it.

Let me speak directly to the issue. Stop looking back. Stop wondering why. Stop regretting. Stop dripping, spilling, or pouring corrosion all over those dreams.

It really doesn't matter how badly you think you missed it. It is time for you to rekindle your dreams, and then ultimately time to pursue them. I am not worried about how corroded you think that dream is. Not only can those dreams be rekindled, they can be restored. And, as I shared before, restored dreams are usually better than we ever imagined, but we aren't talking about restoration quite yet.

We are simply taking about rekindling the dreamer within. At this stage, do not start worrying about the possibility or impossibility of the dream. Do not start trying to figure out the end of the story. Do not start trying to calculate the outcomes and the results.

Somewhere in the dust left over by what you thought was a dead dream are a few embers, glowing orange, even if ever so slightly. Those embers are alive and packed with potential—potential for your life. Those embers are waiting, patiently, for you...

They need your belief. They need your breath. They need your permission. When given permission, those embers can ignite into fully developed dreams. Simply blow a little whispering breeze on the embers of those dreams and let them awaken once again.

REKINDLING DREAMS—A CAUTION

Just as you are having the courage to begin to dream again, here I go issuing a caution. Well, let me simply caution this—don't try to rekindle the dream from an ember to a completed dream all at once. There is a journey that is required, as we have already talked about—and you have yet to learn the three truths of transformational breakthrough you will need in order to successfully take the journey and turn that ember of a dream into a reality. You have yet to truly understand how to unleash the potential of that dream.

Right now, go ahead and rekindle the dream, but don't blow such a wind on it that you flame it right out. Not sure what I'm talking about? You will in a moment.

Once in a while, you have probably rekindled a dream, and for a moment, you can imagine what it would look like without all that corrosion. And, a little motivation kicks in. Ok, so *a lot* of motivation kicks in.

You waste no time. The dream is alive once again, so you better get to it right away, before it dies again, or so you rationalize. You don't wait patiently for the dream to fully reveal itself. Instead, you chase the dream as you used to see it, or maybe as you want to see it now. You feel like it is now or never. So, you go from passive to powered on a moment's notice. Ready or not, here you come. Pedal to the metal. Zero to sixty. Passive to powered.

You subscribe to a goal-setting course. You pick up a book on productivity. You buy a new journal, or better yet, a dream/task journal day-timer thing. Or, even better than that, you spend hours watching YouTube videos and making your own custom-colored bullet journal. Trust me, I have been there.

From there, you start to put pictures of the Blue Angels and the Thunderbirds all over your walls again. No wait, that was me… You start to put pictures of blue skies, scenic oceans, mountain land-scapes, roaring lions, and muscle-bound athletes full of pithy and inspirational quotes all over the walls—the walls of your social media pages, that is.

No longer do motivational posters reside on your literal walls where only you can see them. No… your motivational images and memes must be shared with the whole world—so the whole world can know that you are motivated, so everyone can know you are a dreamer on a mission!

You follow tutorials of how to make the best Instagram images pop. You watch videos of how to curate the best Pinterest Boards. You spend hours and hours creating your visually enhanced and externally shared motivation to justify to yourself and to others that it is okay to dream.

And you lie to yourself that in doing all these things, you are dreaming. Truth is that more often than not, when you do this, it looks less like dreaming, and once again, more like *wishing*, and a lot more like wasting time.

And, you know how the rest of the story usually goes. And so do I, because I have done all those things myself. Give it a few days, weeks, or months, and rarely are we nearer to the dream. Usually we have missed it and squandered it again, or at least we are in the process of missing it and squandering it because of all the time we are wasting.

This time we have arrived at the same result with a different method. We moved too quickly. We chose power over passivity with such aggression that we snuffed out the rekindled fire. We spent so much wasted time online "dreaming" or what we told ourselves was dreaming, that we have a lot of wishes on our walls, but no dreams in our hands. We also have very little chance of re-fanning the flame of that dream, let alone restoring that dream.

Here is why: There is a huge difference between *rekindling* a dream and embracing the journey of *rediscovering* and *restoring* that dream.

Let me say that again…

> *There is a huge difference between rekindling a dream*
> *and embracing the journey of rediscovering and restoring that dream.*

Just as there is a huge difference between having a dream and pursuing a dream, as you now well know. For now, simply rekindle the dreams that have been dormant inside your soul. Give them a whisper, a breath, a prayer, a little wind of belief. Then, let them be. Once rekindled, dreams have a way of heating up.

As for rediscovering and restoring those dreams, much of the rest of this book is about how to do just that—to pursue your dreams, to unleash your potential, and to experience the truth of transformational breakthrough along the way.

In order to take that next step, we are going to have to put the past behind us. We are going to have to identify and overcome the pain that killed the dreams within us. We are going to have to put our history of passive dreaming to a stop. We are going to put a stop to false dreaming and to dream-wishing too. We are going to discover in-depth the journey we must take to reach our dreams.

To do so, we must understand how dreams found, and lost, missed and squandered, once rekindled can be rediscovered and restored.

CHAPTER 3

REVIVE — REDISCOVERING & RESTORING DREAMS

"The future belongs to those who believe in the beauty of their dreams."

- ELEANOR ROOSEVELT

So many times, I have looked back regretfully through the lens of history, shaken my head, and beat myself up. How did I miss the opportunity to attend the Air Force Academy? How were my dreams so clear to me and to those who loved me most, and yet, I completely missed them? I didn't even so much as lift a finger to pursue them.

It was as if I thought dreams just manifest themselves. Or, it was as if I thought that dreams were supposed to be just that—dreams. To have but not pursue. Either way, I squandered any opportunity to become a fighter pilot.

Still yet, at other times, I look back through the lens of history and gratefully offer thanks to God that I *didn't* take that path. I loved the idea of soaring in the blue sky and becoming an elite fighter pilot, but there is a lot that comes with that privilege, and it comes at great cost. It is a cost that all men and women who serve in our Armed Forces understand, a cost for which I am grateful to them for their sacrifice. A cost that I hadn't fully calculated while dreaming about soaring in the blue skies. And a cost I am thankful I didn't have to bear, which makes me even more thankful for those who have chosen the weight of bearing it for me.

Beyond the cost of that journey, it turns out that there too is a practical reality that would have prevented me from my dreams anyway. During my freshman year of college, I was struggling to see the dry-erase board from a middle row in the math lecture hall. It took me a while to realize that it was me, not the Calculus professor's handwriting, and I eventually discovered I had developed slight nearsightedness. As such, I never would have passed the eye exam for military pilots, and I would be "stuck" at the Air Force Academy, the dream of being a pilot totally dashed before flight school. That in itself would have been a very painful corner of stuck and lost.

Combine my slight nearsightedness with the reality that I sneeze three times every time I walk from indoor light to sunlight. Yes, exactly three times, every time—just as my Dad and my brother do, and now my son also. I recently found out that it is actually a condition where your brain confuses the sunlight with a stuffed nose and causes you to sneeze. Everyone tries to offer a tissue, but actually sunglasses would be of more help. Well, in truth, sunglasses don't really help either. Nothing can stop the three sneezes. It just happens. And, I have since heard that it is also a condition that disqualifies you from being a military pilot.

Yet, still to this day and until I get the opportunity, the number one experience on my bucket list is to do an hour or more ride-along in a legitimate fighter plane. Of course, I would prefer it to be while wearing a G-Suit so the pilot can take me through as many aerobatic maneuvers as he is willing to throw at me before I blackout or puke. Or both. Far and away, that is my number one bucket list item; all other experiences stand at a distance in its shadows. Not the blacking out and puking part, but the soaring and maneuvering in the unlimited blue skies… that part.

If and when it happens, I'll probably sneeze three times on the canopy as we get started, but it will be all blue skies from there. I'm pretty sure if I get to experience it and check it off my bucket list, the experience will be so rich, so exhilarating, so amazing, that I will add it to the top of the bucket list again. I know… that's not how a bucket list works, but a boy can dream, err… *wish*, right?

Maybe it is possible to live out the bucket-list dream someday, but the truth of the fighter pilot dream is that it was never going to happen anyway. That dream, as real, transcendent, and soul-inspiring as it was, truly was never going to get off the ground.

Maybe it had been a wish, maybe it had been a dream, but it was long past gone. Time and perspective have healed whatever pain and regret I experienced over missing and squandering the dream of becoming a fighter pilot, and I am thankful for the peace of that healing.

I truly believe that life has a way of working those things out, and when we get a higher view, or elevated perspective of life, we discover that all things, including hard things, can work together for good. I believed it before I ever saw my dreams rekindled. I believed it before I ever saw my dreams rediscovered and restored. I believe it now more than ever.

DREAMS—DORMANT, BUT NOT DEAD

Let's fast forward through 15+ years from that freshmen year of college. My dream of soaring in the blue skies was dead, or so I thought.

So, I moved on. In those 15 years, with no thought of blue sky, other than enjoying the natural beauty of it above me, my life began to take off, not toward any dream in particular, but it took off none-theless. In that time, I had graduated, *cum laude*, from the University of Denver, a local prestigious private university, with a BSBA in Finance & Marketing.

My success in college was funded on the back of a lot of hard work, specifically my parents' love, each working 2–3 jobs at a time, my work-study and paid internship income, a few grants and scholarships, and the maximum student loans you could take for an undergraduate degree. I still remember the days in the field house parking lot, changing quickly from my school clothes to my fitness center front desk work-study uniform, and later into slacks, tie, and pressed shirt to make it in time for my office job/internship at a local investment firm.

For some reason, I always had favor in leadership ranks, and my internship jobs were often paid roles, working directly for CEOs. These environments and experiences provided huge opportunities to be shaped for my future. Despite these opportunities, I chose to begin to grow my career differently than most of my peers.

I observed a lot of things—good and bad, healthy and unhealthy—during those paid internship years in college. I knew that if I set the objective to be my own advancement, then one life (my life) might make it to the top of the corporate ladder—one single life would seemingly shine bright. Based on observation and using my strength to learn from the mistakes of others, I could see that route was often empty and lonely, not to mention a shallower definition of success than I was interested in pursuing.

Much like when I was a child, I could foresee the future, learn from the mistakes and missteps of others, and adjust my trajectory accordingly. As a result of seeing the mistakes of many who chased their own success, I took some time in my early 20s to do some reflection. For the first time, I wrote a personal mission statement—one that directed my life away from the pursuit of personal gain.

The mission statement is as vibrant today as the day I wrote it, and it is "how" I live out my life purpose. My mission was then and is today still the same:

Jeff Rasor's Life Mission
My mission is to use my unique gifts and talents to encourage, inspire, and unleash the unique gifts and talents of those around me.

It was that simple. The aim of my life was to be about the betterment of others. If I could help others become the best versions of themselves, then instead of just one young man on a bright career journey (me), there could be ten, one hundred, and maybe even thousands who are shining bright in their careers and lives.

That could literally change the world, one bright light at a time, or if I was so fortunate, thousands of bright lights at a time. I didn't fully realize it then, but I had tapped into something true at the level of my soul, and it echoed of greater purpose. Years later, it would draw me back to blue sky dreams, but I didn't see it initially.

Leading in the marketplace in my early 20s, using my mission statement as a compass, my career advanced surprisingly quick from one industry to another, one leadership role to another. While I hadn't set that as my aim, it was happening as a result. I found myself, even when I did not see myself as a leader, giving leadership, direction, and guidance to those who needed it, often to those who I perceived to be far more successful than I.

In age, accomplishment, and experience, they were without a doubt more successful. But in heart, understanding, and wisdom, I suppose I had some advanced guidance to offer—my gifts and talents were truly unleashing theirs, and we were all growing as a result.

IN ONE PROFESSIONAL ROLE ON THAT JOURNEY, WHILE STILL ONLY IN my late 20s, I took on the creative programing director role for a nationally recognized nonprofit organization, which produced large-scale events in basketball/hockey/concert arenas all throughout the United States.

Looking back, when thinking of jobs in the traditional sense, it was by far my favorite job. Now today, as an entrepreneur and guide to people and organizations who need to experience the power of a breakthrough, this has been the only professional role I have ever had that has matched and even surpassed it.

As much as the leadership role was a pretty big deal in that industry, I simply saw it as an open door, one in which I desired to serve faithfully, ignoring the accolades and position/title significance others may have craved. I never really did the math of the impact back then. The numbers didn't matter, because that wasn't how I measured success in the first place. The role in that leadership seat was simply the next role in my journey, the next stop where my career led me.

I recognized and took seriously the enormity of the responsibility of it then, but not the status of the role. I was measuring success by a different measuring stick, and this was simply another place to use my gifts and talents to unleash the gifts and talents of those around me. In truth, it is probably that outlook that allowed me to have as much impact as I had.

As I have been evaluating the first half of my life and career recently, I have come to realize that my leadership approach in that role allowed me to influence and impact quite a number of lives. During my four years in that role, I was responsible for and provided leadership guidance to the creative content development and programming for everything that happened on our stage during our day and a half event. That was no less than 12 hours of live programing, planned out quite literally minute by minute, in 16–20 cities each year.

Looking back, I realize now that my work directly influenced and impacted more than 500,000 men who attended our live events during my four short years in that role. I have no idea of the number of how many wives, children, extended family, coworkers, neighbors, and friends those men went home and impacted from there. Without exaggeration, my influence and leadership easily could have directly and indirectly impacted more than a million people.

And, while those numbers are huge, I carry more pride in my heart for the individual lives of people I personally impacted for good—the lives of those on my team, or other staff within the organization, not to mention the various contractors, vendors, and volunteers I was so blessed to interact with. I count them as the most important lives I touched among the million plus that may have been influenced.

Truth be told, those numbers are quite shocking to me, especially given I am the shy, quiet, non-attention-grabbing kid, who became a young man who wrote a mission statement about not setting a course for his own success but for the success of others. You would think that a shy, quiet kid who prefers to hide out and avoid the spotlight, especially one with a mission to make others great, would impact well, not that many.

Yet, the opposite is more likely true. If I had tried to ignite only my own career, I probably would have never been able to impact even 10 people. Instead, by giving my every effort to ignite the gifts and talents of those around me, I was guiding 10,000–20,000 men to breakthrough each and every summer weekend for four years. Without knowing it, or having a metaphor for it, I was soaring in the blue skies within my own career, as I was helping others do the same.

How I got in that role from that work-study job at the fitness center and internship at the investment firm only six years earlier is still dumbfounding. Additionally, my own mission to use my life for the benefit of others had accelerated my career so much further than I could have if my objective had been solely to seek my own advancement. That leadership concept is worth writing about, but that would take us off course for the purposes of this book. The simple truth is this: I was living with this mission before I had truly discovered my purpose, and little did I know it, but I was on to something.

As I said before, purpose is deposited inside of us from an outside source and it also takes us beyond ourselves. If we are more aware, we will realize that purpose has a way of finding us, even if we aren't looking for it. I was truly using my unique gifts and talents to encourage, inspire, and unleash the gifts and talents of those around me. At the nonprofit, I was unleashing the gifts of our music teams, our speaking teams, our video/media teams, and our production teams, to name a few. The whole journey of those four years was a fairly thick slice of heaven, as the saying goes.

You would think my career would have taken off from there, and it very well could have. I most likely could have parlayed that role into any number of concert tours, media programming and

production, or creative development opportunities. Yet, as I shared
in the Introduction, I am attracted to the corner of stuck and lost.
As unhealthy as it can be, I empathize with those individuals,
couples, businesses, and organizations leashed to that corner.

WELL, AS MY OWN CAREER WAS HAVING MORE INFLUENCE THAN I
could have ever dreamed, the church my wife and I called home was
beginning to drift near the corner of stuck and lost, if not already
anchored there. While the senior leadership may not have described
it that way, most of the 5,000 people who attended could feel and
smell the stench of stagnancy just under the surface—hidden just
below the thin veil of size and excitement that existed then.

Don't get me wrong, the church had an amazing legacy of
beauty and rich influence and impact in the community and in my
own life; the church itself didn't have a stench. No, it was the stench
of stagnancy that existed within the fabric of its methods and
culture that was fairly potent.

As such, the opportunity to use my gifts and talents to impact
the gifts and talents of the church's leadership team and the congregation was very appealing, although wrought with career suicide.
True to form, I did not give much concern to my own career journey, especially compared to the opportunity to help the local church
I called home turn its trajectory toward a healthy future.

The senior pastor had been observing my career path from a
distance, and the trail of influence and impact that I was leaving
behind me was not lost on him. So, after a number of months
discussing timing with him, having just turned 30-years-old, I made
the leap—out of corporate executive and nonprofit leadership into
the unknown waters of leading within the context of a local church.

I'm going to spare you the details, but the next part of the story
is this: at the end of nearly five years on the strategic leadership
team at the church, I had made little positive impact on the stench
of stagnancy, let alone on the church's trajectory. Yet, the experience
had made a huge negative impact on my trajectory. Those were the

most difficult years of my career, truly causing me to reach the point of a vocational wilderness—the type of stuck and lost that not even Bear Grylls can get you out of (the book about wilderness will most likely be my next).

I had surrendered my career journey for a dream of what the church could become—a church with the same DNA as its nearly 45 years of history, but a fresh nature, just like grandkids are to the lineage to a family legacy (same DNA, new freshness). Yet, in nearly five agonizing years, not only had my dream for what the church could become died, but so too did all my dreaming. Yes, *all* my dreaming. Again. I was lost in a bad way, calling into question my own leadership, my own track record of impact, and believing to my core that I had no genuine talent, and no longer valuable in the marketplace.

The overwhelming clouds had darkened all my belief and sent a devastating message, delivered to my heart like a poison-tipped arrow. It sounded like this inside my weary spirit: everything I had accomplished and experienced up to that point in my career had been dumb luck, if not a complete fraud. Unfortunately, I began to embrace that message as if it were true, only deepening the sense of wilderness I found myself in.

Not surprisingly, the length of time and depth of this wilderness was impacting other areas of my life too, including my marriage, friendships, and my health. At that point, my only hope was to make it to the next day, and then repeat, accepting even in my mid-30s that being leashed to the corner of stuck and lost was my destiny. I truly felt like the dreamer within had died or been killed. Thankfully, although it felt like it, that is not the end of the story, and I invited a guide into my life to take me on a journey. What I would later discover is that those dreams from my childhood weren't dead, but they were simply buried and dormant.

DREAMS—REVIVED

After absolutely no breakthrough in any way over those five years, and none to be seen on the horizon, I found myself at the same time both further from and closer to my dreams than I ever imagined. I eventually and finally sought the help of a friend and mentor, Pete. He was a guide of sorts, who walked me through a two and a half day LifePlan process that I mentioned before.

In two days of deep and introspective work, my eyes were opened again, to the truth of the beauty and strength of my life—beauty and strength that had been long since buried by the dry sand of that wilderness season. It was clear, beyond a shadow of a doubt, written on flip charts on the walls (literally)—my season at the church must come to an end.

The result of the LifePlan was not just *permission* to resign but *instruction* to resign. It was the final nail in the coffin of an already dead dream of what I could do to help my church's future. And, it was time to memorialize that dead dream and move on.

In that moment, now 15+ years removed from missing out on the Air Force Academy, I was both as far and as close to my dream as I had ever been. Regarding the "as far away as ever" part of that statement, it looked like this: on paper, I was five years removed from a genuine career role in the marketplace and about to resign from a wilderness-inducing, dream-killing, dead-end job on the strategic leadership team at my local church. I was an awful long way from blue sky. So, now what?

Thankfully, the process helps filter what *to do* next as much as it filters what *not to do*. A part of the journey that brings the clarity is discovering your own unique purpose, which came to the surface during the latter half of the second day. While I have word-smithed my Life Purpose statement a number of times over the years to fine tune it, the essence of what was uncovered, I now say like this:

<u>Jeff Rasor's Life Purpose—Why I Exist</u>
I exist to lead people and teams to breakthrough,
to guide them into their unique purpose, and
to inspire them to fulfill their potential.

At least in my opinion, *that* is a powerful purpose statement, loaded with energy, excitement, service to others, and founded on extreme clarity and focus. The clarity and focus of this statement is what keeps it from being too lofty or pithy. It is such a clear statement that I always know when I am living, working, and playing within the context of my life purpose. And, on the other side of the coin, I know when I am *not*. The ability to identify when I am within my life purpose and also identify when I am not actually creates a steering mechanism of sorts that can guide my life, not unlike the three-axis control system the Wright Brothers conceived.

My Life Purpose is not the only steering mechanism that came out of the LifePlan, but it is easy to see how this one sentence describing my life purpose—a sentence which is founded in clarity —is and will always guide me. Imagine the ability you would have if you were able to have that kind of clarity about your unique type of purpose for your life. It's possible, my friend, and we will cover the importance of that work in future chapters.

Bringing back into view the Life Mission Statement from 10+ years earlier also added another guiding mechanism:

Jeff Rasor's Life Mission—How I Go About It

My mission is to use my unique gifts and talents to encourage, inspire, and unleash the unique gifts and talents of those around me.

By combining my newly defined Life Purpose and my existing Life Mission, I had a powerful combination of filters to apply to any future opportunities I wanted to explore. Not only do these statements provide a filter, a mechanism, a system for me to assess my life in any given moment, but they also provide a navigation system of sorts, to evaluate the future.

As a result, a couple exciting things bubbled to the surface as a result of the filtering—both of them leading to the same solution. Leveraging the extended clarity I had discovered, it became apparent that my organizational leadership journey, which covered a depth and breadth of industries, sectors, and settings had given me an extreme confidence.

I knew I could comfortably walk into any boardroom or executive meeting in any sector or industry and lead the team to experience breakthrough, to discover their purpose and reach their potential. Founded on the same clarity, depth, and breadth of my one-on-one personal leadership experiences, I knew I could help any individual or couple experience the same.

The net result of all this clarity and purpose was more clarity—it was time for me to become an entrepreneur and launch my own consulting firm to guide individuals, couples, businesses, and organizational teams to breakthrough, so they could discover their purpose and reach their potential. It just so happened that there existed a few pre-existing consulting tools I could build into my portfolio of consulting services that were in direct alignment with living in the truth of my Life Purpose and my Life Mission.

One of those tools was the very LifePlan process that guided me out of my wilderness season and into my breakthrough. The same idea of guiding people to be restored in their purpose and to fulfill their potential, as well as using my gifts and talents to unleash the gifts and talents of those around me is exactly what the LifePlan is all about.

Not only did I believe this based on my experience within the LifePlan as a client, but the filtering and guiding system the LifePlan provided for my life affirmed the same truth. I knew I could use the very LifePlan process that gave me a hope and freedom to help others experience what it meant to be set free in the same way.

Not long after that extremely clarifying two and a half days, I was trained as a professional facilitator of the LifePlan process. Because of my extensive leadership experience across numerous sectors, I also become certified as a professional facilitator in a companion process, known as the StratOp process. The StratOp process is an organizational series of tools that lead to a strategic, operating, and growth planning solution for corporate executive and divisional leadership teams, entrepreneurial businesses, as well as nonprofits and churches.

In addition to my extensive experience in such a wide variety of one-on-one and one-on-team leadership experiences, I now had two significant tools within my consulting portfolio to go change the world—still while using my gifts and talents to unleash the gifts and talents of those around me. The result would be the ability to lead people and teams to breakthrough, to guide them into their unique purpose, and to inspire them to fulfill their potential.

Walking into the LifePlan, I had been further from blue sky than I had ever been before. Walking out of the LifePlan I realized that I was actually closer than I had ever been, even if I didn't fully know it yet. I was *actually dreaming* again. I was dreaming about using my life for the good of others. The dreamer had been revived. While I wasn't aware of it at that moment, I simply needed to rediscover the dormant dream that had been right under my nose for years, and then go on the journey to see it restored.

DREAMS—REDISCOVERED

As a result of the LifePlan, everything in my life had shifted. I had new perspective, new clarity, new purpose, and a new future on the horizon. Beyond simply navigating, my newly discovered Life Purpose and my pre-existing Life Mission would serve as a significant portion of a steering system that allows me to pilot my life with purpose and intentionality. No longer prohibited by passivity but instead, powered and piloted with purpose.

Leaving the church would require communicating with the leadership, creating an exit plan, and finding a timing that fit their needs. Figuring out the best way forward for all involved gave me some time to get trained in these new consulting tools, as well as to contemplate and move toward my future as a consultant. I didn't see it coming, but all the truth that had risen to the surface in the Life-Plan was just about to help me rediscover and restore my dreams of blue sky.

During this period of transition, one of the steps I was going to have to take was to create and name some sort of business entity. The act of creating and naming things has always been important to me—not only because names carry deeper meaning but because I'm a bit of a word-guy. After having no inspiration for a couple months, I was out on a walk with my wife and two young children, and out of nowhere, I found the blue sky again, or rather it found me.

We were quietly enjoying a family walk on a crisp, beautiful fall Colorado day, and I took some moments alone, away from the playground where my wife and the kids were enjoying their time together. Pondering and praying through this new entrepreneurial journey I was about to embark upon, I was thinking through the naming of the firm I was about to launch. I knew it had a lot to do with people and teams, and I knew it had a lot to do with the purpose and potential of those people and teams. Frustrated that nothing was coming to mind, I simply looked up in wonder. Then, it happened.

Above me on that beautiful fall day in Colorado was a canopy of unlimited blue sky. All of a sudden, without warning, my heart was captured by it again. The expanse of it, the unlimited possibility of it, and the beauty of the blue sky all pulled on the strings of my soul, just as it had when I was in first grade. In a single moment, it all came flooding together. I had it! Metaphorically, figuratively, and even quite literally, the blue sky revealed itself in that moment in my soul. *Blue Sky Potential.*

Yes! That's it! That's why I have been dreaming about the blue sky for a lifetime. It wasn't just a shy, quiet, and kind little boy daydreaming in first grade; it was the wonderment of potential and possibility of what could be. It wasn't truly about the Blue Angels and becoming a fighter pilot; it was the unlimited canopy of possibility I witnessed those pilots perform as individuals and as a team to wow the crowds. And then, in that moment, out on a walk, it wasn't simply the Colorado blue sky I loved so much; it was the endless possibility and potential that blue sky represented. A *Blue Sky Potential* that every individual and team could discover and pursue. I could not believe it. I was speechless. I wasn't even looking for blue sky, and it found me.

As my mind raced through these realities and connected all of these dots, I realized that is what I should name my consulting firm: Blue Sky Potential. Honestly, it isn't that great of a name for a consulting firm. It is better as a metaphor, a concept, a truth–a reality that exists for every person and every organization.

In that moment, and every moment since, Blue Sky Potential represents the unlimited, unending potential that is bound up in every single person and every single team. Every individual has a Blue Sky Potential. It is limitless. Every couple has a Blue Sky Potential. It is boundless. Every organization—for profit, nonprofit, or church—and its leadership, divisional, and project teams have a Blue Sky Potential. Blue Sky Potential… is infinite possibility.

In fact, with this new understanding, I could see that I had been unknowingly living out my dream during most of my career journey. I had been helping the people and organizations I worked for and worked with to actually move toward their Blue Sky Potential, while using my unique gifts, talents, and purpose to unleash the gifts, talents, and purpose within them.

It also explained why the five years at the church were so challenging—most of the leadership of the church believed they were operating the church near the apex of its greatest potential. Believing incremental change, if change of any kind, was all that was necessary, there had been no recognition that the decreasing size of the congregation was saying otherwise.

As a result of that blindness, my ability to lead toward a breakthrough, to ignite and unleash purpose, not to mention the transformation that was required (more on transformation ahead) was severely hindered. Yet, at least I had understanding, perspective, and clarity. It didn't ease the pain immediately of what felt to me like a failed 5-year experiment in my career, but it did explain the barrenness I felt.

Needless to say, that moment in the park under a canopy of blue sky was an unbelievable moment—one of those types of experiences where you feel like the stars have all aligned, where you recognize there is truth to the idea that all things can work together for good. It was one of those moments when I could just stand in awe of God, grateful that He knows what He is doing, even if I don't. It was a moment that connected first grade to the Blue Angels to my mission statement to my career trajectory to LifePlan and to my future. It was a moment I first saw a common connection surrounded by that beautiful, glorious, limitless blue sky that had first captured my soul as a child.

I had rediscovered my deepest and truest dream, in so much *better* of a form than I could have ever imagined.

DREAMS—RESTORED

From that moment forward, I can honestly say I have been living the dream, fully restored and better than I could have imagined. I have had the opportunity to serve so many great people and great organizations along the way. The variety of people and organizations are so diverse, each one of them unique in their purpose, unique in the direction of their potential. And living the dream for others is pure joy for me.

The joy I experience in doing so comes when a husband and wife come to my office with heavy hearts and weary spirits, only to leave with relief and excitement after experiencing breakthrough, discovering purpose, and connecting the dots to see their potential. A personal joy comes over me too when I speak at church gatherings, give a talk at a conference, or a corporate keynote address, and individuals come forward, some with tears in their eyes, thanking me for the impact of the authentic stories I shared and the impact it had on them.

The joy also comes as I wrap up the end of an offsite retreat, when a leadership team stands up with excitement in ovation, high-fiving each other with a passion to get back to the office and change the world by reorienting the trajectory of their organization. The joy comes when I see a church leadership team filled with purpose and noble conviction get on the same page with each other and chart a course to a greater pathway to transform the community in which they are called.

In fact, not long into my entrepreneurial consulting journey, I was even invited back into the executive leadership of the church I called home, the one where I had got stuck and lost in the wilderness. I told you I'm attracted to the corner of stuck and lost, now didn't I? Over a second, nearly 5-year journey together, I was able to embed myself and my guiding leadership style to truly accomplish what I was unable to do the first time around.

The second time around, I was able to help them reorient themselves back to their true DNA, navigate a multi-year succession plan, and ultimately and successfully find, announce, and later install their next senior pastor. He is thriving, and so is the church, now back on course toward a great future. Mission accomplished.

I have been living the dream for nearly 10 years now, simply taking people and teams back to the drawing board, so to speak. I have been leading them to breakthrough, to be set free and unleashed from what holds them back, helping them discover purpose, and inspiring them to soar into the blue sky of their potential.

For me, that dream is a dream worth living for—the thrill of it keeps me up at night and wakes me up in the morning. And, despite the many challenging times, it has been pure joy for me to pursue that dream with powered and piloted with purpose. That is not to say I haven't faced adversity, that I have not run up against challenges, that I haven't failed in many ways. I have, many times over.

Those realities are part of pursuing any dream—they come with the territory. If anyone ever tells you otherwise, I'd question whether or not they truly have experienced pursuing a dream that is bigger than themselves.

Still, without a shadow of a doubt, I know this: I am living the big dream for which I was made, and it is better than I could have ever imagined. That, my friend, is the definition of *restoration…*

RESTORATION IS AN INTERESTING CONCEPT. FOR SOME, THE IDEA OF restoration is limited to the idea of bringing back the beauty that something once held—like restoring an old piece of furniture or rebuilding a classic car. The piece being restored had once existed in its finest, mint condition form.

Time, environment, and quite possibly a good deal of mistreatment caused that original condition to fade, be tarnished, or even damaged and corroded. This applies to you as much as it does to that object. Restoration in this sense simply cleans it up, puts it back together, and if possible, causes it to function again. This is a good result, no question.

However, while those things are important, they would probably fit better under the category of repaired or rebuilt. And, that type of restoration is great for a toaster, or a chair, or even a classic car, but it is not good enough to be worthy of the type of restoration you deserve for your dream. Real restoration goes beyond repairing what has been broken or replacing what has been lost. When I talk about the idea of a restored dream, I'm not talking about repaired or rebuilt.

True, genuine restoration is much different; it so much more than that. True restoration goes deeper. It transcends the simplicity of a fresh coat of paint, or new working buttons. Remember in the last chapter when we talked about dreams that were corroded by pain, neglect, squandered opportunity, and regret?

When it comes to your dreams, restoration removes the corrosion, fixes the broken, replaces the lost, and returns your dreams back to you in a condition and a function that far exceeds the original condition.

Did you get that? Far exceeds! This is *real* restoration. This is the restoration you long for. This is the type of restoration you only dreamed possible for your life. This type of restoration is available to you.

Genuine restoration is the experiential result of overcoming every limitation, discovering and living the big dream for which you were made, and realizing it is better than you could have ever imagined.

I have experienced it myself, and I have helped so many others experience it for themselves. And, I want you to experience it for yourself. Your dreams can be restored—not only to the original condition, but *better*, beyond your original dreams. For me, the work

I do and the life I get to live far exceeds daydreaming out a window, and it far exceeds piloting a fighter jet.

So, why am I sharing so much about *my* story? Isn't this book about helping you?

Yes, absolutely. But if you can't trust that I have walked the road from first grade dreamer to missed and squandered dreams to dead, buried, and dormant dreams, through a significant season of wilderness, only to see my dreams rekindled, rediscovered, and restored, you probably would not think it possible for you. The type of Blue Sky Potential I get to live in is unique to me and I love it, but it isn't any better than the Blue Sky Potential you could be living in.

I can't tell you when it is going to happen for you, but I can assure you that it can. I can also encourage you that it will, but not if you don't allow yourself to dream again. Your dream may not look like you used to think it looked, but I bet when you find it, it will look, feel, and be *better*.

Somehow, in the grand scheme of life, your dream will come to pass fully restored—better than it would have ever been in your wildest imagination. Begin to dream again, my friend, because…

A rekindled dream is the beginning of restoration.

PART 2

DISCOVER: BLUE SKY POTENTIAL

CHAPTER 4

BLUE SKY — SO MUCH MORE THAN POTENTIAL

"I dwell in possibility."

- EMILY DICKINSON

I KNOW I HAVE BEEN STRETCHING YOUR THINKING AND EXPANDING your vision. You know it too. I also know it has been challenging, yet good. And, I hope you know that too. You may have hoped that by now I would have given you a few tips and tricks about how to be set free, so you could set the book down unfinished and start soaring into your future. But instead, I have taken you into some deep waters and into some thin air. If I may say what all the kids are saying these days… *Sorry, not sorry.*

I care for you enough to not sell you an adventure and then give you a kiddie coaster. Oh, there have been and are still going to be plenty of ups and downs, but I'm not going to cheat you out of all that you want and need. This is not a 60-second ride. There is so much more to come.

I have invited you into a journey, and as of yet, I have not given you a map. I have helped you begin to see that overcoming gravity is actually possible, especially when you realize that more power isn't always the right solution. I have exposed my own passivity as a way of challenging yours. I have stirred up dormant dreams and the painful past or regret that almost killed them. In the midst of all of that, I have dared you to believe that the restoration of your dreams could be a better version of life than you have even dreamed. You have already come a long way, and you have already begun to move toward your potential.

I know it may not feel like it, but you are already further away from that corner of stuck and lost than you know. These first steps are the hardest, and you are very doing well, my friend. Way to go! I'm proud of you, and I'm proud *for* you.

Take a deep breath. Because we aren't stopping here. We are pressing forward. I'm going to stretch your mind further and expand your vision higher. There is more to see, and it is time for you to see it. You are ready. You have made it this far, and it has prepared you for this next phase. All things are possible, and it is time to look at the possibility of all things.

BLUE SKY POTENTIAL

As I sit on my favorite bench in my favorite place in the world, I am thinking of you, praying for you, and pondering the idea of blue sky. I have prayed many prayers here on this very bench over the last decade or so, and nearly all of them have been answered. So be encouraged when I say I am praying for you too.

As I gaze out over the seemingly infinite, sun-glistened waters of the Pacific Ocean, the blue of the water outmatched only by the blue of the sky, I realize it would be easy to understand "blue sky" simply as a sunny day. In a literal way, this would make sense, as you too have probably enjoyed a few days of sunshine under some beautiful blue skies.

Yet, I'm not really pondering the weather or a desire for you to enjoy more vacations. Instead, I am pondering how I can best communicate the metaphorical meaning beyond the idea of blue sky. I'm searching for a way to explain the idea that captivated my soul as a child, and how to describe the vision of Blue Sky Potential I attempt to cast to every individual, couple, team, client, audience, friend, and even stranger I find myself in front of. So, is Blue Sky Potential the idea of seeing your own life take flight and seeking to fulfill your own potential, as we have already discussed? Yes, but no —that is part of the method of how we pursue blue sky, but that isn't blue sky in and of itself.

Well then, blue sky must be the term for our deeper dreams, whether rekindled, rediscovered, or even restored, right? To that idea, I would also say yes, but no. Dreams do get us get us closer, but not all the way there. You might be reading that last thought, thinking, *wait a minute… if I were able to rekindle the dreamer within, rediscover the dreams that have been lost, stolen, or squandered, and then see those dreams restored into a version that is better than I could have imagined, how would I not be living in blue sky?*

If you would argue along those lines, I think you would have a great case, and based on the personal stories I have shared, I can see your point. But… blue sky is so much more than that too. Blue sky is so far beyond our dreams that I can actually make a case that *even I am not fully living in blue sky yet…*

"Wait a second," you must be thinking, *"the author of the book that is supposed to unleash me into my Blue Sky Potential, isn't even living in his Blue Sky Potential yet? How can I trust him? I thought he said he knew the way, that he has not only been there himself, but has taken others there too."* I would respond to your argument with a good deal of humility and a good deal of truth.

I would agree with you in one sense that I am currently living in the blue sky of my potential, loving what I get to do every single day, and loving who I get to do it with. I would acknowledge that I am living in a way that unleashes the gifts and talents of others, leading them to breakthrough, guiding them to see their purpose restored and their potential realized—all these are ways I define the Blue Sky Potential of my own dreams. And yet, at the same time, I would say I have *so much further* to go, and that there is so much more blue sky to grab hold of. Here's why:

Blue Sky Potential is Possibility.
Endless Possibility.

Possibility that is more than our minds and hearts can fathom and imagine. Yes, blue sky is the possibility we could live in our grandest dreams, desires, hopes, and ambitions. And yet, *Blue Sky* is so much more than that. *Blue Sky* is more than simply those things we can name, articulate, and describe. *Blue Sky* also represents those things we cannot name—things, feelings, and thoughts that are even difficult for us to perceive.

The possibility found in *Blue Sky Potential* transcends our emotions, our thinking, and even our dreams. Beyond the atmosphere of what we know is a layer of what we dream, and beyond what we dream is a layer of possibility that is represented by the idea of *Blue Sky Potential.*

Have you ever noticed that when you are cruising at 30,000 feet in an airplane, the air out the window is *not* blue, and the blue canopy is still above and beyond you? From the ground looking up, an airplane seems to be literally soaring in the blue sky. Yet from the airplane, looking out the window to the canopy above, there is still so much more above and beyond.

So, it is with your Blue Sky Potential and the possibility above and beyond. Blue Sky goes beyond what we perceive as the reach of our potential; it goes beyond our imagination, to a place of influence, greatness, and impact that is truly difficult to fathom.

I could argue that Blue Sky Potential could be summed up as the total of all of the dreams, effort, desire, talent, passion, values, purpose, and potential unleashed in our lives. And yet, with that definition, we may still fall short of understanding the expanse of possibility found in our Blue Sky Potential. That is because our potential is not just for our benefit. It is also intended for the benefit of others. Did you catch that? It is easy to read and miss, and even easy to read and *dismiss*. The potential and possibility inherent in our blue sky is not only for us, but *for others* as well.

Remember my earlier comments about the emptiness I observed in very successful people that was the result of pursuing their own potential, for their own gain, and their own status? Remember how those experiences early on caused me to point the trajectory of my life in a way that is intended to ignite the gifts and talents in others?

I can't ignore that reality with you. I don't want that emptiness for you. Do I want you to self-actualize your own dreams and potential? Absolutely, without question. Yet, at the end of this book, if all that I have accomplished is to ignite you to pursue *only* a selfish new trajectory to actualize your own dreams and potential, then I have failed.

I will have led you to successful emptiness, or the emptiness of success, or I will have successfully led you to emptiness. However it is best worded, none of those descriptions measure up to true success for me.

On the other hand, if I have helped you begin to loosen the binds on all that that holds you back, so your life can take flight toward your intended potential to inspire, aid, benefit, and change the world by *your* life, then I have truly made the difference I am trying to make. *That* is the possibility found in the blue skies I dream about. That is truly *endless possibility*.

If you get ignited to lead a life of purpose and toward your potential, then I have ignited one life. Because you are worth it, it is also worth it to me. But… if in the process of igniting you to lead a life of purpose and potential, I am also able to create an understanding and a passion inside of you that your life is intended to do the same in others, then I have created in you the ability to touch 10s, 100s, 1,000s, or more. And together, along with a few others, we can change the world for good.

More than you can imagine, I dream that your life would not only be fulfilling and satisfying *for* you but would also be satisfying and fulfilling *through* you. Not only would it be a life of restored dreams beyond your imagination, but I dream that you would experience the joy of living a life that creates and leaves a lasting impact on the world around you. There is absolutely nothing like it on earth. That's because that kind of life doesn't live on earth—it lives in the blue sky of possibility.

I dream you will get a glimpse of something so lofty, so high in the blue sky of your potential, that it might even take your breath away. Begin to envision a life, your life, that exists not only unto itself, but also unto others. Begin to envision your life making a positive difference in the lives of people who not only want *but need* what you have to offer.

Take a few moments to pause and let that sink in…

Dare to imagine the joy on the faces and the hope in the hearts of those your life will touch. Take another deep breath. Close your eyes. Inhale. Exhale. Wait for it… *There it is.* There is a feeling of warmth somewhere deep inside. Embrace it. Maybe you haven't felt that for a long time. Maybe you have never felt that before. *Enjoy it.* Go ahead and smile. Set the book down and take it in for a few minutes. Do you want to know what that feeling is?

That feeling you have… It's *purpose.* It's *worth.* It's *value.* It's *identity.* It's *belief.* And, that feeling is powerful. As you lean into it more and more on this journey, you can learn to wield that power against all that holds you back.

A belief in endless possibility is a direct affront
to the leash of impossibility.

So, close your eyes again. Go ahead and shut out the voices that are coming against the truth that your life exists for a purpose. Even if it is a bit of a battle, don't let go of the feeling you are experiencing or let it be taken from you. Relax. Inhale. Exhale.

That warmth you are feeling is a sense that your life matters. It is a sense that you matter. In fact, it is more than a sense; it is a truth. You are important. You matter. You are not forgotten. You are not invisible. You are not alone. You have value. You have purpose. Undefined purpose as of yet, maybe, but that's ok. No need to worry about that at this point.

For now, simply dwell in the transcendent possibility that your life matters, has purpose, and is intended and designed to make a positive impact on others.

I told you I was going to stretch your thinking and expand your vision, didn't I?

We may not be at the summit on this journey yet, but we have definitely arrived at one of those scenic overlooks. Look out upon the expanse of the beauty of not only what your life could be, but what your life already is—a life filled with value, worth, impact, and purpose.

Don't let the fact that you don't feel like you are currently living in that potential ruin the moment. There is no room for guilt, shame, or regret right now. Just let the possibility of it all continue to warm and inspire you.

Your life is intended for a greatness that goes beyond you and beyond your imagination. The greatness of your life is intended to transcend the traditional understanding of personal fulfillment, and even the traditional understanding of how the world views success. Your life is intended to impact the world around you for good, and when it does, you will feel like you are soaring in your Blue Sky Potential. And, that leads to endless possibilities.

You are excited, aren't you? Maybe a little nervous again, right? That's ok. Me too. And, don't worry about that, either. Every time I come to this scenic overlook with someone, it triggers the nerves. Because it is quite breathtaking, even for me. Who wouldn't feel some nerve-stimulating adrenaline if they were here standing with us. The beauty of it all. The strength of it all. The *possibility* of it all; the possibility of the impact your life could make. As you consider the truth of this scenic overlook—that your life was made to make a positive impact on others—you can see the possibility of your life… and it is *endless*.

Take it in for a moment longer; it is worth the time. The possibility of your life and its positive impact on the world is worth the memory you are making right now. You'll need to remind yourself of the vision of what this looks and feels like during the journey ahead. For now, even if it doesn't have a detailed description, simply embrace the expanse of the possibility for which you were made.

Speaking of reminding yourself, you are coming up on another set of those free downloadable reflective exercises. This is a great moment to write these powerful feelings down, to recall them when the journey of discovering your purpose gets challenging.

We will talk more about defining your purpose later, but for now, understand that your purpose goes beyond your own experience; it includes the ability to send others soaring into their potential as well.

Once you are set free, you are empowered to set others free.

Orville and Wilber Wright had been pursuing the idea of creating a craft that would soar into the blue sky—in truth, pursuing their own potential as inventors, but also the potential of flight itself. They were pushing the boundaries on what was possible, and in doing so, they set in motion endless possibility. Their breakthrough technology set in motion a rapidly unfolding industry of flight. Many advancements soon followed, and still more advancements in flight are occurring to this day, none of which would have ever been possible if the Wright Brothers hadn't taken the approach they had.

The greater truth is this: in the end, it really isn't about me nor even about you or your own self-actualization—it's about using our lives to inspire, serve, and see others soar into their fullest potential. That is when our fullest potential is fully realized, and we are truly living a life of endless possibility. As much as we would like to, we can't fully help others move toward their potential until we are living more fully in our own potential.

To the extent that you aren't pursuing and living in blue sky, not only are you missing out on the greatness of your own life, but you are missing out on the joy of helping your family, friends, and others discover and experience their own greatness—to live in their own potential. Let's keep that in mind as we work on your breakthrough.

Let's start with you, your journey, your adventure, and how to move away from your current state of stuck and lost, remembering that as we unleash you into your potential, you can help others do the same. Now, I want to give you that map and help you begin to understand where your potential and possibility reside.

CHAPTER 5

OPPORTUNITY — IT'S MORE THAN YOU THINK

"Many of life's failures are people who didn't realize how close they were to success when they gave up."

- THOMAS EDISON

IMAGINE FOR A MOMENT THAT YOU ARE FEELING A BIT LIGHTER, A BIT more free, and a bit more hopeful. Imagine for a moment that you are feeling inspired because you have caught a glimpse of your potential, the shimmer of your purpose, and you are believing for the first time in a long time that your future is quite possibly filled with endless possibility. It feels good, doesn't it?

I too am imagining for a moment that is where you are right now. And, it feels good to me too. The truth is that it isn't just your imagination. It's a new view of the life you have been desperately wanting to experience.

There are probably a few voices trying to whisper doubt and

fear, but the scenic overlook was such an awe-inspiring sight, those voices are mostly held back at this point, drowned out by the voice of belief and possibility.

Bubbling up among what you are hearing is some version of, *"OK. So, you have taken me to some deep waters and to some thin air. I'm following you. I'm trusting you. But… dare I ask… how do I get from this scenic overlook to the blue sky of my potential and all that endless possibility you are shining a light on to help me see?"*

That's a great question. Fair and timely. I will answer it, I promise. But, before I do, it is time to pull out a map, or at least a few diagrams, to help you see where "here" and "there" actually reside.

In a sense, I want to allow you to identify yourself in a specific location, in many ways, just like a "you are here" marker on the display in the shopping mall, or the map out on that backcountry trail, or even the blue dot on your smartphone.

To give your mind and heart a better descriptive handle on where you currently are, where your potential and possibility reside, and the journey from one to the other, I want to introduce some additional metaphors with a bit more definition.

Without it, your search for your potential could be hindered or distracted at best. With it… well, it will still be quite the journey, but at least you will have a framework to turn to if you feel lost. As I unpack the framework of these diagrams, I will need to provide some definitions, much like the legend of a map, to help you understand the pictures and the markings. To be fair, they are going to look more like graphs from math or science class, but I will try and make them pretty…

A PRESENT & FUTURE REALITY

Let's start with your potential, way up there in the blue skies. Let's set the record straight—your life has always had a Blue Sky Potential. From the moment you were born, and each second that has passed since, your potential has had a trajectory. I'm sure some positive and negative experiences have impacted that trajectory, but for the sake of argument, let's consider your trajectory to be one of increasing potential, as evidenced by the chart below.

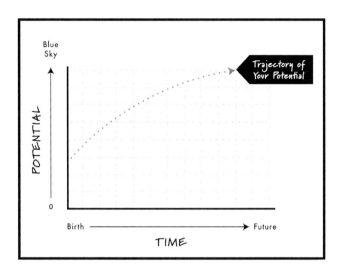

By looking at this chart, and based on how I have diagramed the *Trajectory of Your Potential*, you can see that even at the moment of your birth, you had potential. As a baby, there wasn't much self-actualization (unless you were a very early overachiever), but there was plenty of stored potential (which we will discuss more in the next chapter). As you grew up and developed the basics of walking, talking, and learning, your potential increased right along with those skills.

As you matured and developed through those adolescent years, you began to have a better understanding of your dreams, your desires, your hopes, and maybe even your unique gifts and talents—all of these attributes and character traits continuing to increase the potential of your life.

This same increasing of potential continues through early adult-hood, early career, and for some, throughout your career. Every experience, every learning, every part of your story (good or bad) can actually increase your potential and the endless possibility of the impact your life can make for others.

As I said before, you have probably had some positive and negative experiences that have impacted your potential. What I have experienced and discovered in my own life and in the lives of those I have guided may be surprising to you—even negative experiences can have a positive impact on potential. I will unpack that more in the coming pages, but for now, trust that idea and look back at the diagram.

In the end, even in its most simplistic form, you can see the trajectory line of your potential started at birth and then has been consistently increasing since that moment and is still increasing to this day. In a sense, even reading this book is increasing the height of the trajectory of your potential.

All that potential is residing somewhere up there in the blue sky. Your potential is a *present* reality, in the sense that it already actually exists. Just because you aren't living in it yet, does not deny its presence or existence.

Again…

> *Your potential is not a theoretical idea, but instead*
> *it is a present reality waiting for you to tap into it.*

So, if you can be set free, if you can discover where breakthrough happens and then truly experience genuine breakthrough, the reward of that potential is likely to also be a *future* reality. Your future truly can include the reality of soaring in the endless possibility of blue sky.

CURRENT REALITY

Throughout Chapter 4 and now the opening section of this chapter, we have been talking about the blue skies of potential and endless possibility. Now, however, it is time to talk a little bit about that corner of stuck and lost, through the imagery we are developing in this diagram. Just as much as your potential is a present reality, so too is the truth of the current reality in your life right now. Follow me as I add a new line to this chart.

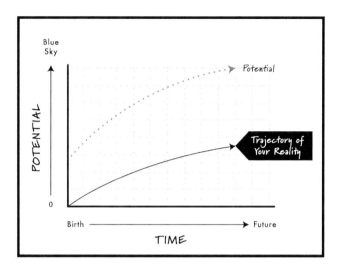

This new trajectory line is the *Trajectory of Your Reality*. You can see that this trajectory line of your reality starts below the trajectory line of your potential. Don't overanalyze. Don't worry that I placed it below the previous line. As I mentioned before, even at birth, you had more potential stored up within you than you were offering to the world. So, at birth, the reality of your impact was less than your potential. Makes sense, right?

As you can see on the chart, however, the hard truth is this… your reality line is *consistently* below your potential line. I'm not being harsh; *I'm being honest.* Unless for some reason, you have lived or currently are living up to or beyond your potential, the trajectory line of your reality is going to be consistently below the trajectory line of your potential. *Ouch.*

I know. It hurts to see it so plainly drawn out like that. It gives new meaning to that phrase *"reality bites,"* doesn't it? The truth is, however, that you would not have picked up this book and would not have made it this far in this book if it weren't so.

Let me keep advancing the diagram before I unpack any more disturbing reality. Let's add *you* onto this chart, as in you, right now. And let "you" be marked with an airplane, signifying that you are in flight, on the trajectory of your current reality.

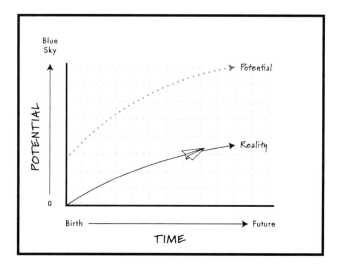

There you are! I see you up there, flying comfortably on the trajectory of your current reality. With excitement, I'm waving to you! You are waiving back too. Yet, as you think about it, you are probably not waving back with all that much enthusiasm (if you are even waving at all).

It's not like you are on the bow of a cruise ship, about to head out on seven days of Caribbean fun, waving excitedly to me and all the other people who are *not* on that ship (that is, unless you are reading this book while on a cruise ship, which is entirely possible, and makes me slightly envious).

In addition to the fact that you are most likely not on a cruise ship right now, the reason you are not excitedly waving back is that you aren't *that* excited about your current reality; even if it is a good reality currently, it just is not the reality you dream of.

Admittedly, there are parts of your reality that are really beautiful, I'm sure. But, there are plenty of areas of your reality that aren't so pleasant. So, waiving back to me from that vantage point might even feel a little exposing or a little embarrassing.

You dream about living in a better reality. That's one of the reasons you picked up this book. You dream about breakthrough, about finding your purpose, about being set free, about unleashing your potential, and now, perhaps, you dream about actually soaring in the endless possibility of the blue sky.

Think about the possibility of this, however… if I had placed your airplane up on the trajectory line of your potential, you would totally be waving back with excitement. Hey, you might even do some loops and other aerobatic maneuvers as you wink from the cockpit, because your life would be so rich, fulfilling, and rewarding that you couldn't help but show off a little. That's my dream for you!

But… you are *not* on the trajectory line of your potential. Your airplane is stuck, or lost, or both. Either way, in your current reality life definitely isn't soaring. Sadly, it likely doesn't even always feel like it is rising (a la the Montgolfier Brothers), let alone gliding or flying.

Sometimes it feels more like it is facing a few bumps, wind sheer, or even vomit-inducing turbulence. Worse, it can feel like life is completely stalling out. And, by the laws of aerodynamics, an airplane that has truly stalled is one that has lost all of its lift and is much closer to a tailspin than it is to rising, gliding, flying, or soaring.

It is not my intention to discourage you, so please don't be discouraged! In the short time we have been on the journey together, the reality of your situation has already begun to improve, which should give you some encouragement and hope. Yet, if you aren't keenly aware of how bad your reality is in comparison to your dreams, you won't be motivated to take the risk it requires to move from "here" to "there."

If you haven't noticed yet, the two trajectory lines I have drawn for you just so happen to split our chart into three sections, or layers of airspace, not unlike the earth's atmosphere has varying layers.

The scientific boundaries in the earth's atmosphere aren't hard and fast, as there is no physical line in the sky that separates one from another. Yet, we are still able to understand the concept that the atmosphere has various layers, each with a unique nature and unique properties. So too are the three layers of airspace in our diagram. Let's give these three layers a name and describe the unique nature and properties of each.

THE POSSIBILITY ZONE

Quite simply, above the trajectory line of your potential begins the layer of the atmosphere that I call the *Possibility Zone*, which exists way up in the unlimited canopy of blue sky. As we have discussed at length, your Possibility Zone is made up of your dreams, the desires of your heart, your potential, and the endless possibility of your life making a positive impact on others. It is the atmosphere of fellow dreamers, where your life is intended to live and soar.

We have already spent extensive time describing the uniqueness and nature of this zone, especially in Chapter 4. So, for the sake of this "you are here" diagram, we now have a name and an image of the location of where this zone exists.

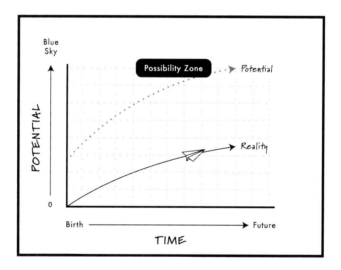

THE COMFORT ZONE

Just as the Possibility Zone exists in the atmosphere directly *above* the trajectory line of your *potential*, there is a zone that exits in the airspace directly *below* the trajectory line of your current *reality*. You most likely have already heard of this area, but you may have never understood it with the help of a diagram like this.

This layer of atmosphere is what I call the *Comfort Zone*.

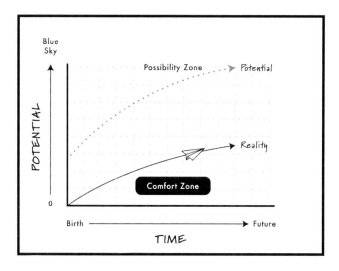

Oh no! It is that dreaded Comfort Zone that everyone always talks about. It is dreaded because most of us cringe when someone brings it up. It can feel so convicting when someone says something about it. And yet, it can feel so cozy and comfortable when we are looking to remain, well, *comfortable* in our current reality.

There is a good type of cozy and comfortable, as in enjoying a hot cocoa, while sitting in your favorite chair near a fireplace at Christmastime. And, there is a stuck and lost type of cozy and comfortable—the type of cozy and comfortable that lulls you to sleep, dulls your heart and mind, and ultimately traps you in the status quo. That is the danger of the Comfort Zone.

Here is how we get trapped. When we experience something that is challenging, it is often uncomfortable. That is because whatever is challenging us in some way is more often that not *actually* uncomfortable. Whether it is a new exercise discipline, a new diet, or a new job, there is a discomfort in the *new*.

In some ways, we work hard to learn the techniques, skills, and knowledge in order to get "comfortable" with that new exercise approach, nutrition plan, or new job. Growing to a place of competency and ability is a good thing, because when we get more comfortable in that way, we can often preform at a higher level. But only for so long.

For most of us, it only takes so long before competency is replaced with complacency. As a level of complacency begins to set in, we are no longer motivated by learning those new techniques, skills, and knowledge. When this happens, we begin a subtle acceptance of the status quo. And, when we accept the status quo, we can get trapped in our Comfort Zone.

When we are in our Comfort Zone, we often rationalize it by thinking things like *"well, I just had that challenging season a few months ago in the new job, so this steadiness is good for me right now. Things are working well, and I don't want to mess that up."*

It makes a lot of sense to rationalize in this way because very few of us enjoy a constant state of challenge or difficulty. Yet, for some reason, we assume that the smooth sailing is going to remain that way, so we attempt to ride it out as long as possible.

That isn't all bad, because there are actually some moments in life when it is healthy to simply sit back and enjoy some calm water for a bit. Yet, little do we realize that most likely there is soon coming another challenging season on the horizon.

When it comes, we are startled, if not frustrated, that it is interrupting our comfort. We then struggle and wrestle through that challenging season until we are back into a place of comfort. When we ultimately navigate back to a place of comfort, we redouble our efforts to maintain that cozy place and not let anything disrupt it. Which over time leads us to focus our life and navigate all our decisions around the motive and preference of *comfort*.

You can probably see where this is headed. We knowingly chose comfort and yet, as a result, we unknowingly choose to be trapped in the status quo of our own fortified Comfort Zone.

As this back and forth plays out from one season to the next, one year to the next, we don't realize it, but a new reality is being defined. It is a reality that is based on avoiding risk, cultivating a reluctance to change (because change disrupts comfort), and an unwillingness to grow (because new growth is challenging and, well, requires change, which disrupts comfort).

So, we cruise through life on the trajectory of our current reality, experiencing disruptions to our peace and comfort, only to fight our way back to our prior comfortable reality. Yet, because we value those smooth seasons, we rarely push ourselves to intentionally be uncomfortable and grow or develop in some way that is new.

As we fight for comfort, but defend against anything that would make us uncomfortable, which includes improving ourselves, the sad reality is that the real trajectory of our lives often begins to flatten. We move forward, but we rarely move upward. Yet, we long for more out of life, and often scratch our heads as to why we aren't experiencing more.

We post a lot of pictures on social media about how good, smooth, and steady our lives are, but it often is just a cover-up to the sense of stuck and lost that we feel in our souls. If we are honest with ourselves, we are spending most of our time and energy trying to stay comfortable and very little time actually going through what it takes to fly higher and soar—which if you haven't put the pieces of the puzzle together yet, requires a serious amount of *discomfort*.

In the end, that is the sneaky dangerous reality of the Comfort Zone. The sneaky part is that the Comfort Zone is comfortable, meaning it is a safe place to exist. Yet, it is also dangerous because when the motivation is to remain comfortable, that motivation will cause us to preserve and protect the status quo.

When we continually make decisions to navigate back to the safe, comfortable status quo, we effectively leash ourselves to the corner of stuck and lost. As a result, the trajectory of your life will be limited by the height of your Comfort Zone. Did you catch that?

The trajectory of your life will be
limited by the height of your Comfort Zone.

Here's the picture… accept the status quo for too long and the the trajectory line of your current reality will flatten, if not start to arch downward, all the while the trajectory of your potential will remain well out of reach. It's time to stop ignoring the dangers of the Comfort Zone and time to prepare to get uncomfortable. Because your dreams exist well outside your Comfort Zone.

If that description of being stuck and lost feels like you, fighting to maintain a level of comfort, all the while discouraged because you can't reach your dreams, well then, let that soak in for a few minutes.

At some point, if you want to reach your dreams, you are going to have to make a decision to leave behind all that is comfortable. There is no way around it. You cannot reach your dreams and remain comfortable at the same time, just as you cannot soar while leashed to the corner of stuck and lost.

THE OPPORTUNITY ZONE

There is still a third zone on this chart, one that separates your Possibility Zone from your Comfort Zone. Do you see that gap between your Possibility Zone and your airplane, stuck on the trajectory of your current reality at the top of your Comfort Zone?

That gap may even feel scary or overwhelming. That is under-standable; it's uncharted atmosphere, after all. It is quite a distance across that gap because it is like a great chasm. There is a lot of airspace that separates your dreams from your reality. Yet as I said earlier, please don't be discouraged. There is a reason to stay posi-tive. You have a guide with you now, and it just so happens that the layer in the middle, the layer represented by all that whitespace… that gap is my specialty.

Remember back in the Introduction when I told you about the passion of my life that keeps me up at night and wakes me up in the morning? It's right there in that gap—scary and overwhelming as it may be. I am here to help people like you. And, teams and organi-zations too. I am privileged to come alongside and guide people and teams to breakthrough, and inspire them toward their potential. It happens in many different forms, like in this book, but there are so many more ways I can help you later in the journey too.

While you might find all this white space in the gap discourag-ing, I am invigorated and motivated by it. That space is why I was created; why I exist. That space too is why we have found each other—because you need to elevate the trajectory of your reality from your Comfort Zone to your Possibility Zone, and I can help you do that. This is not a commercial by any means. It's a simple reminder and encouragement that you are not alone in this journey.

What is even better than that? Remember my opening thoughts, before the Introduction, when I shared my dream, my Blue Sky Manifesto... I'm not the only one you have with you. I have invited you into a community of dreamers who are truly seeking to soar above the clouds together.

You and I, as well as a small but growing community of dreamers, are on a journey together to move from our current realities to the blue sky of our potential. It is going to happen, my friend. For a lot of us, including you. I believe it.

Back to the whitespace... Let me explain more specifically how I see it. But to do so, let me change the focus of the conversation away from something that may be discouraging or scary to you and redefine the gap by something that is motivating and invigorating. Let me give a new introduction to the journey we are headed toward. That gap between your reality and your potential...

I call it the *Opportunity Zone.*

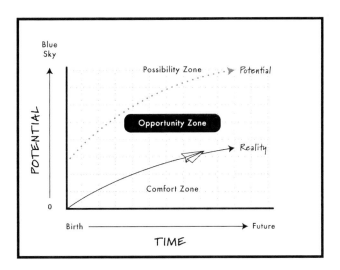

That's right, I call it the Opportunity Zone because it is filled with *opportunity.* No, I'm not just being optimistic. No, I'm not just looking through rose-colored glasses. No, I'm not just trying to spin your discouragement and change it into a positive outlook. As scary as this gap may seem, this is the Opportunity Zone, and as such, it is rich and teeming with the opportunity to learn, grow, develop, overcome, and of course, *transform*.

The reality is this… the Opportunity Zone is part of nearly every journey that traverses between reality of the Comfort Zone and hope of the Possibility Zone. No one who has crossed that gap has done so without navigating through the Opportunity Zone and laying hold of the benefits of growth, transformation, and the resulting courage it takes to make it through.

On one hand, I am hoping that having a name for it gives you a bit of hope. On the other hand, I recognize that being told you have to navigate through an Opportunity Zone, one that results in transformation, in order to reach your potential may not be exactly what you wanted to hear at this moment. But I wouldn't be a worthwhile guide if I didn't shoot straight and accurately describe the journey ahead.

You may also be hoping that it is as simple as giving you a few tips and tricks necessary to cross through the Opportunity Zone. Well, that would be easy, wouldn't it? Well, it's not quite that easy, but you already knew that. Good journeys that become great adventures are never that easy.

The fact is that we are going to spend most of the rest of our time together discussing the rich opportunity that a journey through the Opportunity Zone provides. We will unpack the unique nature and realities that exist in the Opportunity Zone in the coming chapters, but it is important to not leave this diagram unfinished.

CLOUDS OF CONFUSION

Even if you did want to leave the Comfort Zone behind, there still exists a reality that is preventing you from crossing through that gap. This reality predominately exists within the Opportunity Zone and it creates quite the barrier to your trajectory. Even if you are not trapped by the Comfort Zone, this barrier is lurking just above, and most likely is another major reason you have not already crossed through the Opportunity Zone on your own. I refer to the barrier as the *Clouds of Confusion*. Yep, take a look.

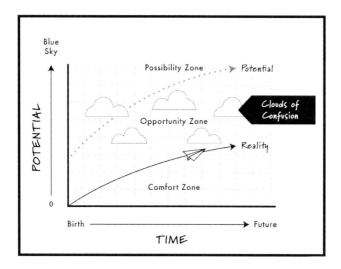

The Clouds of Confusion are simply that—confusing. I'm not talking about dizzied or discombobulated, like getting sucker-punched in a dark alley and waking up on the ground, perplexed and unsure what just happened. Well, actually, it may feel like that at times.

I'm also talking about the type of confusion where things feel uncertain, unknown, and unsettled. I'm talking about a lack of clarity, a lack of understanding, a lack of confidence, a lack of direction, and where it seems that there is no clear path forward.

Sometimes these Clouds of Confusion are created by the external circumstances of life—some of which we can control, some of which we cannot, some of which we created, some of which we have no idea how they came to be. These external clouds that can confuse our ability to see how to move forward can be physical, medical, relational, financial, vocational, and more.

Even if one of these areas of life is slightly off, misdirected, fragile, or broken, the resulting clouds can create enough of a barrier that we choose to keep our trajectory on its current path in our current reality and within our cozy, protected Comfort Zone.

To pursue our potential in the face of some of these clouds creates an inherent risk many are not willing to take.

Even worse, not all clouds are external; often the Clouds of Confusion that create a barrier to our potential come from within. These internal clouds are some of the most challenging to navigate. While sometimes created by or the result of those external circumstances, other times they originate in childhood wounds, doubts, fears, and experiences.

As such, the internal clouds can billow above us like a raging thunderstorm. Internal clouds like doubt, disbelief, fear, apathy, anger, bitterness, unforgiveness, discouragement, and depression can all quickly get out of hand, filling our skies with darkness and blocking most, if not all, of our view of our potential. If we can no longer see our potential, for most, there is no attempting to navigate toward it.

Are there *always* clouds that exist in our lives? No, certainly not. At certain times in life, these Clouds of Confusion are completely absent, and you have an unencumbered view of your Blue Sky Potential. Yet, even during these times, it is still going to take courage and quite the effort to navigate away from the Comfort Zone and through the Opportunity Zone.

Times without clouds are rare, and if that is where you currently are, you have a great opportunity, and the truths about unleashing your potential that are on future pages are going to accelerate you through that Opportunity Zone. Yet, don't skip the rest of this chapter, or the rest of the book for that matter, because Clouds of Confusion can often form when we least expect them.

AT OTHER TIMES IN LIFE, THE CLOUDS ARE SO THICK, SO DARK, SO locked in, for so long, you completely forget there is such a thing as blue sky. After a while, you can even forget there is any potential for your life to be a better reality than you are currently living.

When you are in one of those seasons of life where the dark and ominous clouds have you socked in for way too long, joy begins to wane, and hope begins to evaporate. When it gets really bad, one of the words I use to describe seasons like this is a *wilderness* season.

As for wilderness, I'm not talking about the inspiring, let's take a long weekend to go camping under the stars with a few friends and enjoy the beauty and glory of creation type of wilderness. I'm not even describing the "fun" of the wilderness as seen in the 1980s pop-culture flick *The Great Outdoors* with Dan Aykroyd and John Candy.

Even that version of wilderness would be a welcome experience compared to the barren, dry, empty and often lonely wilderness seasons that life can bring when it is all clouds, all the time, and we completely lose sight of even the idea of our life having potential.

Maybe you find yourself there right now, in some sort of a wilderness season. Maybe you aren't just a little bit confused, or a little bit lost. Maybe you find yourself just barely holding on, feeling stalled out, about to head into a tailspin. Maybe you are already in a tailspin.

Well, hold on. Don't let go of the yoke (the steering wheel in an airplane) just yet. Or, better yet, admit you can't fly the plane alone anymore and surrender to the idea that you need help, not just from me as a guide, but quite possibly something or someone bigger than the both of us.

Whether you want to hear it or not, or agree with me or not, I believe there is a God who loves you, who values you, who accepts you, who desires the best for you, and who longs to be known by you. That same God is the one who planted those dreams in your heart, who foresaw all the potential and possibility of your life, and who will never forsake you. Whether you know it or not, want to believe it or not, I believe God is with you right now and is going to stay right with you as you walk through and out of your wilderness.

And, it's ok if you aren't ready to let "God be your co-pilot" (which is a terrible bumper sticker, by the way). You can still count me in for helping you during your wilderness season. I've been lost in the wilderness seasons of life too, and I can assure you that you are not alone, and that you can make it through this season.

It is going to take a balance of holding on, letting go, and maybe even letting God (if I may be a little corny and cliché). If you can do that, this book is going to help you see blue sky again, but it may not be enough to get you completely out of that wilderness. If you find yourself in a wilderness season in life and feeling like all is lost, or about to be, definitely keep reading, but also consider seeking other professional help.

Whether it be pastors, rabbis, counselors, therapists, rehab centers, or helplines, there are far more people than you can imagine who are soaring in their own Blue Sky Potential by helping people who are in situations like yours. If you need professional help in a wilderness season, turn to those professionals first, and if you reach a point where you are a danger to yourself or others, don't hesitate to call the National Suicide Prevention Lifeline at 1-800-273-8255.

Wilderness-like seasons of life can be excruciating and cause a sense of helplessness and hopelessness, both of which can manifest in extreme emotions and behaviors. These seasons of life are not something to play around with, nor be ashamed of.

By the way, if you are enjoying the journey in this book, and you believe a similar journey on the topic of life's wildernesses would be helpful, I would love to hear about it. Simply reach out by email at jeff@jeffrasor.com and put "wilderness" somewhere in the subject line, and you'll hear back directly from me.

Again, I'm not here to replace those important professionals who are called and qualified to help you directly with the urgent and immediate needs—please turn to them first, especially when you are in need of that type of help. Yet, if I can be of assistance from a guiding/coaching standpoint, I would love to know about that. In the meantime, keep reading, and keep hanging in there. I'm already praying for you.

FOR MOST PEOPLE, THE REALITY OF LIFE IS THAT THEY ARE NOT currently at either extreme, but rather, somewhere between—between unending blue skies and overwhelming, ominous dark clouds. Truth be told, somewhere in between is where most of life is lived. Partly cloudy is where we spend most of our days, or partly sunny if things are going well.

Either way, the atmosphere is a mix of blue sky and gray clouds. There is enough blue sky to believe that there is more to this life than we are presently experiencing, yet there are enough Clouds of Confusion to keep us from attempting to take flight through the Opportunity Zone.

Anytime the Clouds of Confusion exist over our heads, even if they aren't dominating the sky, the thought of even attempting to navigate from our reality to our potential feels daunting, if not downright impossible. When Clouds of Confusion are present in any amount, we are often unable to comprehend that the Opportunity Zone can actually be an opportunity for learning, growth, development, and transformation.

Instead, we see the distance between where we are and where we want to be as a limiting barrier, filled with Clouds of Confusion that offer a high likelihood to get bruised, hurt, or disappointed.

The end result is that we continue to travel on the trajectory line of our reality, accepting a status quo, remaining in the safety of our Comfort Zone. We find comfort in the cozy nature of our reality, even if life isn't all that cozy. Deep inside, we know we are living woefully short of the trajectory line of our potential, but still, we are as lacking in motivation and as we are rich in excuses.

We put off the attempt to break free until the proverbial "someday," when we feel like there will be more time, treasure, or talent to risk the ascent into blue sky, or at least that is how we rationalize our delayed flight.

Well my friend, "someday" is not a day on the calendar, so we never get there. Taking that approach, it doesn't take long before we find ourselves tethered to the corner of stuck and lost, somewhere deep in our Comfort Zone, often trapped long before we ever realize it.

ONE MORE THING

From there, we begin searching for all the wrong things in all the wrong places, desperate to find a way to get unstuck. We attempt to add more power to our lives, as we discussed much earlier, and yet, we rarely break free from the tether.

It creates a vicious cycle of hope, attempt, trial, error, failure, despair, ultimately leaving us stuck and lost. It feels like it repeats, at times for years on end. The end result is that our potential feels well out of reach or even totally out of sight at times.

Sadly, stuck and lost can seep in deep and become a type of *identity*—a negative identity that is not at all like the positive identity we can discover when we find our purpose, as we hinted at in the last chapter. Stuck and lost, trapped in our Comfort Zone is not exactly the type of identity for which we want to be known.

Something needs to change. Something must change. Life was not intended to be lived like this. There must be something else.

Take a look at the diagram one last time and I will share one last thought.

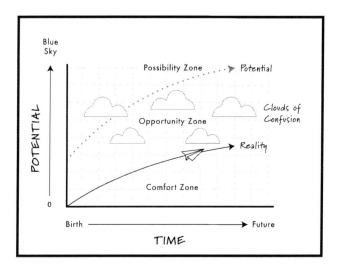

You are currently existing on the trajectory line of your reality, dreaming about soaring on the trajectory line of your potential in an unlimited canopy of blue sky. You know that if you could get up there, your life could truly be fulfilling and also count for greatness with endless possibility to impact others for good. Yet, the Clouds of Confusion are blocking a good portion of both the view of and the path to your potential.

These realties are keeping you leashed down to the corner of stuck and lost, far from being willing to navigate across the Opportunity Zone of learning, growth, development, and transformation that soaring in your potential requires. That about sums it up, now doesn't it? Right now, you are thinking yes, that's it. That explains my life! Now, what?

Well, there is something missing, something you can't quite put your finger on, one missing component. Let me share with you that one last thing that can and will change everything.

You are in need of a breakthrough.

There is no other way to say it. You need a breakthrough. You need both a break in those clouds, and you need to break free from what holds you trapped in your Comfort Zone. Whether you know it or not, you have been looking for breakthrough in a lot of ways and a lot of places, but you have yet to find where breakthrough happens, let alone how to experience it.

That's because a breakthrough can't be discovered, borrowed, bought, or begged for. A true breakthrough must be experienced, and genuine breakthrough experiences occur almost exclusively *while on* the journey through the Opportunity Zone.

This is why you must continue taking the steps to move you forward and upward. The breakthrough won't likely come until you are well on the journey across the Opportunity Zone and through the Clouds of Confusion.

As you continue to journey toward your potential, you will need to be set free from all that holds you back. As you take the risk to cross through those Clouds of Confusion, you are going to have the opportunity to experience a genuine breakthrough, or a series of them, and when you do, you will never be the same.

You are so close, so please don't give up now. Breakthrough is coming, my friend. But, like I said, it usually only comes as your life elevates, not necessarily before. So, let's get your life moving up.

To generate the lift you will need for the journey upward, you are going to need to tap into a fuel source. Fortunately, it has already been provided for you, so let's keep moving ahead and discover that fuel source together.

CHAPTER 6

FUEL — THE POWER OF TRANSFORMATION

"Transformation without work and pain, without suffering,
without a sense of loss is just an illusion of true change."

- WILLIAM P. YOUNG

EVERYTHING WE HAVE BEEN DISCUSSING UP UNTIL NOW HAS LED US TO this moment on the journey. There is more promise, potential, and possibility on the horizon of your life than you ever imagined would be possible at this point. You understand the weightiness of this moment. You are at the edge of the Opportunity Zone, and you are in need of a genuine breakthrough.

You have been needing one, or more than one, for a long time. You are hoping that experiencing a breakthrough is gentle, easy, quick, and filled with joy. I assure you, joy is often a natural result of a breakthrough, but it is not always the first emotion when experiencing a breakthrough. The reason is that there is a required process that must be engaged that precedes the experience of a breakthrough. That process has a name, which we'll get to soon enough.

Taking the next step on the journey is not for the faint of heart. You will be tested. You will be challenged. This is the place where inspiration alone will no longer move you forward. This is the place where you must choose daily, if not moment by moment, to remain steadfast.

As much as the Opportunity Zone is filled with the opportunity to learn, grow, develop, and transform, it is accordingly also wrought with challenges. It is those challenges that present the opportunity to transform. So, as you navigate and elevate through each challenge, you are going to grow in strength and beauty with each step.

Yet, as scary as it probably sounds, you have something going for you. You already have a natural resource that will fuel this breakthrough as well as future breakthroughs. You truly do have potential. And your unique potential is perfectly suited to provide the fuel you uniquely need to elevate through the Opportunity Zone.

As you are already painfully aware, you aren't doing as much as you could with the potential you have, but guess what that means? It means you have a whole bunch of potential stored up as fuel just for this moment and the journey ahead.

One word for the current state of your stored-up potential is *latent*, which means dormant or hidden (not unlike your dreams). Don't miss this… the definition of latent goes even further. In biology, latent also implies that whatever is dormant is only dormant until the right circumstances and conditions for development exist. In other words, it is stored up with purpose, waiting to breakout, so you can breakthrough.

We have talked about restoration already, that even those deepest dreams would come to pass in a better form than you would have envisioned. Part of that process is seeing your dreams reawakened, rekindled, rediscovered, revived, and restored to be sure. And yet, so too is the patience you need in the process of seeing your abilities, burdens, talents, desires, and purpose come to be.

What you must know, however, is that your potential is only

lying dormant or hidden until just the right time, when the circumstances and conditions are most suitable for its development. Remember, the Wright Brothers experienced this too. The science behind aerodynamics had recently been figured out. Small, but powerful engines were being created. And, two brothers were engineering the mechanical systems that would give them the ability to pilot flight—all of this happening at just the right moment in time.

Likewise, at just the right moment in time, all of your potential is going to be like a giant tank of fuel, waiting to be converted into power, so you can successfully experience the breakthrough you need in order to live a life above the clouds.

The conditions of the winds, waves, terrain, and the weather patterns in the Opportunity Zone are the perfect conditions for your potential to be shaped, developed, and put to use. In fact, I will go a step further. The ironic (and at times, frustrating) reality is that your potential *won't* get developed without you entering into the Opportunity Zone. And, that is what makes the journey so challenging and so different from anything you have experienced before.

The most challenging part of the journey is the very part of the journey intended to draw out your very best.

Don't skip over that. Let that sink in for a moment. There is a truth to that statement that is worth tucking into your back pocket and hanging onto. I'm even going to say it again.

The most challenging part of the journey is the very part
of the journey intended to draw out your very best.

This is why this next step is so transformative. You need the challenge of the Opportunity Zone more than you know. For your potential to be fully developed and begin to manifest, you will have to navigate into the challenging barriers that exist there. Then, one by one you will need to break through each barrier until you shoot though the Clouds of Confusion into the unlimited canopy of blue sky. That is going to take quite the effort and quite an amount of energy, and if we are going to need to produce energy, we need to tap into the fuel source of your potential.

POTENTIAL DEFINED

As we begin to look more closely at energy, fuel, and potential, it is necessary to explore some basic physics. Yep, *physics*. If I happened to just name your least favorite class in all of your schooling, please don't tune out now. We aren't going to use any physics equations. There won't be any pop quizzes, chapter exams, or even labs. So, don't fret. Instead of tuning out, simply tune in, lean in, and take notes, because with a few simple principles, you are going to understand more about breakthrough than ever before.

And, by the way, if you are a physicist, or if physics was your favorite class in all of your schooling, don't beat me up on any technicalities if I misspeak. My point isn't to teach physics. Rather, it's to use some of the concepts and principles as a metaphor.

I have said a lot of things already about potential—it's the sum total of your talents, your passions, your dreams, your hopes, and when in the blue sky of your potential, it leads to the endless possibility to live a life of greatness, a life that impacts others for good. Don't forget all that now, but let's take it back down to a simple, basic definition.

In its most simple form, potential generally refers to a *currently unrealized* ability. In other words, *stored* ability.

While that definition can create discouragement, it can also be encouraging, because currently unrealized ability does not have to stay that way. It can change into *future realized* ability.

In traditional physics, the study of energy is one area where the concept of potential is most easily understood. So, let me change a word in our definition of potential from *ability* to *energy*.

In physics, in its most simple form, potential generally refers to a *currently unrealized* energy. In other words, *stored* energy.

Again, *currently* is the key word, because just like with ability, energy does not have to stay unrealized. Is does not have to stay stored. It can change into *future realized* energy, which is often found in the form of *motion*. And, since you are at least somewhat stuck and lost, positive motion is a good thing. In physics, this type of energy is known as kinetic energy. Trust me, after these definitions, it isn't going to get any more technical.

As a review, the two forms of energy we are talking about are:

1. Potential Energy—Stored Energy
2. Kinetic Energy—Energy in Motion

It's that simple. That's all you need to know to understand what I need to share with you.

Just as there are two forms of energy in basic physics, the same is true for your potential, or your ability. Your potential can either be stored or in motion. Maybe stored is a nice way of saying stuck, but you get the picture. Most likely, you feel like your ability is stuck or stored or on hold in some way. Again, I would argue that it is *latent*, or stored up while waiting for the exact right conditions.

Yet, your desire is to see your life moving forward. Great. But to understand how to fuel that forward motion, I want to take this physics lesson a bit further. Let's take a look at a physics example based on a bicycle to help you more deeply understand the relationship between potential energy and kinetic energy, between stored energy and energy in motion, between stored ability and ability moving forward.

LET'S GO BACK TO THE WRIGHT BROTHER'S BICYCLE DAYS, PRIOR TO any thought of flight. Both brothers were known to have enjoyed recreational cycling, and each purchased their first bicycles in 1892. But like many brothers who do things uniquely, they approached cycling very differently. While Wilbur preferred long rides in the countryside of Dayton, Ohio, Orville was considered a "scorcher" while enjoying racing on the road and on the track.[1]

Their pursuit of this recreational hobby led to a growing reputation in their community, not only as skillful cyclists but as skillful mechanics too. Fixing their own bikes as well as the bikes of their friends, the word got out. By 1893, the brothers decided to open a small bike rental and repair shop, known as the Wright Cycle Company to service the needs of the local cycling community.

By 1897, the enterprise had grown to five different locations throughout the west side of Dayton. During that time, they also added retail bicycle sales to the mix of rental and service business, eventually carrying more than a dozen bicycle brands.[2]

During that period of business growth, cycling at large was growing too. By the mid-1890s, more than 24 competing bicycle shops were operating in and around Dayton. Wilbur and Orville needed to find a way to soar above (pun intended) the stiff competition they were facing, so in 1895, they decided to begin to manufacture their own bicycle line with the first model hitting the market the following year, in 1896.[3]

Deciding against the use of modern manufacturing and assembly techniques, the brothers produced hand-crafted originals, touting their high-quality mechanisms and constructed frames in addition to a polished, durable enamel finish. As an aside, a decision to hand manufacture their bicycles is consider by historians to be an important piece of the puzzle that explains why the Wright Brothers had the aptitude to create the mechanism that would help pilot and control a powered airplane.

In total, the brothers manufactured approximately 300 bicycles under their label, and yet, only 5 are known to still exist today.[4] What is rarer than one of their bicycles, in fact, so rare that it is non-existent, is a picture of Wilbur or Orville on or even with a bicycle. Not just one of their bicycles, but *any* bicycle.[5]

So, back to our physics lesson about potential and kinetic energy, using a bicycle to help us understand the concepts. Since we have no picture, we will have to imagine. Imagine their vintage, top-of-the-line model bicycle, known as the Van Cleve, sitting at the top of a very tall hill. Let's assume the bike is chained to a fence, allowing it to remain standing, but clearly resting (i.e., not in motion).

For the sake of this exercise, imagine that you are sitting on that beautiful, brand new Van Cleve, enjoying an amazing view from the top of that very tall hill. As you are envisioning this, remember that the bicycle is remaining still, chained to a fence at the top of the hill.

According to the basic physics definitions that we have covered, the 1895 Van Cleve (with you still sitting on top of it, of course) has a tremendous amount of *potential* energy. Remember, potential energy is simply stored up energy. Based on the height of the hill, the combined mass of you and the bicycle, the force of gravity that is pulling on the bicycle, and maybe a few other things, there exists an inherent stored, or *currently unrealized*, potential energy in that bicycle.

As long as it is just sitting there, the potential energy stored in it remains significant and constant—meaning it never loses its potential energy. You can't deny it, you can't minimize it, you can't change it. The potential energy in the bike simply *is*. Not unlike the potential of your life, really. You can't deny it, you can't minimize it, you can't change it. It has not been damaged or stolen—the potential of your life right now simply *is*. Your potential is significant and stored up, waiting to be released.

Back to the bicycle... You and that bike will simply sit there, forever, not going anywhere. *Unless and until* you are unleashed from that fence and impacted by some force that releases you and the bike down the hill. We will discuss that force in the next chapter, but for now, you are just sitting there.

I'm waiving at you again, *you cyclist, you*, sitting at the top of that hill, decked out in your best cycling kit, looking all turn of the 19th century, so sporty and dapper. You look like you are ready for fun, but life on the bike isn't very fun right now, is it? You aren't even "riding" the bike, now are you?

Nope.

You are just sitting there, going nowhere, and you are getting an intensifying pain in your... backside. There is no arguing though, according to physics, you have a whole bunch of potential, stored energy that is currently unrealized. Lots of potential energy, absolutely no movement or motion. Lots of potential, not much fun.

For now, however, let's assume that something or someone was to set the bike loose, to set it free or unleash it. Why? Well, after all, a bicycle has purpose, and its purpose is usually intended for more than just sitting there, stuck and lost, chained to a fence. And, if a bike, made of metal, rubber, and plastic has more purpose than remaining stuck and lost tethered to a fence, how much more purpose do *you* have?

That was a rhetorical question that actually deserves an answer, so I will answer that—you have *infinitely* more purpose. So, again, let's assume some force causes the bicycle to be set free and move more in alignment with its purpose. As this unleashing force is applied, you and the bike begin to roll down the hill. *This* is where things get exciting.

Now that you and the bike are in motion, a new form of energy is in play—kinetic energy. Remember, kinetic energy is energy in motion. Even with just a little bit of kinetic energy, your bike ride is a whole lot more fun, now isn't it? The pain in the backside you were feeling isn't quite as noticeable. A smile is coming over your face as you feel a light breeze. Yes, this is already much better! Kinetic energy (energy in motion) is so much more fun than potential energy (energy that is stored up and stagnant)!

At this point, imagine you have only traveled part way down the hill. According to physics, you are now experiencing both kinds of energy at the same time. You and your Van Cleve are in motion, and that kinetic energy is creating the fun and joy you are experiencing. Yet, you are still quite a way up that hill, which means the combination of the height of your current location, the combined mass of you and the bike, and gravity's relentless force, you still have a solid amount of potential energy still stored up.

At this moment in the bike ride, you are experiencing both kinetic and potential energy at the same time. You have some energy that is in motion and still lots of stored potential energy. This is not necessarily a bad place to be—at least you are moving forward, with plenty of more fuel to keep going.

With each second that passes, however, your speed increases as you continue down the hill. In the realm of physics, something is happening behind the scenes that you don't yet realize. You are experiencing increasing amounts of kinetic energy (motion), while exhausting, or using up the potential (stored) energy that remains in you and the bike. The physics principle you are experiencing is a transfer of energy.

The potential energy is being transferred into kinetic energy as you race down the hill. With more and more momentum, you realize it's fun, it's fast, and it's exhilarating. As you experience this, your joy is evident, and your face is simply glowing and radiant. Best of all, you have all but forgotten about the pain in your lower extremities.

I believe the physicists out there will appreciate if I go a little further. There is a more accurate word than "transferred" that can be used for describing what happens as potential energy becomes kinetic energy. This exchange of energy is called *conversion*. At the top of the hill, you had a tremendous amount of stored, potential energy.

As you are racing down that hill, the potential energy is being *converted* into kinetic energy, and thus you now have motion, action, and a smile. Let's imagine as you reach the bottom of the hill, the road that continues is perfectly flat.

As you know, the momentum that has been generated will allow you to continue rolling on that flat road for some time. At this point, all of the potential energy (relative to the ground) has been used up or, rather, converted into kinetic energy. Just as at the top of the hill, you had 100% potential energy and absolutely zero kinetic energy, now racing full speed forward on the flat at the bottom of the hill, you have 100% kinetic energy and absolutely zero potential energy left.

All of the stored, potential energy was converted into kinetic energy. What *was* unrealized potential energy *is* now fully realized, manifested energy that is moving you forward, and fast I might add. Truth be told, if there weren't forces like wind resistance, drag, and friction, 100% of the stored energy would result in 100% energy in motion, and you would continue racing ahead on that bike and never come to a stop.

Unfortunately, life can be a drag, as you know, and can inflict resistance on our trajectories, like winds, weather patterns, and storms that push against our forward motion as we attempt to elevate through and above those clouds.

Yet, we can see there is a relationship between stored energy and energy in motion, and that relationship is based on a *conversion* experience. The physics principle of conversion is what helps us understand the concept of realizing, manifesting, and fulfilling the stored up potential energy.

The same is true for us, but for the human journey of turning potential into reality, there is a word and a concept that is better than conversion. For you to experience the process of your potential becoming your in-motion reality, you are going to need to experience *transformation*.

TRANSFORMATION

Like conversion, transformation is the process that describes the relationship between your stored-up potential ability and a future of forward movement, motion, and momentum. Without this transformation of power, it will be next to impossible to reach your Blue Sky Potential. It is transformation that converts your latent potential into fuel, so you can soar upward into the blue skies. As we have discussed, the best place to seek transformation is by leaving your Comfort Zone in order to navigate and elevate through the Opportunity Zone.

I have already made the case—from the moment you were born and every experience since, your life has had a tremendous amount of potential. You have abilities, talents, passions, experiences, desires, and dreams that all contribute to the purpose that is bottled up inside of you, the potential bound up all around and within you. But, for your stagnant life and latent potential to be converted into a new reality, a new form of ability, a new manifestation of all of your gifts, talents, dreams, and desires, you must experience the *process of transformation*.

A simple, albeit limited, definition of transformation is this: a thorough or dramatic change in form or appearance.

As a culture, we love the idea of that type of transformation.

Episode after episode, we consume television shows filled with stories of home, face, and body makeovers. We seek out before and after pictures on social media. We buy cars that give us a new view of ourselves. We order products that help us see ourselves differently, or at least cause others to see us how we want to be seen.

We are constantly on the hunt for a new form or appearance. Yet, we sell ourselves short when we call it transformation, let alone buy a new form or appearance, thinking it will transform us.

To be fair, once in a while, these things are part of a real transformation, but all too often, the "transformation" is only surface deep—limited to a new form, or a new appearance, picked up off the shelf, from the online store, or the facial tutorial video you saw on social media. All fine items, products, and outcomes, but often there is no deeper internal change—only change to the outward form or appearance. Instead, true transformation is much different; it is so much deeper.

True transformation is a change to the very nature of a thing or person into a completely different nature, whether by natural or supernatural means.

A genuine transformation will change *everything*. When we experience transformation, our very *essence* has indeed transformed. The reason our nature is different than it was before is due to the fact that transformation changes us to the core. And, when I say core, I mean deep, as in the soul, the spirit, the mind, the heart—and often, all of it together.

Not only does transformation overhaul us at the core, but because our core changes into something very different, so too does how we see things, how we understand the world, how we see and understand *ourselves*.

In basic biology, this type of transformation is referred to as a metamorphosis. Most often, metamorphosis occurs when an insect or amphibian transforms during its lifecycle from an immature form to an adult form in two or more distinct stages. For us non-insect, non-amphibian types, we do not experience biological metamorphosis like this, but our transformations are often similar in character.

When our essence is changed, when our nature is changed by transformation, it often results in moving us from a place of immaturity to a place of maturity. When we experience a transformation in our lives, usually we can look back over history and see that we "grew up" through the process. Something about our younger nature was left behind, and something about our new nature is very different, often more mature or more seasoned.

For this reason, most transformations are often holistic, or all-consuming, meaning they impact us in many significant areas. More often than not, a transformation changes us spiritually, physically, emotionally, relationally, vocationally, or at the very least, set in motion changes that transform those areas. As a result, our very nature actually matures, shaped by the experience of transformation.

Transformation is not simply change for the sake of change, however. We experience the transformation purposefully—it shapes us, reorients us, and redefines us in order to exist successfully in a new unseen future. Transformation can be hard and painful to say the least, mostly because it involves change on a substantial level. Yet, it readies us for something we weren't quite ready for before.

Maybe you are starting to back away a little bit. Maybe all this talk of change and transformation is too much to bear. Well, let me ask you a couple of questions…

- Do you think the nature of who you are today—stuck on the trajectory line of your current reality, far beneath the trajectory line of your potential, separated by a bunch of Clouds of Confusion and an Opportunity Zone—can that nature magically elevate you to a possibility that you have only dreamed of?
- Do you believe that without significant change, the essence of who are today can successfully soar and thrive in the blue skies of your potential? Or, lead a life of significance, impacting others for good?

Without trying to discourage you, there have been dozens of times in my life when I looked up toward my dreams and realized a bunch of transformation was required in order for me to ascend and thrive higher in the blue skies of my potential. And not, because "I'm not good enough," but instead because "I could be better." I was willing to accept the challenge of transformation, knowing I wold be stronger on the other side.

You see, the transformation process has purpose. Just as a cocoon has purpose for a caterpillar, preparing it for its mature stage of life as a butterfly, the transformation process prepares you for a future stage of life. And, not only does that preparation lead to increased maturity, it develops your wings. And, you need wings to soar.

If your nature does not transform like that of a butterfly, you will never fly, nor express the beauty that your life was intended to express. You will simply stay stuck as an extravagant version of a worm, watching everyone around you transform and soar away.

The transformation process prepares you to thrive in a future reality that you are not even prepared to survive within today.

You have all the potential you need, but you aren't ready to fly in the way you were intended. Release (or unleash) a caterpillar in the sky, and it free-falls to its death (well, unless it just bounces, dusts itself off, and starts crawling again). But a transformed caterpillar— i.e., a butterfly—when released, will naturally take flight, majesti-cally. That maturity, that growth, that development, that *transforma-tion* is not just for your good and the good of your future, but it is also *necessary*.

At the beginning of this chapter, I shared that this step is not for the faint of heart. That's because transformation requires patience, perseverance, trust, faith, and a good deal of risk. Because transfor-mation is the result of the effort you offer during the challenges you face while in the Opportunity Zone, where the conditions and circumstances for converting your latent and unrealized potential into fuel are perfect. In that way, the Opportunity Zone is like your cocoon, if you will.

To fully take advantage of the Opportunity Zone, and the need to fuel your transformation while in it, there is a basic element you must understand. At its most basic level, transformation requires *change*. Some love the idea of change and the experience of change, so they get excited at the prospect of transformation, but others... not so much.

For many, the very word, dare I say it again, *change*... ugh... disgusts them. Still for many more, it even can cause immense fear. But, let's take the bar even lower.

At an absolute minimum, transformation requires you to possess a *willingness* to change. To be candid, you should not even have transformation on your radar if you are dogmatic, stubborn, and unwilling to change who you are at some level. Which also means you should not have blue sky on your radar either. Without a willingness to change, you are destined to remain stuck.

I have a piece of art on the wall in my office that says, "Be true to who you are." It is a bold and self-affirming statement in the face of a world and culture that wants to shame you and tear you down for "who you are." At times, in the face of misinformed criticism, I have needed the reminder that comes with that phrase. As much as that phrase can provide strength, there is also something about that phrase that I really don't like.

I know that sounds odd, especially considering it is on my wall, but it's true. The reason is that many people use the phrase "be true to who you are" to justify a lot of things about them that actually *need to be changed.* I know so many people who wield that statement like a sword to anyone and everyone who suggests that they might need to change something. And, if you have this posture, it will most likely keep you from your dreams.

I meet and talk with so many people who want to soar in their Blue Sky Potential, to live a life of greatness, and to make a difference, but those same people are so set on staying "true to who they are," they rarely become who they are supposed to become. Deep down they want to be someone different and will say as much, but then they will throw "I'm going to be true to myself" in anyone's face who suggests a change. It makes me wonder if they really want to be who they say they want to be.

I meet so many people who say they want a better marriage, but they won't change the way they spend their time, spend their money, or how they communicate and interact. I meet so many people who want to be better parents, or at least have better kids, who won't change anything about how they parent. I meet so many people who want to be seen by their employer in a new light, but they won't grow or develop in a new way. I meet so many people who wish they could dig deep and manifest their destiny, but they just can't get any traction toward that end, because they won't change any of their attitudes, habits, patterns, or how they go about their day.

So, in order to avoid the selfishness-inducing view of this phrase, I have learned to look at the "be true to who you are" phrase in a different way than most. I have discovered I can wield that phrase like a mirror, helping me see what needs to change, which has become very, very beneficial. Here is how it works. As I see that piece of art on the wall and read that phrase, I often add a parenthetical statement and say it to myself like this, "Be true to who you are (unless you need to change; then change)."

By adding that phrase in my head, it is like looking in the proverbial mirror with honesty and humility. The ancient Greek philosopher Socrates is generally credited with sharing the astute statement on wisdom: "Know thyself." He later expounded on the phrase teaching that, "the unexamined life is not worth living." So, when I look in the mirror of "Be true to who you are (unless you need to change; then change)," I am able to examine my own life on some level from an objective perspective.

As a mirror, it allows for a revealing of the good, the bad, and the ugly. When I find any bad and ugly in that mirror, and I am honest and humble about it, having at least a willingness to change, I can encourage myself to seek opportunities to change. Unfortunately, not everybody looks in the proverbial mirror this way, and therefore, many do not have the ability to healthily identify areas of necessary change.

With only a rare exception, what I have discovered is most people who are stuck have one thing in common: they are simply unwilling to change. Yet, they wonder why they can't transform, why they can't reach their potential, why they aren't thriving in life. They won't change the way they see the world. They won't change the way they see their circumstances. They won't change the way they see others. They won't change the way they see themselves. They won't change *anything*, as if *change* is a threat to their existence. Well, actually they have got that one *right*.

Change is a threat, of course.
Change is a threat to a stagnant existence.

If this is hitting too close to home, you may need to take some time to process this. You may need to put down the book and take an internal inventory. Ask yourself, "If I am not willing to change—if I am not willing to transform—then what?"

May I suggest an answer to your question? You may need to answer yourself with this, "Quit whining and accept that life as it is right now as the *best* my life will ever be."

If you aren't willing to transform, then go ahead and "be true to who you are." Go ahead and look in the mirror and fall in love with your current status quo. The life you have now is the life you love and is the life you will love the rest of your life, until you don't love it any longer. Forget about that eventual reality for now—at least you will never have to change a thing. That is, of course, not changing anything other than changing the name of the intersection from "the corner of stuck and lost" to "the corner of being true to myself right here leashed to this bench of my current reality for like, forever."

If you feel like I'm being harsh, I too am realizing that I am. I didn't plan to be harsh. But the truth is I have unintentionally changed my approach, for this moment, specifically for a reason. Up to this point, I have been kind and gentle, tending to the garden of your soul, delicately waking up dreams, speaking about your potential and endless possibility. These are very fragile things, kept deep in the soul. As such, I value the gentle truths that need to be unpacked to bring them to light and into reality again.

But, this issue of not being willing to change... It is not a delicate issue. It is a fortified wall, a fortress around your heart, mind, and spirit, established to protect yourself from criticism, judgement, and shame. If you have a major wall up, it is likely your heart has been under assault a good deal of your life and you simply decided to "be true to yourself" as a way of protecting your heart. I get it. At times, life hurts, and more often and more deeply than we ever imagined possible.

Other people are a part of that hurt, and too often the source of that hurt, especially when and how they tell us to change. Even if they don't say it with words, they say it with their attitudes, decisions, and actions as they walk out on us, abandon us, choose someone or something instead of us, betray us, or forget about us. You never intended to put that wall up, but you did—mostly because you were hurt so deeply.

Nearly everyone who spoke to your need to change with words or actions did so from a place of selfishness, anger, judgment, misunderstanding, hatred, drunkenness, guilt, religion, or shame. Unfortunately, few, if any, of those mandates to change were delivered with the motive of love. So, your wall went up and was fortified with pain and bitterness. For good measure, you likely made some version of a "never again" vow to yourself.

Yet, unlike your prior experiences, I'm delivering a blunt truth to that fortified wall out of the motive of love. Blunt is not always mean. I'm simply being blunt because I care. And because that wall of "I will be true to myself and never change" needs to be knocked down if I'm going to help you find freedom and begin to soar.

As much as it is protecting you, that wall is holding you back. I have seen too many people get stuck behind that wall, never wiling to change and, therefore, never able to transform to reach their potential.

For all the people I have guided to discover and pursue their potential, I have met just as many who have chosen to turn away, to fall short, and who too often complain about it. For years. Yes, I have watched people, people I love and care for, mind you, spend multiple decades not changing, yet always complaining about how life doesn't change for them. While the wall was built to keep others out, sadly, the wall-builder too often gets trapped behind that wall in the shackles and chains of bitterness, blame, and regret.

My friend, I love you enough to tell you that it is time to change your unwillingness to change.

Because I care for you enough to want to see you transform. Here lies a difficult reality associated with transformation.

Transformation is a choice—it is a choice of surrender.

I imagine that wall was built, so you could defend and at times simply survive, but it wasn't built because you were planning to surrender. No, you planned to set up camp behind it and hunker down, maybe forever. Yet, now that you can see a glimpse of your life and your dreams being restored, that fortress is keeping you from moving ahead and keeping you from launching into the blue sky.

My friend, the wall needs to come down, and the fortress needs to be surrendered. If you want your life to change, you are going to have to change how you live your life, beginning with how you see your life and see the world around you. You are going to need to be willing to change. You need to be willing to be transformed. Surrender your right to "be true to who you are" and change. You will be better, stronger, and more beautiful for it.

THERE IS ANOTHER WAY THE "BE TRUE TO WHO YOU ARE" PHRASE works like a proverbial mirror for me, helping me reflect on my current reality. I truly believe there is a deeper truth at work in the statement. It is another reason I keep it hanging on my wall. When you dream of blue skies, when you dream of living out all of your potential, when you dream of the endless possibility of living a life that impacts others for good, I assume you envision you are living out what it means to become and be the very best version of yourself. I know I do.

I assure you that when I think of soaring in the blue skies of my potential, and the endless possibility that follows, I envision becoming and being the best version of myself. And, when I envision living out the best version of myself, I know the blue sky will hardly contain my trajectory. So, when I look at the piece of art on my wall, sometimes I add a different parenthetical reference than the one I have already shared.

Sometimes I say, "Be true to who you (*truly*) are," as in the very best version of your future self. The phrase is still working like a mirror, but this time, instead of reflecting the good, bad, and ugly of my current reality, it reflects something so much better, so much brighter, so much more hopeful.

It reflects back to me a vision of the unlimited possibility that the future holds for me. What I discover in that moment is that I am simply *not yet* the version of myself I see that I can become when I envision my life soaring in the endless possibility of blue skies. Now, *that* is inspiration to change and motivation to transform if I have ever seen it.

When you can get a glimpse of the best version of yourself, nothing should stand in your way, not even that fortified wall of self-preservation.

You see, I love the "be true to who you (truly) are" version of the mirror because I love the better version of me I see in that mirror—the best version of myself I have yet to fully become. I also love the "be true to who you (truly) are" version of the mirror because I love the better version of *you* that you have yet to become. For you to get from "here" to "there," it is going to take a transformation—a transformation filled with purpose.

If change is a threat to a stagnant existence,
then transformation is a gateway to an unlimited future.

What will it be for you, my friend? Stagnancy. Or, unlimited future. It's your choice. Fortress wall. Or, surrender. I will answer for you. You want an unlimited future, and therefore, you want surrender. Surrender is a choice to let go of who you are (unchanging) to become who you truly are (transformed).

Since you are beginning to surrender (which is a good thing), let me share another quick secret—transformation must become an *ongoing* reality. Remember, transformation is the process that converts the fuel of stored, unused, unrealized potential in your life into forward moving, realized, and manifest ability.

One experience of transformation will only get you so far. You will not easily get the blue skies of your potential without continuous transformation. Therefore, transformation is not only a *now* thing but is a *future* thing too. Once you surrender, it's good you keep that posture because it will accelerate your journey through the Opportunity Zone. Here's why:

Transformation happens not only *before* you soar, and not only *as* you soar, but so that you will *actually* soar.

Since it is the process that converts unused ability into forward motion, transformation will be necessary for the entire rest of your journey, as you continue to elevate to new levels of seeing your potential realized. When I meet someone who is no longer willing to transform, even if they transformed before, I can already tell you, they have decided to stop pursing their potential.

Oh, they will tell you otherwise but watch closely. Their acceptance of stagnancy will halt the conversion of unused potential, and they will not have the fuel to elevate any higher into blue sky. They will tell you they want more, but they will not live like it nor actually reach for it.

I encourage you to take a few moments, and really process this —spiritually, emotionally, relationally. Dig deep and make sure somewhere deep inside your heart you are at least willing to change. If you are, then take a few extra moments and simply surrender.

Whether surrender is best accomplished for you through a journal entry, taking a walk, saying or writing a prayer, or talking to a trusted friend, it doesn't matter. Simply find a way to come to a place of surrender, a willingness to change and be transformed. Without it, it will be all but impossible to experience a genuine breakthrough. But…

With a heart surrendered for a lifetime of ongoing transformation, well, my friend, breakthrough is right around the corner and once you experience it, there will be no stopping you.

CHAPTER 7

BREAKTHROUGH — LIVE ABOVE THE CLOUDS

"A breakthrough is a moment in time when the impossible becomes possible."

- TONY ROBBINS

To this point, I have been leaning heavily on the visuals and metaphors associated with flight and blue sky, with a few added visuals about you on a bicycle. I have also been leaning plenty into the visual of taking a journey, allowing for whatever version of a journey comes to your mind. I have done so with great purpose, trying to use visionary and imaginary language to allow your heart and spirit to fill in the blanks and the pictures.

Of course, we will continue working with the metaphors of flight and blue sky because it is most fitting to how I personally see the pursuit of potential. But that metaphor only speaks to the journey upward and into the sky. So, what about using some metaphors that speak to the journeys that can be taken over land or by sea?

Many a great journey and adventure have occurred this way, and these images and descriptors will be useful for those who better identify with these types of journeys.

If you follow ancestry and lineage, you may appreciate knowing that my 14th generation grandfather on my father's mother's side was named John Alden. He was the barrel maker on the Mayflower that sailed from Plymouth, England, in 1620. It's true: my "grandfather" had a major role in one of history's most well-known adventures. Risking it all as one of an estimated 30 crew members, along with 102 documented original Mayflower passengers,[1] he sailed the open seas in search of the possibility of what could be—not just for him but for those on the ship, and unbeknownst to him, for millions of others who would follow over the next few hundred years.

As a child, I was able to visit Plymouth Rock, in Plymouth, Massachusetts, the site and actual stone traditionally held as the landing spot of the Mayflower. While there, I even had the opportunity to walk in a few tourist shops named after him, which was a surreal experience.

Surprisingly, that may not be my only relation to a historical adventurer. While I have not personally seen the documentation yet, according to family lore, my wife's family is descended from Pocahontas, another definitive historical figure, partly credited with influencing peaceful relationships between English Settlers and Native American tribes. Those in the family that claim it are believable people, but I haven't gotten my hands on the documentation yet. Regardless, it is neat to consider the possibility.

With all that potential heritage from a pioneer of the sea and an adventurist of the land, it's funny that I identify more with flight and blue skies. Unfortunately, to my knowledge, I have absolutely no lineage flowing from the Wright Brothers, or even the Montgolfier Brothers, or anyone related to flight, rockets, or space. But, I digress… let's get back to the journey.

BLUE SKY VISUALS

For now, let me take the diagrams and concepts we unpacked in Chapter 5 and describe for you a couple different but similar metaphors for taking a journey into your potential. You may wonder why I'm doing this. My motive is simply to allow you to grasp these concepts with the most meaningful metaphor for you.

I imagine not everyone is moved by jets soaring in the sky as I am, and not everyone has a fighter jet ride-along on their bucket list. So, I want to expand some of the visionary language into other relatable metaphors with the hopes of deepening the inspiration and motivation you have right now.

Additionally, more than just the imagery and metaphors that relate to different people, another reason I want to expand to a wider variety of pictures and metaphors is as you begin to pursue your potential, the inspiration and guidance isn't going to come from this book alone. I want to help you connect to a world that is calling out these same themes that you are experiencing.

Pop culture, fine art, other fiction, and non-fiction literature, poetry, scripture, music, movies, and the like are expressing many of the themes you are discovering on this journey with me. If I were to categorize all of the above areas of focus into 3 general categories, I could easily make the argument that art, literature, and culture are screaming the realities and truths we have covered.

From feeling stuck and lost to down and out, to dreams being dashed and laid waste, to feeling like the underdog, to overcoming, winning, and finding restoration, to turning the tables on our circumstances, to seeking our potential and manifest destiny…

All of these are common themes. The human journey is that of drama, plot twists, joys and sorrows, celebration and mourning, success and failure. The best books, the best movies, the best documentaries, the best sporting events, the best theatrical productions, the best poems, the best short films, the best music, the best paintings, the most inspiring narratives in scripture and ancient texts truly speak to these realities.

They tap into something deep within us—we see the stories in those forms as our story, and we see ourselves *inside* of those stories. When we connect deeply with them, it gives us hope, inspiration, and motivation that our lives could count for, dare I say, greatness?

And guess what? Art, literature, and culture are all saturated with the use of imagery and metaphors. Metaphors of life broken and stuck, free and soaring, and the battle and the journey in between the two. So, if I can help you associate this journey in a number of new ways, then the environment around you is going to come alive to support and inspire you on your journey.

As you have been reading along, you may already feel like songs on the radio, movies, even inspirational quotes on social media are "stalking" you, "haunting" you, or in a more positive light, "whispering" to you. Nonetheless, they all seem to be reiterating what I have been communicating with you. If you haven't felt it yet, I believe you will soon, and when you do, I want to have shared two additional blue-sky visuals to help you connect more deeply—one by land, and one by sea.

BY LAND

If you are more of a back-country type, you have made it through some interesting territory and landscapes in life already, but you find yourself at a new trailhead, looking at the topography of what it will take to truly pursue your potential.

Your potential is on the horizon, high on the summit of a great peak of discovery. It is a peak you have been wanting to climb for a lifetime. You have climbed other peaks and have known the beauty from the top. So, you know at the top of this peak is overwhelming beauty as well. In this case, it is the endless possibility of living a life of greatness, a life of impacting others for good.

You know there is quite a journey between you and that peak, but you haven't committed to leave the trailhead yet. Whether by foot, or by horse, depending on your preference, that journey will take you through the valley floor, through the dense forest, and a wide variety of terrain, all filled with opportunities for learning, growth, development, change, and transformation. It is filled with unknown steps and unmapped trails. It will take time, effort, and new skills, to be sure, turning that stored potential into realized ability.

Yet, you also know there are plenty of potential barriers around the next corner when on a backcountry adventure. The Clouds of Confusion exist out here in the backcountry, creating surprising wind and storms that make the journey feel impossible at times. There are even natural pitfalls that come in the form of mistaken paths, lost trails, and dead ends. You are stuck, wondering if, when, and how you will ever summit or even find your way back to the trail.

You need a breakthrough, you need to be set free, you need to be unleashed, so you can begin your quest of discovery and transformation.

BY SEA

If you resonate more with the idea of the sea, imagine your life represented by a ship instead of an airplane. Realize you have sailed a few smaller seas and have experienced the wind in your hair as well as the taste of the saltwater in your mouth. You embrace those realities fully, and yet, right now, you find your ship comfortably nestled in the harbor of your current reality, unable for some reason to set sail again.

Out on the horizon, way out at sea, across the deep waters is where your potential resides. It's blue too, and you dream of sailing to the horizon, where the blue waters of potential, fulfillment, and success exist. For you, there is still more. Beyond fulfillment and success is a place of impact, of living a life of greatness that impacts others—this is the place on the horizon where the blue sky and the blue waters meet. *That* is the place of endless possibility for you.

As you know too well, there is quite a gap between your present reality in the harbor and your potential and possibility out on the great sea in the distant horizon. You know too that the distance between the harbor and the horizon is truly an opportunity for transformation, filled with learning, growth, development, and an invitation to change your very nature.

These are waters that, as of now, you have yet to cruise upon. It seems risky, even in good weather, because you inherently know fog, clouds, gale force winds, and treacherous storms can roll up on the open sea out of nowhere, creating a barrier to your future, and sometimes creating devastating consequences.

This barrier has the same Clouds of Confusion—whether external or internal—that create the weather patterns that keep you stuck in the harbor. You too need a breakthrough, to be set free, to be unleashed, so you can begin to sail toward discovery and transformation.

No matter the imagery, it is clear… there is quite a distance between "here" and "there." And, I know you feel ready to move ahead, to continue the journey, and to get going. But, not so quick. There are just a few more concepts I must share before I give you the all the tools you will need.

Hang in there with me. Don't stop now. Stay with me because all that we have been working through is going to come together nicely. Once it does, we are going to quickly get to the very practical truths that will set you free from your current reality, move you toward your potential, and help you reach your dreams.

FORCES & MOTION

We ended Chapter 5 by pointing out that you need to experience a genuine breakthrough in order to journey through the Opportunity Zone and past the Clouds of Confusion. Then, in Chapter 6, we learned the importance of being willing to change and transform into a better version of yourself, a version that living in your Blue Sky Potential will require.

We also learned that transformation is the process that fuels the conversion of potential ability in to realized ability. As a result of all these learnings, we are almost to that breakthrough. But it is going to take a little bit more. It is going to require you not just to be willing to transform, but to actually do so. Here's why:

An experience of genuine breakthrough almost always
occurs simultaneously with an experience of transformation.

That is because it is the process of transformation that converts our stagnant and latent potential into realized forward motion. Without that forward and upward motion, there is hardly a chance to break free. Remember, the conversion process is challenging because it only happens as we journey through the challenging terrain of the Opportunity Zone, which as we have discussed, is often thick with Clouds of Confusion—both external circumstances and those internal thunderstorms.

As you elevate through the Opportunity Zone, each cloud you are confronted with will be an opportunity to learn, grow, develop, and transform. Those clouds are the very conditions that need to exist to present you with the opportunity to transform, to convert your potential into reality. Again, your potential is *latent*, lying dormant simply until the conditions and circumstances necessary for transformation occur.

Transformation will require you to operate in a new way—in a way that is consistent with your new nature yet *inconsistent* with your old nature. This will be a battle. Your heart will tell you that you are ready, but your mind will slow you down. You will want to get in the cockpit and soar, but your mind will convince you that you aren't ready and that you need to stay in the training simulator.

You will put on your hiking boots or climb up on that horse, but your mind will tell you that you feel lightheaded. You'll rise to the position of the helm, standing ready to sail, but your mind will tell you your stomach feels seasick. There is a "stuckness" that is overwhelming. Everything else about you is all green lights, but something invisible is holding you back, and you are leashed to your current reality.

To get to your breakthrough, it is best if you are in motion while in (or even after) the transformation, and yet, to truly push through, you are going to need to be impacted by a force (or forces) that will set you in motion even higher, ultimately setting you free. To understand this, we are going to go back to physics, but only for a moment. It all goes back to Sir Isaac Newton and his first law of motion. And, since you know that by heart, you know what I'm talking about… just kidding, no pop quizzes, I promised.

Newton was able to discover and articulate a number of truths about physics that had eluded description prior to his work. His first law of motion reads something like this, "Every object remains in its state of rest or uniform motion in a straight line *unless it is compelled to change that state by forces impressed upon it*" (emphasis mine). I have always wanted to say, "emphasis mine." Fun! Anyway…

In other words, he is saying if an object is just sitting there, it will remain there unless and until something applies a force to it, which will then set it in motion. He is also saying an object in motion will remain perfectly in that exact motion (velocity and direction), unless and until something else applies a force to it. That force will change its motion in some fashion, whether changing the speed and direction or both.

At times a force can actually cause an object in motion to come to a complete stop. In nature, it is rare for a single force to deliver an exacting blow to cause a moving object to come to an exact, perfect stop. The reason it is rare is because that force would have to be in the perfect direction and strength to exactly negate the previous force and direction, with a net result of "zero," leaving the object in an exact state of rest.

While rare in nature, this experience is not so rare in life. You have probably experienced this on more than one occasion, and that exacting blow stopped you in your tracks. You were moving forward in life, heading in a certain direction at a certain speed, when all of a sudden, the force, brought on by internal and/or external circumstances, moved in the exact opposite direction of your life with just the right amount of force to bring you to a complete stop.

Sometimes you have the inspiration, motivation, and desire to apply force to yourself to get you going again, but then another exacting blow happens. Another force opposing your dreams and opposing the positive direction you are making as you pursue your potential comes along and brings you to a stop once again.

After too many experiences like that, it's only natural to give up, and one day look up and see you are at the intersection of stuck and lost. It's not long before you realize you've been there longer than you care to admit, leashed or chained, if you will.

So, if you are at rest, at the corner of stuck and lost, and you don't have the energy, drive, or inspiration to apply force to yourself, you are going to need an outside force to impact you and set you free from that reality. Let me encourage you with this. So few people actually have the hope and drive to apply force to their own journey. Just because it looks like everyone else is doing it doesn't mean they actually are.

Most likely, you will need an outside force to dislodge you. I hope and pray that the inspiration and truths in this book do just that—impact you in such a way that set you in significant motion toward the blue sky, or the blue waters, or the blue horizon on that great peak.

Maybe you aren't quite as stuck as I have been describing. Maybe you are on the move a bit, but you aren't so excited about the direction, speed, and trajectory line of that movement. As Newton points out, you are moving in a straight line of the trajectory of your current reality, and that will remain your current reality unless and until another force is applied to your life.

If that is you, according to Newton, it is still going to take a force to compel and impact you in a way that reorients your trajectory and sends you soaring into blue sky.

Similarly, I hope and pray that the inspiration and truths in this book do just that for you too. These very thoughts about force are what I personally have experienced over and over again through the transformations I have experienced in life, especially the transformation I have been experiencing over the last few years.

MORE THAN A YEAR AND A HALF BEFORE THE PUBLISHING OF THIS book, my family and I picked up and moved across the country from Denver, CO, to Newport Beach, CA. It is quite the story of why and how this move came to be, but suffice to say, it was quite possibly the most significant decision in the life of our family to date.

You see, I am a third generation native of Colorado, and my wife is a forth generation native, making our kids fourth and fifth generation, which is extremely rare. While we are fairly well-traveled, Colorado has always been home, and nearly all of our family lives there too. Additionally, because of a very specific burden and calling, if you will, we spent the entire adult half of our lives (20+ years) pouring ourselves into the local community, our local church, and the people of our suburban-Denver city, Arvada.

That investment in that community was beautiful. We have impacted and been impacted by thousands of lives, and as a result, we were nearly unable to enter a coffee shop, restaurant, or supermarket without running into someone we knew, and often more than a few someones.

As much as we had an impact on others, we were also the beneficiaries of love and investment so many others offered to us. We did not have any intention to move away from Colorado, having long before already begun to envision the future pictures that would get taken in our home—homecoming, prom, and wedding pictures, ultimately pictures of grandkids and even great grandkids running up and down the stairs, enjoying meals, and playing in the backyard.

Without getting into all the details, we reached an amazing finish line with regard to our calling to our local community and church, as I described a little bit previously. It was a job well done, mission completed, you've-crossed-the-finish-line-so-stop-running type of experience. It was exciting and fulfilling during that 20-year journey, and it still brings warm memories as we reflect on all that had been accomplished for the good of others.

Over the latter 10 years of that journey, most of the lifetime of our two children, we had been taking time away from the investment in our community by vacationing annually and often semiannually (or more) to visit a number of friends who lived in Southern California. We loved the work we were doing in our community of Arvada, but we needed regular times to refresh and renew in order to stay on course as a family. Taking time to enjoy friends, fun, food, and the sunny and sandy beaches along the Pacific Ocean always did just the trick.

Over the course of those 10 years, and because of the blessing of buddy passes from a family member, I was fortunate to make some 20-25 trips to Southern California, whether to see friends, visit clients, run marathons, attend conferences, or simply vacation with the family. Thankful for this buddy passes, we were often able to travel as an entire family for these endeavors.

These times were always so rich and restful for our family as we would use the time to stay "off the grid," so to speak, keeping the emails, phone calls, and texts to an absolute minimum. We even had the opportunity to spend a 4-month sabbatical in our favorite coastal village along the Southern-Californian coast. We didn't know it then, but those times of respite grew roots in our hearts that ultimately began to sink into the soil, climate, and culture of Orange County.

About a year after my 10-year church staff journey had all wrapped up, things began to change, and a force was at work within our hearts. The force was not big at first, but it was disruptive. I love subtle, disruptive forces, and I have learned to "lean in" discerningly when I sense those subtle forces creating motion. My wife and I began to sense a whisper of change and felt an unexplainable sensation of being too close to our own corner of stuck and lost.

After much prayer, many conversations, and a lot of soul-searching, we realized there was a greater purpose behind that small but disruptive force. Instead of just a whisper, or simply a disruptive call to change, we began to hear a genuine invitation.

As we began to listen more intently, we discerned an invitation to risk and even to transform. We hadn't known it but disguised in all the beauty of and the work with the people in our community, my wife and I as individuals had come to a place where our growth was pushing against a lid, or an invisible ceiling of sorts. You see, we are the growing types, always looking for the challenge of changing and becoming more—pursuing the best version of ourselves.

As we pressed in to this whisper and continued to pray, we

began to see a picture of a terrarium, one of those beautiful mini-gardens contained within a small glass jar that are like a dry aquarium for plants. However, the terrarium of our lives had a glass lid on it. We realized that in our 20 years of pursuing our own growth in the community in which we served, we had reached a growth lid. And, to stay pressed up against that lid would eventually lead us to our own corner of stuck and lost, if we weren't there already.

Additionally, we began to realize that the soil of the territory of our influence, which had been so rich and full of vibrancy for us, had gone stale. In fact, it wasn't that the soil had lost its quality, but that we had derived, squeezed, and taken up every bit of nutrition the soil our local community had to offer. In the end, we began to discover that the invitation was not only to transform, but to do so by transplanting into new soil, for a future of new growth.

It was a hard realization, because we knew that kind of transformation and the resulting transplant would require us to leave everything familiar and journey into an unknown new future. Behind that invitation to transplant and transform was a belief that new soil (not better, but new) would offer different nutrients for a different type of growth. We also knew that new soil meant new location, which would help us get outside of the limiting terrarium we had found ourselves in.

Don't get me wrong—we loved our lives in Colorado, and we loved the people there and were loved by them. And as beautiful and clarifying as these discoveries were, they were equally as challenging and scary. As we continued to seek and discern what transplanting meant, we began to realize that the whisper was actually an invitation to move to Southern California.

Even though only a whisper, it created a wind that was very disruptive, acting as an outside force on us, wooing us to cross a new Opportunity Zone and enter into a new season of stretching, growth, development, and yes, *transformation*. Just maybe, on the other side of all those Clouds of Confusion, God was revealing a new level of Blue Sky Potential for *our* lives, for the lives of our kids, and for our future. In the end, we finally RSVP'd a "yes" to the invitation, allowing the subtle wind of disruption to blow into the sails of our lives and carry us to the West Coast.

The move was wrought with risk in all sorts of areas, and it would prove to be the greatest financial step of faith we have ever taken. But the invitation was clear, and our desire to seek our potential and that of our kids was an unrelenting motivation. The force of that whisper was significant, and it set in motion a great chain of events that led to a lot of motion, moving, transplanting, growing, and ultimately transforming.

Now, on this side of the move, I can assure you, the transformation was and still is off the charts, which means that there have been times that have been tremendously challenging and times that were other-worldly beautiful. We have and still are soaring upward in the face of so many unconquered Clouds of Confusion—both the internal and the external. And yet, as we navigate through, around, and over each cloud, we see new opportunities to transform into the best version of ourselves by converting unused potential into realized and elevated forward motion.

In fact, this book is specifically a result of those steps of faith and the transformation that ensued. Without that move, this book would still be buried somewhere deep in my heart, a dormant dream, with the risk of my "passive dreamer" squandering and missing out on the opportunity as I did with the Air Force Academy.

The dream of this book, and my potential to write it was latent of course, waiting for the right circumstances and environment to be transformed. The conditions and circumstances in Colorado would have never been the optimum conditions for this portion of my potential to be realized.

That's no fault of Colorado—because it had been the perfect conditions for growth during the first 40 years of our lives (what we affectionately refer to as Volume I). Colorado was a place where the conditions were perfect for our potential to be discovered and put to use. For Volume II, however, those same conditions would have never become the conditions needed for the remaining latent potential in our lives to be transformed into realized potential and endless possibility.

You have probably already considered the thought, but I want to point something out to you. The ideas, concepts, and truths shared in this book are not theoretical, nor are they something I simply came up with on a whim, attempting to enter into the spotlight as an author.

These thoughts, ideas, principles, and truths are something I have lived out over and over again throughout my entire life, each breakthrough an experience of finding freedom from the gravity that holds me back. Not only my life, but I have consistently used these truths and principles to guide others to experience that same freedom in their lives. They are time-tested and proven.

It would be easy to simply stop the story short and say we have lived happily ever after, but it would not be an accurate description of the journey. Truthfully, our family is thriving like we never have before, our marriage is beyond healthy, more than it has ever been. Our kids have matured in so many ways, especially their talents, character, and their faith. Opportunity and open doors exist for them like never before.

Is there still more blue sky for us in the future? Absolutely! Yet, we have had (and still have) some serious Clouds of Confusion to overcome as part of our transformation process. But we aren't going to let a few clouds stop us from becoming the best version of ourselves.

When in California, our family has always moved more by the time of the sun than by the time of the watch. Maybe it is a beach thing, maybe it was a SoCal thing, or maybe it was a vacation thing. Even though we now call home the place where we vacationed, and real life goes by real watch time (rather than vacation time), we still move and flow with the movements of the sun as much as we do the watch.

For example, nearly every evening, we take a family walk as the sun sets. When we are home, we stop what we are doing, turn off the oven or the burners, hang up the phone, turn off the television, gather ourselves up, and head out the door. We put everything on hold to take a family walk along the coast, waiting for the sky to be painted however the artistic creator is feeling for that evening.

The walks are a time of joy, friendship, love, and reflection, and we all cherish it together. If I or my wife don't recognize the sun is about to set, one of our kids will come running through the house, like an alarm sounding off that it is time to go for a walk. Sometimes we take a football, a scooter, or a remote-control car, but most often we just take ourselves.

There is always some sort of camera to capture the beauty of the sunset. Sometimes we walk for 15 minutes; sometimes it turns into an hour and a half, and the half-cooked dinner back home gets ignored because it comes second in priority to our time together.

The walk gives us a chance to share stories, spend time together, and be specifically grateful for another day of life that is coming to a close. No matter how long we are gone, usually just before the sun disappears, we take a moment simply to pray together, thanking God for our health, for the love we experience, and for the sunset's reminder that each passing day is precious, valued, and to be cherished.

UNLEASHING FORCE—TRANSFORMATIONAL BREAKTHROUGH

In the early days after our move, while out on one of these walks, we noticed something on the end of the block, four houses down. There was a bicycle chained to a palm tree, and right around the corner is a hill that heads straight down to the coastline. A bike chained up isn't totally out of the ordinary given it is an active community, but what caught our attention is that it *never moved*. We didn't think much of it until one night, we observed that there was a spotlight shining on it. Odd, right?

Closer inspection was needed, and as we walked up to it, we realized this wasn't just a bicycle chained to a palm tree; this was a piece of art, intentionally put on display by the homeowner. It's an interesting piece of art, looking like a bicycle from a bygone era, almost frozen in time.

It's cool and confusing at the same time, but either way, it is thought provoking. It is rusty, worn, tired, and well, not going anywhere soon. Even if you could break the industrial-sized chain and padlock that secures it to the palm tree, both wheels are secured to the ground with thick pieces of bent steel rebar.

For fun, let's go back and connect the imagery of this bicycle to that hypothetical bicycle that you were hypothetically sitting on. Let me remind you that in the example from earlier, you are sitting on a Wright Bicycle Co. handmade bicycle at the top of a very tall hill, and the bicycle happens to be chained in some fashion to a fence, and of course, you are decked out in your mid-90s cycling gear (and I'm not talking spandex, my friends—remember, we are back in mid-1890s).

Remember, there is a tremendous amount of latent potential stored up in you and that bike, simply waiting to go down the hill and begin to convert, or transform, that stored up potential into forward motion.

Stay too long on that Van Cleve, leashed to that fence, and you won't stay looking as dapper as when you began. No, after a surprisingly short amount of time, you too could grow old, tired, rusty, and ultimately become petrified. Not unlike that bicycle four houses down, you would have no ability to go anywhere.

Would there be reason to hope? Of course. It is going to take some considerable time and work to get that bicycle (and you) out of its (and your) dilapidated condition and functioning again, but *it is possible*. Restoration is not out of the question, but to see a future that is greater than its past, it is going to need a whole lot of tender, loving care. Even once restored, though, we need to remind ourselves of Sir Isaac Newton and his first law of motion.

No matter how good that restored bicycle looks or actually is (or your life, for that matter) or how well its functionality has been restored, as long as you are chained to that fence (or maybe a palm tree if you are so fortunate), your life, your trajectory, and your potential are still at rest and immobile.

Restoration, or even transformation for that matter,
isn't taking you anywhere without a breakthrough.

Likewise, experiencing the freedom of being set free, or experiencing breakthrough without experiencing restoration or transformation is like cutting the chains that are holding an old, rusty, dilapidated bike in place. Cut the chains, unleash the bike, and it still isn't going anywhere. It's barely going to roll, and it may even break down if you try and ride it. Here is my point.

You actually need both transformation and breakthrough.
You need transformational breakthrough.

Transformational breakthrough is the totality of the unleashing force that your life needs in order to be truly set free from all that holds you back and at the same time transforms you and sets you in motion toward your Blue Sky Potential. I shared it earlier in this chapter, but I will share it again.

An experience of genuine breakthrough almost always
occurs simultaneously with an experience of transformation.

When these two powerful experiences work in tandem—breakthrough and transformation—the result is *transformational breakthrough* which changes the essence of your very nature into a new nature, equipped and ready for the blue skies nature AND launches you through and above the clouds in to a new realm of endless possibility.

If you have ever been in an airplane that took off from the ground on an overcast day, you probably can remember what it feels like when the plane ultimately pokes through and above the clouds, into the unlimited beautiful blue sky. The clouds and storms are below and the horizon if full of pure thin air, perfect for cruising and soaring in endless possibility. That exact experience can happen in your life as you experience the power of transformational breakthrough. When this happens, the impossible truly becomes possible.

THREE TETHERS HOLDING YOU BACK

By now, you may have been hoping I would tell you what exactly you need to do to transform your life, but the truth is, I hardly know you. And, even if I did, and I pointed the changes out, you may not believe me, because what needs to be transformed is usually hard to see when we look at ourselves. Sure, others can tell us, but we won't believe it until we experience a revelation of sorts, like scales falling off our eyes.

I have worked with thousands of people, helping them unpack the things that slow them down, hold them back, or trip them up, and nearly every time, the types of things that come up are unique to the individual. Yes, there are themes, but the way each of those areas of needed transformation manifests is unique to each person.

I'm not even going to attempt to predict what areas of your life need transformation. At the same time, however, I can give you a clue how to discover them yourself.

The *clouds* will tell you.

I know that sounds mystical and vague, but it is true.

Even in the uncertainty, created by the Clouds of Confusion you are trying to navigate, you are going to find some answers. I am not a clinical psychologist, but as I have shared a few times, I observe trends and patterns and learn from them. This is what I have observed: What seems like the real challenge of the confusion and uncertainty in the clouds you are facing (whether it be finances, relationships, vocational issues, etc.), the challenge isn't really the clouds or circumstances themselves.

The true challenge is the necessary internal transformation that the cloud is showing you. Think about it. Think about your life. Think about multiple challenges you have faced recently. Think about how you feel about those challenges. Think about any possible resolutions to those challenges. Are there overlapping themes? Is there a common underlying issue coming to mind? Most likely, yes.

For now, it's good that you are looking at those things. When you see the same patterns emerging from a variety of clouds, you are onto something, and as you lean into it, you can discover exactly what needs transformation. You are going to need to continue that journey of inward searching often.

Truth be told, however, I don't want to take too much time unpacking this, because as you ascend through the Opportunity Zone throughout a life of ongoing breakthrough, you are going to be regularly facing challenges that reveal areas of necessary transformation. Taking too much time here would bog us down in the specifics instead of keeping our minds on the greater picture and the greater journey.

I'd rather move on to the next pattern I observe: too many Clouds of Confusion, too little transformation, too much "stuck and lost," too little breakthrough and most people fall prey to three overarching themes, three realities that wrap themselves around us like shackles and chains, tethering us to the ground:

- *Doubt*
- *Fear*
- *And apathy*

Not buying it? I'm not surprised. I'm not a betting man, but if I were, I'd be willing to make a significant bet that when we began our journey together, if I had asked you to write down the three things holding you back, you would not have identified these three themes.

Most likely, you would have named the circumstances that are troubling you. You would have written down things like lack of finances, lack of time, lack of energy, broken relationships, or no support from loved ones, or… so many things like that. The list could go on and on.

You'd be right that many of those things are standing between you and a life of greatness, soaring in the blue sky of your potential. But, you would only be right because those are the Clouds of Confusion and uncertainty—the winds and weather patterns that are blocking your view and path to the blue sky. You would be wrong because those circumstances and realities are *not* the chains holding you back. Certainly, those clouds can be challenging, diffi-cult, and sometimes downright overwhelming, but the truth is they are not impassable, in and of themselves.

They are currently impassable because you are leashed to the ground by the tethers that are created by these challenges, not the challenges themselves. Whatever challenges you are facing, the ongoing inability to conquer and move past or above those chal-lenges creates devastating shackles of doubt, fear, and apathy. Even some of the early things we talked about like pain, regret, and feeling like dreams have died all lead to the chains of doubt, fear, and apathy.

Think about it.

I would love to start that business, but I'm not sure I have the skill (*doubt*). I can see myself leading that new initiative, but what would others say (*fear*)? I dream about helping with that nonprofit, but maybe it would be better after I graduate (*apathy*). I wish I had a place to use my talents, but I'm not even sure I am talented (*doubt*). I have always dreamed about adopting, but I'm not sure we can afford it right now (*fear*). I would love to get in shape, even run a half-marathon, but work is really busy right now (*apathy*).

Now add back on the challenges and confusion found in the clouds, and if you can't overcome the doubt, fear, and apathy that hold you back in general, you will never do it in the face of those challenges. That's why pursuing your potential has felt all but impossible. So again, you find yourself at stuck and lost, and prob-ably depressed by the status quo of going through the motions each day. This is why I told you in the beginning that I can't solve all of your problems. But I did assure you I could show you the way on the journey.

THE HIDDEN POWER OF PERSEVERANCE

As we have discussed already, transformation is a journey, and jour-neys require something of us that the Comfort Zone doesn't not require. Transformation requires something of us that your current trajectory does not. The journey of transformation, especially one that is going to work in tandem with a much-needed breakthrough, will require *perseverance*.

Perseverance can simply be defined as a steadfastness in continuing despite difficulty or delay in achieving success. It is hard work. It is laborious. It requires diligence and grit. But there is something hidden in the word I want to point out. A good friend of mine, Vince, was encouraging me during my most recent transformational season and made this point, which was tremendously helpful to me.

I'm going to take his original line of thinking and expand it a bit, but not without a caution. Now, I may have already annoyed the physics majors, but I'm about to upset the English majors too. But, just as I asked for some grace from the physics experts, I am asking for that same grace from the linguists.

Look closely at the word, perseverance. Buried and hidden in the word "perseverance" is the word, "sever." There is an important correlation between these two words, but it is not based on the etymology of these words.

To cover my bases, I looked up the origins of both words, and while they both originate in the early- to mid-14th century, with middle English and middle French origins (perseverance includes some Latin origins), they do not come from the same source or root word. So, maybe I'm out on a limb here because the etymology isn't related, but I'm going to keep going with it.

I see a correlation in how these two words work together, especially when considering our conversation about chains, tethers, and leashes holding us to the ground, which I'll explain in just a moment.

First, let's take a look at the word sever. It is such a blunt and aggressive word. It means to cut ties with, to abandon, to divide, to put an end to, especially suddenly or forcibly. Depending on your imagination, a multitude of images are going through your mind as you picture the brutal and blunt act of severing, and all I have to say is... Ouch. Yuck. Cringe. Oh Man.

Don't shy too far away from that imagery, because that is the type of intentional force you will need to deliver to those chains that are keeping you from freedom.

Severing is a part of the journey of perseverance, a part of the journey of breakthrough, a part of the journey of transformation, a part of the journey of pursuing your potential. And, this journey will require you to sever a number of things you no longer need, which are right now holding you back.

No matter what metaphor you prefer—air, land, or sea—there are chains holding you back. Like a jet, tethered to the tarmac or the flight deck of the aircraft carrier, or like a pioneer whose horse is tied to the post, or like a ship anchored at harbor or still tied to the dock, you have significant leashes holding you down, keeping you from truly soaring.

To get moving and unleash the process of transformation in your life, it is going to require a tremendous amount of force, if not multiple significant forces to separate you from and break the chains that bind you. There must be a severing—a parting of ways.

When you sever something, you must do so with force. If it was not the case, I could simply say, unwind, cut, separate, release, but that is not what I am saying. I am saying you need to sever some things in your life with an aggressive, intentional, forceful blow or series of blows. This is what it means to *unleash* your potential.

You must sever the things that hold you back—the chains of doubt, fear, and apathy. Now, it's ok to be a little uncertain if or how these three things are holding you back. For now, trust me, and know that I will unpack each leash more deeply in the upcoming chapters. For now, trust me that they are formidable foes, and you will need to sever them in order to breakthrough and experience transformation.

Here is where the perseverance part comes in. Doubt, fear, and apathy are relentless enemies. You can and will sever them, but they will come back. And, you will have to sever them again. And again. And again. Like sci-fi jungle vines in a horror movie, doubt, fear, and apathy have a way of regenerating.

They are always chasing you, attempting to trip you, and attempting to tie you back down to the ground at every turn. Therefore, you are going to need to understand, value, and wield the truths that deliver a severing blow to those vines.

WE HAVE SPENT SIGNIFICANT TIME TALKING ABOUT TRANSFORMATION, and now you have only been introduced to true breakthrough, which we will unpack more in the coming chapters. For now, break-through is brought about by o*ngoing severing of doubt, fear, and apathy.* Transformation by *a constant willingness to change.* You need both —*ongoing transformation and ongoing breakthrough.*

These two things are what you need most to unleash your life, for you to be set free to reach your dreams, and to soar into your Blue Sky Potential and the endless possibility that awaits.

We must remain willing to change. We must remain willing to transform. We must continue to sever doubt. We must continue to sever fear. We must continue to sever apathy. We must do so with ferocity and consistency, with grit and perseverance.

When we learn to live this way, the result is truly an experience of *Transformational Breakthrough.*

Transformational Breakthrough is what crafts you, redefines you, and changes your nature into the best version of yourself, which is the version you need to be to reach your potential. It is the new you. The best version of you. The transformed version of you that has broken through doubt, fear, and apathy and became a new person in the process. It is the version of you that is willing to go through that transformation and severing process anytime life requires it.

You aren't alone in this. Others have gone before. And, others will come after. I am on the journey with you too. Truthfully, I have never met someone who is living their life to the fullest who made it into the blue sky of their potential, who soars in endless possibility impacting so many other lives, who has not truly experienced trans-formational breakthrough. And, those that do so consistently make it a lifestyle to regularly seek out opportunities to experience trans-formational breakthrough again and again.

Will you accept the invitation to be among
these courageous and daring dreamers?

It all hinges on this reality, this mentality of seeking transformational breakthrough. You don't cut through the clouds without it. You don't learn, grow, develop, and change in the Opportunity Zone without it. You don't soar above the clouds without it. You don't find the best version of yourself without it. You don't live a life of greatness—the endless possibility of impacting others for good —without it.

The chains of doubt, fear, and apathy are industrial sized, to say the least, based on a whole bunch of lies that continually whisper: you can't, you wouldn't, and maybe later.

To truly break those chains filled with lies, it is going to take a mighty blow of truth. In order to soar, you are going to have to discover and wield the three simple truths of transformational breakthrough.

WIELDING THE TRUTH THAT SETS YOU FREE

I am thrilled with the progress you have made up to this point. You are an inspiration to me. From where you were when we began this journey up until now is a sign of significant progress—progress that should be celebrated and honored. Let me be the first to say you have made it further than most. At some point along the way, many people choose to turn around and give up on a genuine pursuit of their potential.

The journey I have taken with you up until now simply requires too much for some—too much introspection, too much stirring up pain and regret, too much dreaming, too much stretching, too much perseverance, too much change and transformation. There is something different about you. You are so hungry for the endless possibility of living a life of greatness while soaring in the blue sky of your potential that you have journeyed well and willingly to this point. You have so much going for you, my friend. So, let's go the rest of the way, shall we?

You have been waiting for this moment our entire journey, and I thank you for waiting so patiently. The payoff is here. I'm going to change my approach ever so slightly. Instead of playing the role of a guide who is stirring up things within your heart, spirit, and soul, I'm going to move into a guide who is more of a coach/teacher.

I'm going to be telling it to you straight and challenging you to discover, understand, and value the three simple truths of transformational breakthrough. In doing so, I'm going to address one truth per chapter for the next three chapters.

In the Introduction, I shared with you that completing this book is the first leg of a greater journey we can take together. So, as we complete this final phase of the first leg of the journey, I want to leave you with more than inspiration alone. I want to leave you with three practical, undeniable truths that can change the trajectory of your life.

I want you to know these three truths inside and out. I want you to be able to quote them to others. I want you to reflect on them when your mind wanders while you are in the car, in the shower, while you are exercising, or in a meeting. I want these truths to be on your mind anytime you are deep in thought, journaling, or being reflective. I want these three truths to be on the tip of your tongue any time you are facing a challenge, taking on a difficult project, or even when you need to have a difficult conversation.

These three truths are *that* powerful.

They are the three truths that can unleash you from what holds you back. These are the truths that are going to fuel and guide you through the Opportunity Zone, as you move from your reality to your potential. These truths that will help you navigate the Clouds of Confusion, the internal things you wrestle with, and the external circumstances that are in the way. These three truths can be wielded to sever the leashes that hold you to the ground. These three truths are so powerful they are going to help you in nearly every situation you are going to face in life.

Remember how the Wright Brothers created the 3-axis-control system for steering and controlling their flying machine? Remember that without that revolutionary approach, they would have been just like the rest of their competitors who were focused on power? Remember how I made the case that your life needs a similar "system" for piloting it, so when power is added, the power does not simply power you into a crash landing?

These three truths are just that—your 3-axis control system. These three simple truths of transformational breakthrough are going to work together as the mechanism that will help you pilot your life with intention, balance, and direction. These three truths have been developed over a lifetime of personal trial and error, a lifetime of leading and guiding others, a lifetime of observing and gleaning from the wisdom and the success, as well as from the mistakes and failures of others. These three truths of breakthrough are time tested and proven.

That's why it's so important for you to discover them, understand them, value them, and absorb them into the core of who you are.

When someone asks you why you seem to soar above everyone else, these three simple truths will be your first thought. When someone asks you how you stay so focused in a world of uncertainty and confusion, a warm smile will rise up inside because you know you are piloting your life through all that uncertainty with these truths. And, because I believe you are going to find a Blue Sky Potential that is filled with the endless possibility of a life that impacts others for good, I want you to be able to point them to the journey we took together and the truths that set you free.

These three truths will deliver the unleashing force necessary to sever what holds you back and will also set your life in motion toward blue sky. These three truths are dismissively simple yet deeply profound and powerful. Wield them like a mighty sword, using them to combat the lies. Use these three simple truths to deliver the unleashing blow, severing doubt, fear, and apathy from your life.

Just like the Wright Brothers, there was a right moment in time. Everything had come together for a specific moment, for a specific reason. When they applied their three principles of piloting flight at the right time, the impossibility of powered, piloted flight became possible. That is breakthrough, my friend, the type of breakthrough of latent stored up potential, transformed into realized ability, resulting in the impossible becoming possible.

Now, the timing is becoming right, and everything is coming together for you, at a specific moment, for a specific reason. As you apply these principles, these three truths, you are going to experience transformational breakthrough.

For possibly the first time, you are going to have the ability to experience your life in a way that is powered and piloted. And, when you experience this type of transformational breakthrough, blue sky won't be theoretical, but reality, and in your life, the impossible will become possible.

PART 3

UNLEASH: THE THREE TRUTHS OF TRANSFORMATIONAL BREAKTHROUGH

CHAPTER 8

PERSPECTIVE — CLARITY PRODUCES CONFIDENCE

"For me the greatest beauty
always lies in the greatest clarity."

- GOTTHOLD EPHRAIM LESSING

AT THE CORNER OF STUCK AND LOST, THE VIEW AND PATH FROM your reality to your potential is clouded—clouded with the darkness of internal feelings of inferiority, failure, and discouragement, not to mention the dark clouds of the external circumstances and challenges you face. The long-term result of those clouds is a leash of *doubt*, holding you back from even beginning that process of transformation.

Doubt is preventing you from tapping into the fuel source transformation provides. Doubt is holding you back from converting that stored potential of energy and ability into realized energy and ability in the form of forward and upward motion.

You need to sever doubt, and you need to wield a new truth to do it. Therefore, in the face of doubt, and to unleash your Blue Sky

Potential, you need to understand, value, and wield the unleashing force found in *clarity*. Here is "Part A" of the first simple truth of transformational breakthrough.

Simple Truth of Transformational Breakthrough #1

(Part A)

YOU NEED CLARITY...

Clarity, simply defined, is the quality of being certain or definite. When was the last time you felt certain or definite about anything in your life? It's been a while, hasn't it? At least it has been a long while since you felt certain about anything *good* or *positive* in your life.

Yet, the uncertainties feel certain. The doubt feels certain. The confusion feels certain. That's what caused you to pick up this book, right? See how that works?

You had clarity about being stuck and lost, and you took action, looking for a guide to direct you away from the certainty of being stuck and lost. We need to flip that reality.

We need to help you get clarity about the uncertainties of your life. We need to begin to help you find clarity about the future trajectory of your life. Clarity you have needed for a long while. Clarity you need right now.

Clarity is not only important. *It is paramount*, which is to mean that clarity is supreme, and nothing is more important to your future than clarity.

Now that we have made it all the way here, through the journey of rekindling and restoring dreams, seeing a deeper understanding of potential, and the change and transformation required for fuel, the pursuit of clarity is the most important part of the journey.

Without clarity, all the potential, purpose, passion, and perseverance will likely be misaligned, off course, and off trajectory. So, the question becomes, how do we pursue clarity?

SEEKING PERSPECTIVE

We pursue clarity by seeking *perspective*. Without proper perspective, we cannot see clearly. Seeking perspective in this case means seeking a new way of regarding something, or evaluating a new point of view, or even seeking a particular attitude toward something. It should be obvious, but in case it's not, please allow me to point it out.

> *Seeking perspective*
> *requires a willingness to change.*

Drawing back from our last chapter, where I made the case that a willingness to change is required to transform, I will tell you now that it begins much sooner than that. It requires a willingness to change to even have an interest in seeking a new perspective, which needs to happen well before any transformation is possible.

Why is a willingness to change required to seek a new perspective? Simple. Because a new perspective means you might have to see the world, your circumstances, or yourself differently than you do now. And, that means you would need to change, even if that means only changing your mind before you actually experience personal change.

> *A changed mind is the beginning of a changed self.*
> *A transformed mind is the beginning of a transformed self.*

If you haven't noticed, most people who are unwilling to change themselves are also unwilling to change their minds or their perspective on life. They aren't willing to see things through a different point of view, and therefore, they're unwilling and unable to change. For them, because their mindset is on lockdown, the opportunity for transformation, let alone transformational breakthrough, is all but impossible. And, much of that goes back to their unwillingness to seek a new perspective and, therefore, an inability to arrive at clarity.

But that's not you. You want a new perspective. You picked up this book with the hopes that it would reveal something new to you. And it has already, many times over. You have a new perspective on your dormant dreams. You have a new perspective that despite what felt hopeless before, you believe you can be restored—to a better version than ever before.

You now see the clouds you have to navigate not simply as challenges or roadblocks, but as opportunities to learn, grow, develop, and transform. There are probably many other areas of perspective you have gained so far and, hopefully, so many more to come. So, let me tell you about a few other areas of perspective that will help guide your journey.

Perspective begins with getting wisdom from others, especially others you trust or who are gifted at helping bring about a new view. It could be loved ones, close friends, co-workers, community leaders like pastors or rabbis, or even professional guides, whether leaders like me or other professionals like counselors or therapists.

If you didn't invite a few friends to read this book with you and join this journey with us (as I had suggested in the opening Invitation), you may want to do that now. Ask them to get this book, read along to catch up on the journey, and then walk together through the deep waters of seeking perspective together.

Outside of the perspective that trusted people can provide, there are a lot of resources available to you for getting a new perspective. But, it shouldn't be a blind search for perspective. It should be intentional—piloted, if you will. Because of that, my recommendation is that you need to start with yourself and look within to see what you can discover.

In order to take the journey into the deep introspective waters of your heart, spirit, and soul, it will require one thing—that you *slow down*. Like an archeologist looking for clues in a dig site, you are going to have to tend carefully to the subject matter of your heart to truly discover the beauty of what is there. You are not going to easily get perspective if you are moving full tilt. Remember, power didn't lift the first flying machine off the ground; a new perspective did.

First, however, you are going to need to set some time aside. Whether that be for time with some of the aforementioned guides, the friends who have joined you in reading this book, or even to be alone to journal, pray, or read, you will need to take time to find ways that will help you mine a new perspective within. And not just slow down for a few minutes once or twice. You are going to need to set aside regular portions of time to slow down and search within for true discovery.

Again, as you slow down, there is no better place to start than your own life. It may seem easier to start on the external problems —the problems with your finances, your relationships, your career, etc. There are many books and guides to help you do that. The truth is that you may fix, remove, or get around one of those clouds, but rarely are you different for it; rarely does it transform you; and therefore, rarely does it move you anywhere closer to your Blue Sky Potential. It simply, and hopefully successfully, gives you the chance to remove well, *one* of the clouds in your path.

As you know, however, life has an endless amount of clouds to bring your way, so you may not have solved as much as you thought. Instead, as we focus internally on our search for perspective, we begin to get clarity within, which will much better inform how we should approach those external clouds now and in the future.

You may remember the passionate, if not slightly poetic vision I offered in the early pages of this book, titled "Blue Sky.... A Manifesto." It was nearly seven years before I even had my first thought about writing this book that I originally crafted those words—it was and is a manifesto of sorts. And now, years later, it is surprising even to me how true to the core my message was, even then.

Without even attempting to align the content of this book to those words, it is uncanny how much alignment is there. That tells me I'm onto something. All the introspection I was walking in when I wrote that manifesto has come full circle as I have searched deep within to draw out the words that are hitting these pages for you right now.

Whether you read that manifesto as if it were a personal letter, or a poem, or even a spoken word piece, there is a line at the end I want to point out: "I invite you to join a community of dreamers—a community that examines what was and what is, with the purpose of truly discovering the possibility of what can be." See the pattern there?

First, we examine what *was* (past). Then, we examine what *is* (present). Why? Because, when we have a better perspective on what was (where we have come from) and what is (where we are now), we can truly discover the *possibility of what can be* (our purpose, our potential, and the endless possibility of impacting others for good as we head into the future).

Seeking perspective is accomplished by *examining what was* and *evaluating what is*, to discover the *possibility of what can be*.

PERSPECTIVE—WHAT WAS

To seek perspective on what was, we are going to have to look back over and examine our own life story. I know. That can be scary. In your story, there are probably more experiences than you can remember, and some of those memories have left a mark, a scar, or a memory that is going to be challenging to enter back into.

There are going to be plenty of positive memories to walk through too, but even some of those may have a lining of hurt. Nonetheless, it is worth slowing down, taking some time, and looking back to gain a new perspective.

Pete, that mentor and friend of mine who facilitated my Life-Plan, used to always say something like this: "Children have incredibly accurate memories but can have terribly inaccurate interpretations." Think about it for a bit. Think about the difference between a memory and an interpretation. If you have ever been a parent, you may already understand the difference, but I'll give a simple example.

Imagine you are the parent of a young child, say a kindergarten-aged boy. Imagine now that the child just went running out of the room with a steak knife that he picked up off the dining room table. Assuming you sense the inherent danger of a young child running with a sharp object, you would chase after him with vigor, right?

As you race around the corner and approach him at full speed, you stub your toe and begin to fall chaotically toward the child, tumbling and fumbling through the air. In some mighty experience of serendipity, fortune, or luck, somehow you are able to grab the knife out of the boy's hand, while at the same time crashing to the ground. The fall knocks you both across the floor, leaving you piled up on each other like a tangled mess, not to mention, creating quite the scene for your dinner guests in the other room.

Shockingly, you were able to snatch the knife safely, and neither you nor the boy are injured outside of a few rug burns, messed up hair, and some embarrassment. You stand up, thankful for the relatively safe outcome, brush yourself off, help up your teary-eyed child, and then return the knife to a safe place. Mission accomplished. Danger averted. Great job. Way to go.

You win acrobatic parent of the year for that move. You explain the chaos by telling the story to your dinner guests and will probably tell the story to a few friends, if not *many* friends over the years. By and large, your memory and your interpretation of the series of events are accurate.

Now, imagine this scenario through the eyes, memory, and interpretation of the young boy… And, for the sake of this example, let's call him Little Jeffrey. Little Jeffrey's memory is just as accurate as yours. His memory is that he snagged a steak knife off the table, ran out of the room, and all of a sudden, you came running into the room in a crashing calamity of humanity and took the steak knife out of his hands.

After getting yourself up and helping him up, you promptly set the knife in a safe place. At first, a play by play of the series of events is the same. The memory is accurate, for both of you. But the interpretations are going to be drastically different.

Your interpretation of the memory as you tell the story to your friends is something like: You are so thankful that out of the corner of your eye, you saw Little Jeffery grab the knife and leave the room. Your friends would nod and agree and maybe even compliment your keen eye for avoiding disaster. You would continue to interpret the story to your friends about how lucky you were to pull your kindergartener out of harm's way (somewhat heroically perhaps), at all costs (including your own safety and dignity). No, no, no, not in *this* house do we run with knives.

You might even add and point out for good measure that you had to lean on your natural athletic prowess and yoga-based flexibility, so you could turn your stubbed-toe crash into a dramatic and acrobatic one-handed pirouetting knife snatching rescue of your child. Not only would you tell the story to your friends over and over again, but you might even post about it on social media.

Better yet, you might even write a blog post about it as a way to promote the benefits of yoga. No judgement here. It was quite the feat you pulled off, and you got over 100 likes, by the way, so high-five. I only wish you would have selfie-videoed it. That would have got upward of 200 likes… Nice work, super-parent!

Let's remember that Little Jeffrey's *memory* is similar to yours, but that his *interpretation* of the same series of events is quite different, because as I said before, a child's ability to interpret can be terribly inaccurate.

Have I mentioned that it is possible that Little Jeffrey's imagination is something you as his parent still haven't quite found the boundaries of? Anyway, his interpretation and, therefore, how he tells the story to classmates on the playground or to his therapist some 30 years later goes something like this…

Little Jeffrey's favorite meal is steak, and on that particular evening, the steak pirates were about to come barreling through the front door seeking the greatest treasure in all the land (medium-rare ribeye) and sail off with the loot (garlic-mashed potatoes and fire-grilled shrimp side dishes). By the way, this Little Jeffrey is no relation to me, and this is *in no way autobiographical*…

Back to the interpretation. The steak pirates are on the loose, and as is common knowledge, every swashbuckling, pirate-fighting, sea captain needs a steak sword to defeat the steak pirates who have come aboard the ship (via the front door). Little Jeffrey to the rescue! He quickly and valiantly pulls the best and sharpest steak sword (knife) from the dining cabin, racing to meet the steak pirates up above on the deck to eliminate the threat.

All of a sudden, in the middle of Little Jeffrey's heroics, you come running onto the scene—chasing down Sea Captain Jeffrey, with such ferocity that you tackle him, steal his sword, and foil his rescue all at the same time.

Not only did you ruin the scene, but you bruised his bottom (and ego) in the process. Whose side are you on, anyway? Are you a steak pirate too? "Probably," Little Jeffrey determines.

During recess the next day at school, Little Jeffrey tells his friends about how mean you are and that you "don't even get him" or "get his creativity" or you "don't support his imagination." In the end, Little Jeffrey's interpretation is that he isn't even sure if you love him. A doubt has been cast which will frame the rest of every interpretation Little Jeffrey makes about your parenting for the rest of your life. And it also cast a doubt about everything Little Jeffrey thinks about himself, his creativity, and his imagination.

Did you catch that? A doubt… multiple doubts aimed multiple directions… Doubt is a leash, my friend, so easily entangling us and holding us back from our potential.

As I shared before, the memories of the event are fairly similar. However, your interpretation is that you are a *hero* parent, and Little Jeffrey's interpretation is that you are a *zero* parent. Parenting is hard, isn't it?

Ok, so while this story is completely fictitious, and I have set both interpretations at opposite ends of the interpretative spectrum, I have done so for good reason. Because this is how life works. Children are not the only poor interpreters of memories. *We all are.*

Over our lifetimes, we have nearly unlimited memories, and many of them are shared memories with others. Most of those memories, however, come with interpretations that have some element of inaccuracy, if not blinding inaccuracy altogether. None of us are exempt from this blindness. It is because of this that we need to seek a new perspective on our past. We are going to have to examine what *was* and see the good we can draw from it.

We are going to have to look at our memories, our own interpretations, and see if there are any other perspectives that will help us understand where we have come from, who we are, and how we arrived at stuck and lost.

This has happened to me over and over again. In the moment of a situation or a circumstance, I interpreted the memory as one thing, but as I was able to get a greater perspective over time, I realized the situation I was facing was something different. Often God would take that pain and turn it into good in my life.

Without a new perspective, I would look back with frustration, bitterness, and regret. With a greater perspective, I could see a greater picture being painted in my life. Not only have I seen this in my life many times over, but almost without exception, I see it happen over and over again in every person who I have helped guide through a perspective-seeking process.

LET'S LOOK AT THE WRIGHT BROTHERS AGAIN, THIS TIME AS AN example of how perspective makes a huge difference. During the bicycle boom in the 1890s, it is estimated that approximately 300 bicycle manufacturers were producing over one million bicycles each year.[1]

Successful businessmen in their own right, the Wright Brothers decided to venture into manufacturing, adding their own line of bicycles to their business portfolio, along with offering parts, service, and retailing a variety of bicycle brands. In the years they produced their own handcrafted bicycles, they only made and sold 300 bicycles, which equates to about 50-60 bicycles a year out of a market of one million or more bikes produced annually. Not great numbers, right?

This is where interpretation and seeking perspective come into play. One interpretation they could have easily come to is that they are not good at manufacturing things or at least not any good at hand building things.

While I have no knowledge of it, it is possible that friends, family, peers, colleagues, creditors, and others would have offered well-meaning advice to stay out of manufacturing of any type and simply stick to repairs and the retailing of other "better" manufactured bicycles.

Using today's language, well-intentioned advice might sound like this, "You need to stay in your lane," "You need to focus on your wheelhouse," "You need to find your sweet spot," "You need to be true to yourself, and what you have been up to the last few years really isn't you."

All well-intentioned comments, but without perspective, they are more likely doubt-creating comments. Based on their lack of success in selling their custom-made bicycles, it would have been easy for the Wright Brothers to let doubt be cast, creating a chain-like tether that would hold them from their potential.

Yet, history tells us they viewed their experience with a different perspective. History tells us their perspective was that they highly valued the effort, time, and energy that went into building those bicycles by hand. Not only did they value what went into it, but they valued the experience they received from it.

The time they put into hand manufacturing the bicycles was also time invested in manufacturing and hand building the mechanisms that controlled the powering and piloting of the bike (the pedaling and steering). They studied such things with impeccable attention to detail. Then they custom built the mechanisms to do it better, and then they studied and tested it more.

What may have looked like business or manufacturing ineptitude was more likely and more profoundly the laboratory for a greater reality on the horizon, their Blue Sky Potential if you will.

Now, think about your life. Think about all of the memories you may have interpreted slightly or wholly inaccurately. That is going to take a long time, isn't it? That's why you need to slow down, take some time, and dive in deeply. Invite a friend or a guide to walk with you through these memories and see if there is new perspective to be gleaned.

As you seek perspective, I know clarity will follow, and as it does, it will help you understand where you are now and where you are headed in the future.

Just maybe, what looks like a history of failure, missed opportunities, or even ineptitude in your life has been more profoundly the laboratory for a greater reality on the horizon and your Blue Sky Potential. To begin to get clarity in your life, you need to begin to seek perspective on what was.

PERSPECTIVE—WHAT IS

Speaking of where you are now, the new perspective I have been bringing you throughout this book has already begun to help, I'm sure. Admittedly, I have really only scratched the surface of the perspective you can begin to get about your life in this very moment. There are many, many great tools, resources, and assessments that can help you evaluate and discover a new perspective on who you are right now.

I have used many of them and will continue to use many of them because I'm always seeking a new perspective—a new understanding. Just to describe a few categories for reference, you'll find a wide variety of personality assessments, strength discovery tools, temperament, and decision-making tests. And, with each one I take, I seek new perspective in my life, and as such, I am able to see myself with a new level of clarity.

Most people have experienced some of these tools, and still others seek them out regularly. In fact, some people are resource, tool, or assessment junkies. You know who I'm talking about—those people who are taking a new tool every other day and posting the results on social media. Like what is your spirit animal? How does your favorite type of ice cream describe your approach to dating? Based on how much water you drink each day, predict your likelihood of entrepreneurial success.

I'm sure you have seen the crazy variety of assessment tools out there. At times, it can leave us cynical about how useful assessments are altogether. Even some of the good ones can leave us questioning the validity of any tool—a question I often hear is, "How can every human fit so nicely into 1 of 18 categories?" Based on these experiences, a lot of people simply give up on seeking perspective.

Let me encourage you in this. Don't give up. Not all assessments, tools, and resources are created equal. Do your homework, ask trusted leaders and guides which ones have been useful to them, and then begin to seek perspective. If one resonates, glean what you can from it.

If you seek one out, and it isn't sinking in well, ask someone you trust to help you interpret it, and if it still isn't landing, then toss it out, and move on. Just don't give up on seeking perspective.

Beyond just the encouragement, let me offer you some advice as well. Start with the people around you who you look up to, admire, or esteem. Then within that group, look for those who seem to have a well-rounded sense of self-awareness. Seek them out, ask them for a few minutes on their calendar, or offer to take them to coffee.

Then start asking questions.

Start asking them how they came to such a depth of self-awareness, how they are able to separate themselves from the drama and cut through chaos and lead with quiet confidence. Find out what books they have read that gave them the strengths you admire in them. Ask them what tools have helped them discover the perspective they have.

From there, I would expand the search beyond those who are immediately around you to those you admire from a distance. In this case, I'm talking about authors, speakers, or public figures who seem to have a balance, wisdom, and perspective in life that you seek. Of course, you can read their material, follow them on social media, and become a groupie of sorts, but that isn't where I'm going with this.

There's an interesting twist here that many people have never thought of. Listen closely to them in their books, speeches, blog posts, articles, not for their content only, but for their comments about others who have impacted them. No doubt you admire this person, but if you want to know how they got there, I would advise you to begin to look at who shaped them.

When an author drops a hint about a book that impacted them, make a note. When a speaker shares an excellent point about an area of their own growth and refers to the fact that it began when they read a chapter from another author's book, there is a clue.

When you see well-rounded, perspective-based people you admire, it is most likely because those people sought perspective, and if you like how they turned out with that new clarity, then you need to get perspective from the same sources that impacted them. I do this all the time.

You have to pay attention and listen closely, but once you do, you will start to see those clues. Many authors of non-fiction books will even leave a bibliography in the back of their books, and many bloggers will have a section on their blogs that highlight their favorite resources.

These are all great places to consider that take the search for perspective and clarity a layer deeper than simply following your favorite author or speaker.

SEEKING PERSPECTIVE—NEXT STEPS

If you are still feeling a bit unsure where to begin, then let me remind you of a healthy sequence, and then give some categories that may help you get started. I would highly recommend you begin with examining what *was*, as we already discussed.

Starting with seeking a new perspective of where you have been and where you came from is going to give you a great foundation and help you begin to align how you got to where you are right now. Then, as we have talked about, turn next to evaluating what *is*, as in right now.

You cannot move into the endless possibility of what can be from a place you are not yet, so start with where you are. When looking for the right assessments, tools, and resources, whether on your own, or by seeking advice from people you admire, or even the clues being offered by your heroes, there are some specific categories you may want to target.

I have mentioned many of them throughout this book, but not through this lens of perspective, so let me simply make a list. I would look for tools, assessments, and resources that help you get perspective and clarity in a wide array of areas. Find tools, resources, and people that will help you:

- More accurately interpret and understand the positive and painful experiences in your life
- Discern the seasons of life that you have experienced and are experiencing right now
- Understand how to navigate life with your personality, character traits, and temperament
- Discover your how your level of tolerance for risk, change, and uncertainty impact your decision making
- Be conscious of your communication methods and style
- Articulate and define your core values
- Define your strengths and your talents

I know I have listed quite a few categories here, and to some, it can be overwhelming. Yet, your life is so unique, so different than any other life, that each one of these facets of your life is going to bring a new perspective. Over time, with the right guide, that perspective is going to lead you to clarity—a clarity that you have needed for a long time, and a clarity that is required to truly be unleashed from uncertainty and doubt.

I told you that you were going to need to set some time away to begin to truly seek perspective, didn't I? I want you to know it is worth it. As I said before, clarity is not only necessary, *it is paramount.* Without clarity, and often without heaps of clarity, doubt reaches out of the ground and pins us down like bent steel rebar on that artistic bicycle chained to the palm tree that is right now still sitting four houses down the street from me.

I share these thoughts based on my own personal experience and based on the experience I have in guiding others to discover perspective and clarity in these very same categories. Whether through keynote addresses, workshops, seminars, books, webinars and online courses, or private retreats, I guide people through perspective and into clarity in all of these areas. I know the power of clarity personally, and I have seen the power of clarity unleash others into their Blue Sky Potential. You need clarity, my friend. There is power in it. More power than you know.

You see, we don't seek perspective to get clarity simply for clarity's sake. Clarity has the power to produce something we desperately need: *confidence*. Check out "Part B" of this first simple truth of transformational breakthrough.

Simple Truth of Transformational Breakthrough #1

YOU NEED CLARITY
because

(Part B)

CLARITY PRODUCES CONFIDENCE...

You can't fake confidence. You can't muster it up. You can't even mine for it. It is either there, or it isn't. You are either confident, or you are not. There is no in-between. But there is a source that produces confidence. I know what produces a genuine fountain of confidence. It's *clarity*. Like an apple tree produces apples, a kernel produces corn, and a bulb produces a flower, clarity produces confidence. Said another way...

A genuine confidence is the naturally produced result of clarity.

I'm not talking about arrogance, hubris, or cockiness. I'm not talking about being puffed up, filled with pride, or big-headed. I'm not talking about faking it until you make it. I'm not talking about covering up your insecurities by acting over-confident. I'm also not talking about confidence that comes from money, position, power, authority, or strength of resources.

None of these things are forms of genuine confidence. Instead, I'm talking about a quiet confidence that is certain about the trajectory of life. *That* is the type of confidence I believe you are looking for. Think about that.

When was the last time you walked through life with the quiet confidence that your life was headed in the right direction and that you were on the trajectory toward your Blue Sky Potential? For many, even for those who are cocky or who have a wealth of resources, a genuine confidence about the trajectory of life is a rare experience—if they have ever felt it at all.

There are a couple definitions of confidence that are fitting for our conversation. One is that confidence is the state of feeling certain about the truth of something. I want you to discover and know a quiet confidence about the beautiful truth of your life, based on the perspective you have discovered and clarity you have uncovered.

A second definition is that confidence is a feeling of self-assurance arising from one's appreciation of one's own abilities or qualities. Yes! When was the last time you understood or defined those special abilities or qualities about your life? Sure, you have had people affirm and confirm them here and there, but how long has it been since you walked with an appreciation and steady unwavering confidence in them?

I want that for you *so* much. And it can be possible, but rarely can it happen without seeking the perspective in the categories I listed a few pages back. Those are the areas of life that will help you begin to discover, value, and appreciate through a new perspective about yourself. And that new perspective is going to lead to a clarity that you have been needing for a long time. That type of clarity, that which is bathed in perspective and the beautiful truth about who you are and what you have to offer, is going to produce a confidence you have not yet even imagined.

I HAVE SO MANY GREAT MEMORIES IN A WIDE VARIETY OF experiences where I have helped people get perspective and clarity. No matter when and where it happens, it is always an exhilarating experience for me. Sometimes I see it in the audience's reaction when I unpack a new thought while giving a talk. I see it in the eyes and words of an attendee at a workshop who pulled me aside after a session. I get to witness it firsthand with a one-on-one client who invited me to guide them through a transitional season in life.

One of the stories I love and remember the most comes from a client of mine, named Mike, who is someone I now consider a dear friend.

When Mike and I had our first coffee, we had already known each other from a distance for a few years. He had seen me speak a number of times and was an observer of one of my more public leadership roles, which was an extended season of transition and succession planning that required immense amounts of internal and external cultural change in the organization I was serving. I didn't know it, but he had been watching.

When we first sat down, I remember him sharing a bunch of flattering and kind words and that, for quite some time, he had been feeling the need to reach out and ask me to mentor him. Funny thing because I am about 15 years his younger, and I actually looked up to him as I had observed and followed his impact in the world too.

Mike was already extremely successful in his professional endeavors. Specifically, he had become a nationally recognized leader in fundraising, donor engagement, and planned-giving in the higher education sector. As much as he was looking for me to mentor and guide him, I knew there were a few things I could learn from him as well.

He had grown his career though some amazing colleges and universities. Because of his track record, and his ability to navigate the complexities of working with some of the most generous philanthropists and their families, he was regularly courted by the most notable and prestigious universities in the United States.

He finally reached out for coffee for a very specific reason: the university he loved and served had recently experienced some signif-icant leadership change, which was causing some cultural and prac-tical realities to change and shift around him. He continued to share that even though up to that point, he absolutely loved his work as well as the university he was a part of, within a few short months of the changes, he was quickly finding himself at his own version of the corner of stuck and lost.

I listened and encouraged him, and we stayed in touch. We met a few times for coffee and lunch over the next six months, and during those chats, I must have said a few things that piqued his interest in my highly personalized one-on-one professional develop-ment work. He eventually reached a pain-point, or crossroads of sorts, and invited me to guide him through a two and a half day intensive LifePlan experience.

I say *invited*, because while it is a highly valuable consulting service I offer to individuals and couples, I don't view it as a product to "sell." It is too powerful and too sacred of an experience to sell, convince, or otherwise twist someone's arm into doing, and there-fore, I don't use phrases like, "Mike *agreed* to do it." Using terms like that would imply I convinced him to do it, and that is not my approach.

Anytime I have the opportunity to guide someone in any setting, I see it as an invitation to me from that person to join them on their journey. That is true even for this book. Since you decided to pick it up and read it, I consider it a privilege and an honor, and in many ways, as an invitation from you to me to join you on your journey. And in response, I have invited you into a journey of soaring into the blue skies with me, so the invitation is reciprocal.

Nonetheless, Mike invited me, and maybe more practically speaking, hired me to guide him through the a private LifePlan experience. I had communicated the value of a LifePlan, knowing it would help him discover and map out a path to his Blue Sky Poten-tial, both in his life and his career journey. And, thinking ahead of how this story ends, I assume that over those months together that I kept using various phrases that tied the idea of clarity to confidence. I didn't know that I was doing that necessarily—I just assumed everyone saw the connection, so I assumed I was using common language.

What I do know is that I did assure him that I would guide him into more perspective in those few days than he had likely experienced in the totality of his professional development and leadership journey put together. I know that sounds like a big statement, but it's true. I haven't met a client yet who hasn't agreed that inviting me to guide them through a breakthrough experience wasn't one of the, if not the single most, revealing, clarifying, and impactful experiences they have ever had. In going through those early conversations with him, I guess I had talked about the value and connections between perspective, clarity, and confidence.

During this season, Mike was being courted by a number of organizations, and we were regularly talking through those opportunities as our time together was approaching. Interestingly enough, just prior to the time we had set aside for the LifePlan, Mike had secured an interview for a VP role at a nonprofit, and the date of the interview was within a week or so of our sessions. Adding some pressure to the upcoming interview were two interesting twists to the opportunity.

The first twist was that the nonprofit was not in the higher-learning and education sector, but rather a Christian-based nonprofit. In fact, this wasn't just any Christian nonprofit but an organization that has an impact on upwards of 20 million people weekly and is nationally regarded as a leader and innovator in media and broadcasting.

In Mike's career journey, he had twice tried to make the leap from higher education into executive level leadership in a Christian-based nonprofit and had both times made it to the last round of interviews, only to fall short each time in the runner-up position.

In some ways, he was excited about the interview, and in other ways, he was doubtful and apathetic toward it (there are those words again). The previous experiences had each cast a leash of doubt, and the clouds of his current work environment were preventing him from seeing the opportunity for what it was.

The second interesting twist was that despite this organization's legacy and its widely successful direct fundraising efforts from its constituency, it had never established a true long-term strategy for fundraising, donor engagement, and planned-giving. So, as a result, the role Mike was interviewing for would create a new seat at the executive table and would include the responsibility of pioneering, establishing, and building out the vision and a fully functional team from the ground up.

Despite Mike's extensive career and collaborative approach, Mike had never held a role like this. He had run very successful donor engagement programs with larges teams and talented staff, but never had been asked to build one from the ground up. So, mix all of that in with the combination of doubt and apathy Mike already had about the opportunity, the scheduled sessions were extremely timely to say the least.

We have talked about uncertainly, now haven't we? And this is exactly where Mike found himself as we had breakfast on our first morning together. Mike was as uncertain as he had been in years. The university he loved was changing; the result was very uncomfortable; and it felt like it was no longer a place he could give his best. The most immediate opportunity in front of him filled his heart with a combination of doubt and apathy. The other opportunities were interesting, but not compelling. Stuck and lost were clearly intersecting in Mike's life.

In the two and a half days together, we were able to unpack his life story, seeking perspective by mapping his major turning points and how those impacted him and his trajectory. We mapped out how the variety of seasons he had lived were leading to this moment in his life right now.

We were able to chart out the passion, desires, and dreams that had been on his heart for most of his life, as well as unearth and articulate the unique and inherent talents that he alone possesses. We mined out and defined the core values that guided his life like river banks and charted his communication and decision-making style based on his threshold for risk, change, and opportunity.

With all of that perspective, and so much more that came in our time together, we were able to get clarity on his unique life's purpose and vision as well as the strategies to which he would need to hold fast to see that vision come to pass. In fact, as usual, we did not initially even discuss the opportunities that were on the horizon.

Instead, we spent the large majority of our time seeking immense amounts of perspective and regularly arriving at increasing levels of clarity. At the very end, we used a quick filtering process, and the wide and deep moments of clarity we had achieved all converged in one moment.

With that filtering process, in light of the new clarity, we evaluated his current role at the university, the new opportunity at the nonprofit, as well as the other possible job opportunities, and the next steps began to reveal themselves.

Based on the evaluation and filtering process, we discovered that it was very clear that his role at the university needed to come to an end. Not only that, but he most likely only had about three to six months of internal staying power and fortitude. The good news is that the nonprofit was a very viable opportunity and potentially an amazing fit based on all we had discovered in the LifePlan.

We knew that we would soon need to map out an exit plan for his current role, but it would sure be good to first know how the upcoming interview at the nonprofit would go. Because he had already been vetted by a trusted consultant in the industry, the first interview was a fully immersive interview with the executive team at the nonprofit. Given all that we discovered together, we both knew there was a lot riding on this interview.

Not much more than a week after our time together, as he was preparing to board the airplane for that interview later that day, he called for some encouragement. I simply pointed him to all the tools, charts, and clarity that came out of the LifePlan. I even emailed him a cheat sheet of sorts that highlighted the biggest discoveries of clarity from our time together.

Over the years, I have helped a lot of people prepare for interviews, but it is so much easier when I have all the perspective and clarity of a LifePlan as ammunition to encourage them and give them substantive talking points like I could with Mike.

I imagine that story has already been encouraging, but by now, you might be wondering why I took the time to share it. First, I hope that story is a bit inspiring and gives you a glimpse of how perspective and clarity help. But second, and more importantly, all of that was really for the purpose of telling you my absolute favorite part of the story.

It was later that evening when I checked my phone and realized I had a missed call from Mike, and I saw that famous blue dot signifying that I had a voicemail waiting for me. I picked up my phone and hit play, wondering what Mike's reflections of the interview would be.

Well, I'll describe the sound of the voicemail like this: Imagine a rollercoaster junkie had just got off the most adrenaline-pumping, awe-inspiring, best ride he'd ever had on a roller coaster and left you a voicemail to tell you about it—blood still pumping and voice still shaking because of the speed, loops, and twists he just experienced in pure roller coaster joy. I'm not even sure that describes the excitement in Mike's voice.

Better yet, try to imagine the sounds of a competitor at the X-Games, who was the last competitor to go in his discipline and who had just nailed the landing on the craziest, most dangerous, and acrobatic trick he had ever tried.

As he made it to the bottom of the hill, he saw the scoreboard light up with a gold medal score and now is being interviewed by the also-hyped X-Games TV journalist.

Imagine the sense of adrenaline but also the sense of victorious relief. Now, put the roller-coaster junkie and the X-Games gold medalist together, and that's what Mike's voice sounded like.

For me, listening to that voicemail was the payoff. No matter how much Mike had invested financially for the LifePlan, no amount of money could equate to the payoff of experiencing such joy in Mike's voice. And yet, the payoff was not only in his joy and excitement, it was in the words that he shared.

I'm not able to quote it word for word, but it went something like this:

"Jeff! You are never going to believe this, but that was the best interview I have ever given! I'm a perfect fit for them, and I really believe this role and organization are a perfect fit for me! Wow! It was an incredible conversation and an amazing couple of hours together with the executive team. I didn't even prepare my normal notes that I usually use for an interview. I just simply read through the notes from our time together in the LifePlan and the cheat sheet you sent me and affirmed to myself the clarity we had discovered."

"Man, Jeff. You weren't kidding all those times when you said clarity led to confidence! I can't even believe it. I had so much clarity about who I am, the talents I have to offer, and the dreams in my heart that I just confidently shared the vision of how I could bring all of that to their organization. It was so easy and natural. Clarity really does lead to confidence! I have never had so much confidence in the truth that I am ready to make the leap in my career into a new executive role and even one in an organization as successful and significant as this one. I can really see myself in this role, and I know the team can see me in it too. Thank you for the clarity! Thank you for the confidence, Jeff!"

A huge smile rushed across my face then, and rushes across my face, even now, as I remember listening to that voicemail. As I said before, I guess I had assumed that everyone knew that clarity led to confidence, and I hadn't realized I was revealing a foreign concept.

At times, I too easily forget how uncertain life is for most people who do not have clarity. It was in this moment that I more fully realized the value of this truth. It locked in for me in a much greater way. While I had seen it often in my life and in the lives of those I have guided, I had never had it said back to me with quite that level of excitement, and it is a memory I will never forget.

I have pondered that moment many times over since it happened, and I have made another connection that is just as important as the connection between clarity and confidence. There is also a connection between confidence and doubt.

Just like before, I believe this new connection was something I knew inherently, but something I hadn't fully codified without more intentional thought. So, it is time I share it with you. Not only does clarity produce confidence, but confidence has a greater impact than confidence alone. Confidence severs doubt.

This leads us to "Part C" of our first simple truth of transformational breakthrough.

Simple Truth of Transformational Breakthrough #1

YOU NEED CLARITY
because
CLARITY PRODUCES CONFIDENCE
and

(Part C)

CONFIDENCE SEVERS DOUBT

REMEMBER THAT BICYCLE LEASHED TO THE PALM TREE WITH THAT thick chain and pinned down by that steel rebar? That was Mike's doubt regarding his two prior experiences in interviewing for a position like this. For Mike, the confidence that came from clarity dealt a mighty blow to the doubt of his prior experiences.

The confidence-producing clarity was the force that unleashed Mike from his doubt that he couldn't make the leap into executive leadership, let alone in a new sector of the marketplace. In all of the journey of growing, changing, and transforming he had done throughout his career, Mike was still held back by a leash of doubt that was limiting his potential.

For him, through inviting me to guide him into breakthrough, by first seeking deep perspective, he was able to gain immense clarity, and that clarity produced confidence, which, in turn, severed his doubt.

Within a short time, we were mapping out Mike's exit plan at the university and preparing his entrance into his new executive role in a new industry. Beyond the friendship, I have had the privilege of continuing a professional relationship with Mike and have been serving as his executive coach in his new role. Did Mike have some clouds to navigate in the transition, moving his family across the country, and transplanting his leadership style into an existing executive team? Absolutely.

As he elevated from the trajectory of his reality (stuck and lost at the university), toward the trajectory line of his Blue Sky Potential, he did run into a number of clouds filled with confusion, uncertainty, and frustration. Did he have to persevere and sever doubt as those clouds entered the picture? For sure.

Yet, as those clouds attempted to slow him down, we were able to leverage all the clarity we discovered together in our sessions to keep up his confidence, to keep severing doubt, and to help him navigate around, through and over those clouds. There were plenty of areas in which Mike developed and grew during his journey up and through the Opportunity Zone, and of course, as expected, he even transformed in the process.

As of today, Mike has grown his division from a nonexistent team to more than 20 full-time staff members. Beyond the fundraising success his team is having, they have created a fundraising environment that places a priority on the people in the constituency over the money held by those people.

As such, under Mike's leadership, they are pioneering the ability to create community, friendship, and ministry within the constituency of donors like has never been done before. Not surprisingly, focusing on people has let to a lot of goodwill and ultimately to increased levels of fundraising as the byproduct. Talk about the endless possibility of impacting others for good!

The entire journey from our first coffee near the corner of stuck and lost, to soaring on the new trajectory of his potential took about two years, but Mike is truly soaring in the blue sky. In fact, with all the capital his team is raising, this nonprofit will have the resources and funds to expand its reach and impact well beyond the 20 million people it reaches each week for generations to come.

Mike was already doing amazing work in higher education, but now that he is soaring in the blue sky of his potential at the nonprofit, he is elevating his life to a life of endless possibility, a life of greatness that is impacting millions of other lives for good. Mike has truly experienced the *transformational breakthrough* that we have been talking about.

Just one of many, Mike's story is one of the reasons I keep encouraging you that the pursuit of your Blue Sky Potential is a journey—a journey that takes time. It is why I didn't promise to fix every problem you have or find an answer to your every question.

Yet, I did assure you that I could give you a map, or a flight plan, and begin to guide you into your potential so you could reach your dreams. It begins with clarity, my friend, which is founded on perspective, which is established by being willing to see yourself, your experiences, and the world around you differently.

THIS PRINCIPLE OF SEEKING PERSPECTIVE IN ORDER TO ARRIVE AT clarity and, ultimately, a clarity that produces confidence is one I believe the Wright Brothers knew well. As I shared before, many may have considered Orville and Wilbur's venture into handcrafting and manufacturing their own bicycles as a failed experiment.

Yet, I believe how they looked at this season of life, and the type of perspective they gained from it, is what made it possible for them to ultimately create the first flying machine.

It was in this "laboratory" of manufacturing bicycles that the Wright Brothers honed their patience and expertise for perfecting mechanical systems that created balance and maneuverability in human-controlled machines (first the bicycle and later the flying machine or airplane).

Their perspective gave them clarity, and the clarity gave them confidence, which gave them the ability to overcome any doubt that could have attempted to make its way into their minds. I believe their perspective and clarity were so fortified that this is what truly got the first airplane off the ground.

All of their competition from other scientists and inventors in the race for the first airplane was focused on building more powerful engines, convinced that the power would make flight more likely.

However, because of their experience building the mechanisms to make the perfect bicycle, that confidence convinced them that the answer to the question of flight was to be found in building better mechanical systems that would bring balance and control to the flying machine that already had plenty of power.

Their ability to handcraft, test, and adjust the balance and control mechanisms on the first flying machine is what gave them the ability to get that plane off the ground in a way that could be piloted (flown).

It was those very skills of handcrafting, testing, and adjusting the mechanisms on the bicycle that gave them the perspective and clarity and, therefore, the confidence that the same truths would help them solve the problem of flight.

The same is true in your life. As you seek perspective, you are going to have the opportunity to arrive at a place of clarity. That clarity—both in terms of your past and your life as it is right now—can bring about a confidence that can sever doubt and unleash your potential.

While everyone around you is seeking more productivity and power, you are wisely seeking perspective. You know a greater perspective will reveal clarity, and that clarity will produce the confidence you need to sever doubt. It doesn't mean that Clouds of Confusion won't accumulate and even at times bring full on thunder and lightning storms.

The difference is that when they do, the perspective and clarity it provides will help you keep your eyesight above the clouds, where you can clearly envision the blue sky of your potential. It will also fuel your perseverance as you transform through the Opportunity Zone.

A confident certainty can mute all the questions, criticism, and lies that attempt to create doubt and thwart us from our potential. The confidence you can experience in the journey will give you a mighty sword, to deliver the forceful blow to sever and unleash you from doubt when it attempts to ground you.

As a final reminder, here is the first simple but profound truth of transformational breakthrough:

Simple Truth of Transformational Breakthrough #1

YOU NEED CLARITY
because
CLARITY PRODUCES CONFIDENCE
and
CONFIDENCE SEVERS DOUBT

You Begin the Journey to Clarity by Seeking Perspective

CHAPTER 9

MEANING — PURPOSE CREATES COURAGE

"If you're alive, there's
a purpose for your life."

- RICK WARREN

ONCE YOU HAVE EXPERIENCED THE POWER AND POTENTIAL FOR transformational breakthrough found in discovering clarity in your life, you will have a sense of freedom you may have never had before. As you continue to climb through the Opportunity Zone toward your Blue Sky Potential, the clarity you have discovered will propel you to new levels of growth, development, and additional transformation.

Sure, clouds and circumstances will still attempt to interfere with, and at times succeed at slowing your trajectory, but because of that clarity, you'll have a natural source of confidence inside of you. That confidence will fuel your journey around and through those confusion-causing clouds.

You will be able to wield the truth of clarity to continue to sever doubt anytime it attempts to rise up and strap you back to the ground. In a sense, you have been unleashed into your Blue Sky Potential like never before.

Yet, clarity will only take you so far. Clarity gives you the confidence to move away from that corner of stuck and lost. The trouble is that you will eventually run into one or more challenging Clouds of Confusion, which are going to reveal another leash that's holding you back.

The leash of doubt may be slayed, but the internal feelings of failure, pain, and even simply the risk of soaring in the blue skies is likely going to show you a new leash—the leash of *fear*. Fear is a dangerous leash, my friend. It comes after us in so many forms, from so many directions, and often with deadly, trajectory-stopping accuracy.

No matter how much clarity you have discovered, or how much doubt you have overcome, fear can bind you with chains and can keep you tethered to the ground. As I'm sure you have experienced before, fear often leads to a sense of immobility and paralysis, especially emotionally, if not even physically. When fear confines you and stops you in your tracks, it can completely eliminate any chance of soaring further into the blue sky of your potential.

Early and regularly throughout our journeys, it is often fear that leads us into doubt, and as a result, we get trapped by doubt. Then, as we experience transformational breakthrough by discovering clarity, we get free from doubt. Yet, we often forget it was fear that stopped us in the first place.

So, guess what this means?

Even though we have begun to experience the power of clarity, it means we are going to have to face those fears again. I know, that's tough to hear. Especially when you were beginning to imagine and maybe even feel the wind in your hair brought on by the freedom that clarity is bringing into your life. Unfortunately, those fears did not go away, but instead, they simply hid out behind the clouds of doubt, which those very fears created in the first place.

In order to continue your journey of transformational breakthrough, you will need to sever fear. And, fear is a difficult leash to sever, my friend, not unlike that industrial-sized chain and steel rebar that has that bicycle leashed to the palm tree a few houses down the street from where I now write. But there is hope.

Fear in our lives can be defeated, and you need to wield another new truth to do it. To continue to unleash your Blue Sky Potential, to be set free to reach your dreams, you need to understand, value, and wield the unleashing force found in *purpose*. Here is "Part A" of the second simple truth of transformational breakthrough.

Simple Truth of Transformational Breakthrough #2

(Part A)

YOU NEED PURPOSE…

Maybe more accurately, you need to *discover* your purpose. The reality is that you already have purpose—you just may not know exactly what it is yet. Purpose, simply defined, is the reason for which something is created, and the reason for which it exists. More personally and more practically, *your purpose* is the reason *you* were created, the reason *you* exist.

I believe that no matter the story or circumstances that brought about your conception and birth, your life is not an accident. Not at all, my friend. You see, I believe there is a reason you were born, a reason you have breath, a reason you are alive, a reason you have a future, a reason you were created. Within all that reason is *your unique purpose.*

Not only were you created to live, but you were created to live with and for a purpose. In fact, to me, the very reality that you exist is evidence of purpose. Sure, right now, a purpose maybe you have yet to discover, but a life intended and destined for purpose, no less. Now is the time for you to discover your unique life purpose. You are not going much further without it, or at least further in a way that is both fulfilling and impactful to your own life, not to mention to the lives of those around you.

Remember that clarity is paramount, meaning a priority and a necessity. Likewise, purpose too is important. Yet, it is not only important, *it is transcendent:* it is beyond the range of normal or merely physical human experience. The transcendent nature of purpose is what makes it so very illusive to us, often difficult to perceive, grasp, and especially difficult to discover with any amount of detail and clarity.

Yet, without purpose, life can feel empty, shallow, and insignificant. Without purpose, we have no way of evaluating if our lives are heading in the right direction. Without purpose, we have no way of evaluating if our lives are "successful." Even more than those big picture concepts, without purpose, we have no way of truly evaluating the merit or success of each day, let alone the merit of our actions, behaviors, and decisions.

Sure, maybe we can measure and justify the direction and success of our lives, or the behaviors and actions the way so many do. Maybe we can measure the size of our bank accounts, or the size of our houses, or the size of our muscles, or the size of our waists, or the size of our online following, or the size of our status, as some do, and allow those to either define us as successful or not. Yet, at the end of the day, most who have experienced success in those areas would reflect that the merit of those measurements of success leaves them empty and still lacking purpose.

You have likely heard the Beatles famous song, "Can't Buy Me Love," and it is just as true that you "can't buy me purpose." Even the ancient King Solomon, who is recorded in history as having as much love, fortune, and even wisdom as any human being in history, felt the pain of lacking purpose. History records many of his words, through which it is evident that he wrestled with these realities and definitions of success.

After spending a lifetime piling up immense fame and fortune, following and status, Solomon reflected on how his life felt completely meaningless and how it left him wanting more.[1] I believe his search for purpose had been wrongly aimed at all those material things that eventually left him without meaning and, therefore, without purpose.

As I said before, purpose is transcendent. Purpose transcends the material world because the material world will never help us answer the question of why we exist—a question that so many of us find ourselves asking when we feel stuck and lost. Yet, genuine, unique, transcendent purpose that answers the question of our existence is so difficult to truly discover.

I'm guessing that even if you have dared to go on the search for your purpose, you most likely feel like you have come up empty. It very well could be, however, that like Solomon, you have been looking in all the wrong places. Maybe you have been looking in the right places but had no idea how to search and discover purpose. Either way, the obvious question is how do you begin the journey of finding your unique purpose?

SEEKING MEANING

We discover purpose by seeking *meaning*. Without finding meaning, we will likely never discover purpose, at least not one that transcends the material world and its empty measurements of success. Here's why:

> *Purpose always results from discovering meaning,*
> *and purpose offered to the world results in something meaningful.*

Did you catch that? That is the transcendent nature of it—your purpose comes from meaning *and* results in meaning. As you seek to discover your purpose, you will see it is going to be derived from a sense of meaning, *and* it will impact the world around you in a meaningful way. Meaning and purpose are as tied together as perspective and clarity; that is, one leads to the other. Just as seeking perspective leads to clarity, seeking meaning leads to purpose.

Seeking meaning requires a willingness to look *deeply within* ourselves and *widely beyond* ourselves.

Again, even in that statement, you can sense the transcendent nature of purpose. Not only does purpose transcend material things, it even transcends us as individuals. What I mean by that is that when you find your purpose, it is never limited to just an impact on you as a singular benefactor. When you find your purpose, it is going to make a meaningful impact on the world around you.

If you recall all the way back to Chapter 4, I spent quite a bit of time unpacking what the concept of Blue Sky Potential really means. I made the case that beyond self-actualizing, the potential of your life has an endless possibility of impacting others for good. The reality of that endless possibility is more realistic if and when you can find your purpose. So, if endless possibility begins with purpose, and purpose is derived from finding meaning, we need to understand where and how we need to search for meaning.

MEANING—LOOK DEEPLY WITHIN

Seeking meaning begins when we are willing to look deeply within ourselves. The good news is that if we have already gone on the search for clarity, we are well on the way. What I mean by that is if you were willing to take the time to slow down and seek the perspective of what *was* and what *is*, then you are already postured to take the time to seek meaning deeply within. Because the pursuit of meaning also requires us to slow down, to reflect, and to search.

Yet, we are going to have to go a number of layers deeper in our hearts, spirits, and souls. This search isn't simply for a more accurate interpretation of our stories, or a clearer understanding of our core values or talents. Those discoveries will point the way but won't get us all the way.

While all of those things are important in the search for perspective and clarity, the search for meaning and purpose goes much deeper. That said, they are a great place to begin, especially now that we have clarity, and with that clarity, we can go deeper in the search for meaning.

Let's first consider our life stories. If we have done the hard work of seeking perspective and clarity, then we have a great starting point for seeking meaning. As we unpack the various experiences, we have most likely uncovered a whole bunch of positive experiences as well as a whole bunch of negative experiences.

The fascinating reality is that both positive and negative experiences leave an imprint of sorts on our hearts, which cause us to feel a certain way. Those feelings leave traces of meaning, like fingerprints on our souls. If we can take the time to search within, we are going to be able to piece together all the fingerprints that have been left on our souls and identify the source or, in other words, identify what is meaningful to us.

A positive experience will leave a fingerprint of richness, joy, beauty, and celebration. These types of experiences often leave the type of mark or feeling that we would love to see repeated in our lives again and again. We often find ourselves reminiscing about the good old days or that moment that brought us so much joy. Somewhere wrapped up in all those positive memories and positive feelings are fingerprints of meaning.

We would love to have a daily dose of those positive experiences, not just because we are gluttons for positivity, but because they provide a dose of meaning that brightens our souls. More than just our lives, however, when we experience something positive, we often want to see that same experience repeated in the lives of others—those we love and even those we believe we can help.

Think about it. If you have experienced a work environment with an ultra-supportive boss who spent as much time listening and caring as he did managing, you leaned into that. And, over time, because it was meaningful to you, you realized you want to lead others in the same meaningful way.

Maybe you have a friend who just always knew when to drop by with the right words, a small gift, a warm coffee, or a note card with encouragement. Their care brought a great deal of meaning to you and to the friendship. Over time, you learned to notice those moments of needed encouragement in others and offer the same meaning to them.

Why do we do this without even thinking about it? Because we inherently want to bring the type of meaning and value we have received in life and deliver that same type of meaning to those we care about.

Even negative experiences work in this same way, albeit in reverse. When we have an experience of pain, and especially when we get perspective, little fingerprints of meaning are left as a result. Yet, unlike positive experiences we want to see repeated, negative experiences leave a mark we'd rather avoid, never to feel again. The interesting reality is that we can often find meaning by helping others avoid those same negative experiences.

If you were bullied on the playground a few too many times and have done the hard work of finding healing from that, you may find meaning in being a champion to underdog types, with a desire for helping them avoid and overcome similar situations. And, when you come to the aid of others in that way, it is a rich and fulfilling experience for you.

Maybe you were treated unfairly at work, and it left you hurting and bruised for a long while. That leaves a fingerprint of meaning as well, and as you get a healthy perspective on it, you will often notice that you try and anticipate how your leadership impacts those around you, wanting to avoid making others feel the way you were made to feel. Leading that way gives you meaning and even small (or significant) glimmers of purpose in the workplace.

As we seek perspective and clarity from our life stories, we can discover a rich field to explore and search for meaning. We can search deeper into those special times in life when positive experiences left their meaningful fingerprints on our hearts, spirits, and souls. Likewise, when we search for perspective in our negative experiences and it leads us to see them with more clarity and health, we can begin to draw out meaning from those as well.

If you are willing to look deeply within, just in your life story alone is quite a reservoir of meaning. Yet, it is not only in our life stories where meaning can be found. There are so many other areas of our lives we can begin to search for meaning. There are so many areas that make up our interior worlds.

IN THE BREAKTHROUGH EXPERIENCE THAT I GUIDE PEOPLE THROUGH, I use a set of categories that provide clues to meaning, which you will see described in a few pages. To be transparent, I didn't come up with these categories, let alone package them in such a compre-hensive set.

Yet, you can easily find these categories, themes, and concepts as well as study them in any number of periodicals, journals, and books, both modern and ancient. I have been fascinated by how people think, feel, and are motivated, and as such, I have been studying these concepts since as early as middle school. Yet, this list of categories in this form was originally developed by someone else, and much credit is due.

The LifePlan process was originally designed and developed by Tom Paterson, a wonderful sage of a man. His strategic consulting work way back in the day with the Disney Brothers as well as corpo-rations like RCA and IBM all led to a Nobel Laureate prize for his work in rebuilding China, as commissioned by President Ronald Reagan and his administration.

During his career, Tom got to lead and be part of some amaz-ingly positive experiences like filing the patent for the first ATM and helping design Space Mountain, to name a couple. As much as experiences like those define his legacy, Tom also endured many painful experiences and life tragedies which left their mark on him as well.

Through that journey, Tom saw fingerprints of meaning inside himself and realized he could use his same strategic philosophies to help people in the way he was helping corporations and govern-ment. Based on discovering that meaning, Tom pioneered and created the Paterson LifePlan process.

As his legacy continued to be established, Tom poured his life's work into a couple of men, one of them I mentioned earlier: Pete. Pete has been a friend and mentor of mine for 15 years, and his influence on me has been life changing. I am eternally grateful for his generosity of time, friendship, and wisdom to me and my family.

Through Pete, I have been fortunate to have been one of a small number of people who have inherited the legacy of Tom's strategic brilliance in guiding people and teams into discovery, growth and breakthrough. In fact, I even had the opportunity to help develop and write some of the early training manuals for the Paterson Center almost a decade ago.

As I said, I don't claim to have any corner on the market with regard to putting these categories together in this list. What I can claim is I have spent decades helping people go deep in these categories, whether informally in a conversation over a cup of coffee, giving a talk or keynote, hosting a workshop or seminar, facilitating a LifePlan, and more recently through the breakthrough coaching and courses I offer online.

When I guide people to look within through the categories listed here and other categories like them, it is easy to see certain patterns emerge from which we can discover the fingerprints of meaning. When patterns and trends of meaning emerge, we begin to see purpose reveal itself.

With this list, I won't be able to take you as deeply as I can in my breakthrough coaching experiences, but it will be helpful to you nonetheless. I encourage you to allow this to get you started down the right path as you seek meaning within.

- **Passions**: *Passions in this sense align with desires (we will talk about another form of passion in the next chapter). Suffice to say, passions include things we enjoy immensely, seek out and pursue, and derive pleasure from. I'm not necessarily talking sensuality here but rather more pragmatic items. It could be anything from fly-fishing to building spreadsheets. Passions could be anything from baking cupcakes to rescuing kittens. I'm not even kidding. For every person I have ever had this conversation with, or guided in a breakthrough experience, I have never seen the same set of passions. And, if there ever has been an overlap in a subject, the why, how, and what behind someone's passion is always different than another.*

- **Needs**: *Needs speak of things we value, care for, and at times simply need in order to feel like we can function. It can be anything from alone time to adventure, from order and cleanliness to belief and affirmation from others. The motivation behind someone's list* *of needs is as different as every individual, and as you search within for your needs, ask yourself why do I need that? And, what lies behind that?*

- **Drives***: At times, you might feel that your drives are similar to passions, but if you go deeper, you can see the differences. While passions often speak to the experience of the subject of our desire, drives can be compared to our motivations. Said another way, what motivates you or compels you to start something new, or keep going when it is hard, or simply keep showing up when things are confusing. You might discover you are driven to provide, and that keeps you motivated at work when nothing else does. As you seek meaning, you might sense that you are driven by the opportunity to offer encouragement, and that explains why you are attracted to the down and out people in your office or neighborhood.*

- **Obsessions:** *Obsessions are not always filled with vanity, as in I obsess about my hair, or I obsess about my weight. Instead, for this exercise, obsessions are those things that are frequently the last thing on your mind when you go to bed as well as the first thing on your mind when you wake up. In other words, what is consistently "on your radar?" For some, the idea of productivity or efficiency make the list. For others, the ambience or the beauty of the environment around them is always on their mind. Still others might obsess about the well-being of others or how people are feeling. Again, every obsession varies from person to person, but as you dig deeper into what fuels that obsession, you will see hints of meaning.*

- **Characteristics***: Characteristics are the tendencies and personality traits that someone would be able to easily observe as a first impression when meeting you for 15 minutes or so. If people first notice your gentle spirit, there is probably meaning behind that. If people notice your intellect and ability to speak intelligently to many areas of the conversation, there too is meaning. If you are gregarious, humorous, bright, and bubbly, people will probably notice that when they first meet you. And, if you are willing to dig* *deeper into what is behind those first impressions, you will probably find meaning hidden there too. By the way, if it is uncomfortable thinking about yourself like this, it's okay. Stretch yourself and be comfortable in your own skin for a few moments. Even smile.*

- **Qualities:** *Qualities are similar to characteristics, but instead of the traits that are noticed as a first impression, qualities are the endearing and enduring truths about your character that are experienced over longer lengths of time. Loyal, generous, compassionate, unwavering, long-suffering, genuine, humble, authentic, faithful, and truthful are just a few of the many beautiful qualities that are stored within people. As you allow yourself to embrace the reality that these qualities are inside of you for a purpose, you will begin to see there is a greater meaning behind them than simply the belief that you've "just always been like that." Because if you have always "just been like that," then there is probably meaning and purpose behind why you were created that way or even purpose as to why you became that way through the experiences in your life story.*

- **Yearnings**: *I really enjoy unpacking yearnings with people because more often than not, no one has ever asked them about their yearnings, let alone dug into the deeper meaning behind them. Yearnings are illusive because they usually exist below a layer of awareness, often hidden at a gut level. Yearnings hidden deep within the "belly of a person" usually represent something they once had or experienced but have since lost. If not that, yearnings represent something they have never had or experienced but long to have or experience in the future. For some, it is as practical as yearning to not struggle with finances. For others, they yearn for some reality to exist in the lives of those around them, like yearning for harmony— whether in the family, the workplace, or in the world. Still for others, the yearnings are more complex, like yearning for confidence, or yearning for a sense of freedom, or yearning for impact and influence. Under the deep layer of yearnings are often strong themes of meaning.*

- **Hopes:** *Hopes are similar to yearnings, but lie just a layer above, which makes them much easier to sense and articulate. For example, you might hope to enjoy retirement with your grandkids at the lake house. There is a lot of meaning there that goes beyond the finances, the lake, and the house. While you hope for retirement, someone else might hope to author a book or write a song. These hopes are also covered in fingerprints with deeper meaning, which can be found by seeking what type of book or genre of song, and the impact that would flow from its creation. People too easily dismiss hope and do not realize there is meaning to be found within those hopes.*

- **Achievements**: *Not all of us have a physical trophy case with trophies, plaques, and awards for our achievements in life or in our professions. Yet, all of us have a trophy room in our hearts filled with events, accomplishments, projects, or experiences we are most proud of, even if we have never had the chance to identify them. For some, it is a long-range project they supervised and saw to completion. For others, it was the fact that even though they were shy, they prepared for and delivered a speech to a large audience. Still for others, it was nothing they did individually but rather something they experienced with a group or team of others; simply contributing to a shared success was so meaningful, it made it into the interior trophy case of the heart. When we look within our hearts for those things we can quietly pat ourselves on the back for, there is deeper meaning to be found.*

With this list of categories, you can already imagine that no two people would have a similar list when completing an exercise like this one. Even if there were a few similarities here and there, the meaning behind those items would mostly likely be derived from or experienced in a unique way. There is a reason for this. Remember the definition of purpose? The reason *you* were created, the reason *you* were made?

You are created and, therefore, I believe have a creator—a creator not only of your life but of your purpose. And, whether you believe the same way I do or not, those clues of meaning are not there by accident. Those clues of passions, needs, drives, obsessions, characteristics, qualities, yearnings, hopes, and achievements are there for a specific and unique purpose. That purpose, once discovered and lived out, has the potential to have an impact on your life *and* the lives of those around you.

Of course, there is more to each of these items than simply a list of clues. Behind each answer lies even more deeply buried clues. For example, if fly-fishing made the list of "passions," why is that? Maybe it is the strategy of it that you love, the puzzle of figuring out the right fly in the right conditions, for the right spot on the river, for the specific type of fish you are looking for.

When you get underneath these clues by exploring them more deeply, you might begin to see some common themes. Maybe another seemingly unrelated clue will reveal a similar pattern. For example, in addition to listing a passion for fly-fishing, maybe you listed in your "achievements" category that you consider that big project from your previous work situation as one of your trophies in the trophy room of your heart.

If I were to ask you why, you may describe the complexities of the various departments involved, maybe even a difficult relationship with a vendor, but in the end, you solved the puzzle that brought a strategic solution to your firm's client. When you think of that experience, no matter how difficult and challenging it was, you have unknowingly awarded yourself a "trophy" for your strategic problem solving in that situation.

You would not have known it before going through this type of exercise, but fly-fishing and that challenging work project have more in common than you could have imagined. There is a theme in the meaning you find when you can be strategic, problem solve, and find a solution (i.e., catch a fish hiding in the current of the stream or create a unique solution to meet a client's need). What you are seeing reveal itself, jumping off the paper if you will, is a theme.

If I were there with you helping you draw out meaning and looking for themes, we would see together that you find meaning in problem solving, offering solutions, and being strategic. You may have always known you liked being that way or that it came naturally.

Yet, when you see it all over the clues, especially when looking through the filter of meaning, you begin to realize you are finding meaning or evidence of a purpose—a purpose to use for the good of others. If we were to work though this exercise together for a couple of hours, I know there would be more clues that would lead to you to discover meaning. By the end of the conversation, we would have a much deeper understanding of your purpose.

Pretty amazing stuff, right? Well, we have spent a lot of time looking deeply within ourselves, and now is the time to move the search for meaning to look widely beyond ourselves.

MEANING—LOOK WIDELY BEYOND

As much as you need to look deeply within for meaning, there is another place you need to begin to search next. As you are discovering your purpose, you will also need to look widely beyond your life, searching for meaning in the world around you.

Looking for meaning around you is a much simpler part of the journey than looking within. Looking within requires time, depth, often a guide, and a desire to discover. Looking beyond and around simply requires you to open your eyes. You may have noticed, but in case you haven't, there exists an unending supply of brokenness and neediness in the world. Simply watching five minutes of the local or national news will reveal the desperation found both near and far.

Fewer people observe the news on television these days, but that doesn't mean they aren't in touch with what's happening in the world. With the onslaught of instant access through social media, the brokenness and pain in the world are served up to our laptops, tablets, smartphones, and even smartwatches, quite literally as it happens, at all hours of the day and night. It takes a lot of work to be unaware of the difficulties so many in our world are facing.

The process of looking widely beyond you is just that—open your eyes and look for opportunities to make an impact and look for open doors to serve the needs of others. As you do, you will discover many opportunities to impact and plenty of opens doors to serve the needs of others immediately near you and around the globe.

There is no limit to the number of people who are experiencing brokenness, hurt, pain, loss, and desperation. As you look around you, you are going to be drawn to certain people, certain opportunities, and certain needs in a unique way. There is meaning in that, my friend, and there is a reason for that too.

You have been given a unique purpose because you are the only person who can make the impact in others in the way that you make an impact.

No one else has your life story, talents, passions, desires, dreams, abilities, and therefore, no one can make the impact that *your* life is intended to make—there is no one other than *you*.

The world is waiting in need for you to discover your purpose and move toward it. Until you do, the world is missing out on the impact you alone can make. On one hand, it is really as simple as that.

Open your eyes, look around, and find opportunities to impact and look for open doors to serve. Really, just get going. As you do, more doors to serve will open, and more opportunities to impact will be brought to your attention. On the other hand, there are some cautions I want to offer before you prematurely put the book down and start to get ahead of yourself.

MEANING—CAUTIONS

I have seen far too many people get derailed by either focusing too much on looking deeply within or naively leaping ahead and looking around too soon. Without a healthy balance of both and a healthy process, it may feel like you have found purpose, but you may find yourself a lot further from purpose than you could imagine.

Some people spend a lifetime looking within, never realizing that purpose is not intended to become self-serving. Those types of people can tell you all the deep truths in their hearts and how they are better for it, but they still have not found a genuine purpose because they have yet to connect those truths to something beyond themselves.

Looking within is important, but if you don't look around, you can slide down the slippery slope of pride, ego, and even narcissism. If you are the type who is in tune with your inner world yet out of touch with the outer world, it is time to take the next step and begin to search for meaning by looking beyond yourself.

On the other hand, there are far more people who are fully in tune with the world around them yet have not done any of the searching work to discover meaning within. Just as much as I caution against only looking within, I would caution against only looking around.

Some people start by looking around, but it can be a sneaky type of dangerous if you do. The reason this is especially concerning is because when people look around first, they often dive in and take action well before they have any perspective, clarity, meaning or purpose from searching deep within.

I see this especially in entrepreneurial, visionary, leader types. For them, and people like them, they see the world through the lens of opportunity. And, they often see a lot of opportunity. When they see opportunity, they move toward it with fervor, maximizing, and at times, exploiting the opportunity.

Usually this leads to businesses being started, products being developed, and jobs being created, which are often very good things. But, because of their natural bent toward maximizing, for them as individuals, the pursuit becomes more about the efficiency, productivity, and profitability of the venture than it does about the meaning.

When this happens, profit usually skyrockets and purpose plummets. The reason is due to the fact that when the purpose of life is to profit, the few tangible fruits of that purpose are money, status, and power, which can be demanding taskmasters. Live this pursuit of opportunity out over a number of years, and your life will likely look a lot like Charles Dickens's famed Christmas character, Ebenezer Scrooge, which is a life steeped in self-affirming piety and profit, but empty of meaning and void of purpose. If this is feeling like it is a little too close to home, let me offer something that will bring a truth to you through the filter of grace and hope.

Living in alignment with your unique life purpose
should be as generous to others as it is fulfilling to you.

Not only is starting by looking around is risky for those who see opportunity, but it is also tricky for those who experience the world around them with empathy. Instead of *seeing opportunity*, some *feel empathy*, and as a result, they do not pursue profit but instead pursue only compassion. The compassionate types see all the open doors to serve the needs of others, and as a result, they participate in all sorts of nonprofits and causes. This is a good thing in the big picture, but rarely is it anchored in a personally discovered purpose.

You are probably wondering what is wrong with doing this. Nothing is inherently wrong with this, other than when you lack an overarching personal purpose, it can cause you to lack focus, and therefore severely limit your impact.

The struggle for compassionate people is that a lot of things tug on their heartstrings, so they find themselves moved emotionally by outward meaning and pulled in every direction as they find it. Often this results in an experience of turning around and around in an unfocused manner, trying to meet the needs of the world that are so evident to them. Follow me on this…

If this is you, and you are moved by every glimpse of brokenness and every evidence of need, you most likely get distracted often. One month you are writing letters to orphans in a third-world country, the next month you are attending a talk on human trafficking, the next month, you are signing up to help tutor English as a second language, and the next month, you are being begged by your church to volunteer in the kid's ministry.

With each month that passes, you know you did good in the world (and by the way, thank you for helping my daughter on her Sunday School craft last Sunday morning), but over time, you don't feel like it is amounting to anything or that you were living life with true purpose.

Not only does this happen to empathetic types who are generous with their time, it also happens to compassionate types who are generous with their treasure. Givers, donors, and even philanthropists often feel pulled in every single direction with every newsletter that comes in the mail or donor meeting and fundraising ball they attend.

When you look back over time, you see a whole bunch of time and money donated that did good for a little while, but it can leave you personally feeling empty, not to mention possibly used and abused by the needs and demands of others.

As much as I have made the case that your purpose is for others, which I firmly believe, I also need to make the case for the other direction. Living a life of generosity (whether giving away time or treasure) that isn't founded in the uniqueness of your specific clues of meaning that reside deeply within you, can also leave you supremely unfulfilled, empty, and lacking purpose.

Living in alignment with your unique life purpose
should be as fulfilling to you as it is generous to others.

A whole lot of good has been done in the name of compassion and generosity that lacked purpose, focus, and genuine, lasting, fulfilling impact. If you are generous with your time, talent, or treasure, it's time you discovered your life purpose in order to maximize the impact of your generosity.

No matter where you fall on these spectrums, I want to ensure you get this right, so I offer this reminder—as you seek meaning in order to discover your purpose, search deeply within yourself, and then widely beyond yourself.

FINALLY, THERE IS ONE TYPE OF PERSON WHO IS AT A SUPREME RISK of leading a life that looks to others like it has been an amazing life of impact, but the experience can leave a void of purpose and fulfillment in the end. This may only apply to a certain part of the population, but it is worth exploring for just a little bit.

I would label this type of person as the entrepreneurial compassionate leader. Greater is the risk for those who exemplify both sides of this coin at the same time, who also start to pursue purpose from an externally focused, compassionately entrepreneurial standpoint.

These leaders are often found leading a lot of worthy nonprofits, ministries, and even churches. Not only does this caution apply to people in those roles, I offer it to those entrepreneurs who have hit the end of the road of business, whether by age, energy, or interest, and discover that profit is empty of purpose. As they do, they often get reenergized by compassion and begin to chase compassionate opportunities with the same fervor they chased profitable opportunities.

At first glance, these examples do not sound like such a bad thing. After all, maximizing compassion is something we need more of in our world. And, great nonprofits, ministries, and churches need great leaders to see opportunities for impact and see open doors to serve the needs of others. If we had more entrepreneurs and more leaders at more organizations that are intended for good of others, it would seem the world would naturally become a better place. And, I believe it truly would.

So, to be clear, I am not critiquing the outcome, I am cautioning the starting point and the motive. Because of how visionary, entrepreneurial, natural born leaders who have or discover a compassionate bent are "hard-wired," it's important for them to take extra caution. For these types of people, to start and finish well, it will require the hard work of looking within and discovering their unique purpose and role in the world, and just as importantly, where that purpose begins and where it ends.

Without that perspective, clarity, and the resulting accuracy of self-awareness that allows you to understand the scope of your purpose, the pursuit of success can be dangerous to you and to those around you. Entrepreneurial compassionate people have both entrepreneurial and empathetic tendencies, which tempts them to exploit opportunities and be moved by every whim of compassion.

Compared to entrepreneurs, they are very similar, seeing opportunities everywhere, with the only substantive difference is the specific measure of success. Instead of measuring success based on profit, they measure success on things like connecting with larger donors and increased giving or more attendance and more programs. In business, too often the ends justify the means, but in terms of compassion, I believe that should never be the case, but too often, it is the reality.

These types of leaders are in danger of looking at the outward fruit or impact that looks good to the world around them but is rotten to the core because it is built on the back of poor internal ethics and a lack of honor to those who actually do the work of producing the fruit. That might sound harsh, but I have observed and experienced it in more leaders and more organizations than I would care to admit. Sadly, it gets worse.

As I shared before, these types of leaders have a compassionate side too, aware of many of the open doors to meet the needs of others. Again, at first glance, this is a good thing, but just like non-entrepreneurial compassionate people, these leaders and visionaries are also moved (or distracted) by each thing that comes across their desks.

In this scenario, every compassionate whim the leader "feels" gets communicated to the staff as "new vision." This purposelessness and lack of focus that gets regurgitated as "vision" constantly creates instability, disunity, and burnout for those who are giving their lives for the very leader who is benefiting from their sacrifice.

One month, they are telling the staff we are going this way, the next month, telling the staff we are going this other way. As this plays out month over month, year after year, leaders like this get frustrated and grumpy about why the staff isn't following, let alone going anywhere.

Here is the truth: staff members can sniff out lack of focus in leadership as easily as someone standing in the kitchen would smell bacon frying on the griddle. Staff will sniff out lack of focus before leadership 99% of the time. Nothing else smells like bacon, and nothing else smells like lack of focus at the top.

The difference is that instead of running to the scent, staff run from it. When this happens, the staff begins to become subconsciously self-absorbed as they lose energy, passion, and ultimately buy-in, knowing all their effort is just going to be redirected, changed, or scrapped in a month or two anyway.

Sadly, at the end of this road, the organizations led by entrepreneurial compassionate people often look like unkempt zoos filled with "live animals" without fences. Staff members begin to roam freely, do whatever they want or don't want to do, and step on the toes of others.

The result can be outwardly great looking fruit, but fruit which is often produced from a rotten core. If not an unkempt zoo, conversely, these organizations can look like tightly managed institutionally zoos, where the "live animals" have absolutely zero freedom, doing exactly what the leader tells them to do in the exact way the leader wants them to do it. That is until that leader changes his/her mind.

In this case, the staff are simply "exhibits" to make others look in and gawk at the leader's prowess of creating a great staff. Again, often there is a lot of good looking fruit and impact, but produced from a core of dogmatic, my way or the highway leadership.

Sometimes, these types of leaders can create an environment and culture that is an odd combination of tightly managed and unkempt zoo at the same time, which is the most painful of all experiences for the live animals, err the exhibits, err the staff.

Nonetheless, organizations led by people who are entrepreneurial and compassionate are at the risk of pointing to the end (impact) to justify the means (unhealthy culture), which ultimately hurts the people *and* the cause in the long run.

While masked by compassion and cause, this type of leadership pursuit is actually a self-serving pursuit. Not unlike a charitable version of the same Ebenezer Scrooge, it can lead to a lot of distinct moments of impact along with the awards and plaques to prove it, but no real friends, no true influence, and in the end, no genuine purpose either.

If you are an entrepreneurial compassionate leader, please head my observations and cautions—for the sake of your life and legacy, for the sake of the cause, and for sake of the team that supports you. Drawing from the previous chapter, and in order to avoid some of these risks, I would recommend not going on this journey alone. Invite your spouse, a trusted friend, or a qualified guide to help you get perspective and clarity on the meaning you need.

If your purpose (or lack of awareness of the specifics of it) has a direct impact on the organization you lead, this is especially important. If that is the case, leverage the beauty and safety of an advisory or legal board, and regularly allow them to speak into your life and decisions—even, candidly and bluntly.

Allow them to also speak into whether your personal purpose is remaining in alignment with the direction of the organization or vice versa. Your humility to the wisdom and authority of others in all these areas will help to keep your entrepreneurial ego in check and your empathetic compassion focused.

Finally, know when to walk away. When our purpose as leaders no longer aligns with the cause of the organization we lead or if our leadership itself has run its course, we need to acknowledge it. Sometimes the best thing we can do for ourselves and, even more importantly, for the organizations we lead is to let go and move on. When we place the cause above our ego, and trust the candid truth of those around us, we are free to leave with honor, dignity, and with grace.

If this little section didn't apply to you, that's okay. I know it is going to save more than a few entrepreneurial compassionate leaders from fumbling their legacy. So, thank you for taking side path on the journey with us. Let's continue forward.

MEANING—NEXT STEPS

Let me summarize the search for meaning so we can gather ourselves and take some further steps. Whether with a guide, or a team of guides, begin by searching for meaning deep within, which will allow you to draw out your own uniqueness and the specific themes that begin to evidence purpose.

Once you are in tune with the meaning you find deeply within yourself, you can truly begin to look for meaning beyond yourself. The world around is full of opportunities to impact and full of open doors to meet needs. It's simply waiting for you to take a step of faith, and when you do, you can make a huge difference living out your unique purpose in a way that impacts others for good.

So, to take those next steps, let's take a look at the transcendent nature of purpose again—transcendent being that purpose crosses many layers in many directions. In this case, I want to bring together the ideas of seeking meaning deeply within and widely beyond yourself. If I were to take all those clues from all those categories from seeking deeply within, I would attempt to capture an overarching concept into the idea behind a particular word —burdens.

I'm not describing the type of burden that speaks of a heavy physical load. I'm talking about the type of burden that feels like it gives you a sense of personal responsibility, or a sense that you have a specific aim, role, or achievement to meet.

Quite honestly, however, when you find those types of clues in your heart, you do sense a type of weightiness to them, a sense of calling, or personal purpose. Look within for a sense of meaning, one that begins to feel like *your* burden, and it is going to move you closer to your purpose.

Let's take a look at the world's most immediate needs. There are so many, I know. But there are some specifically that are immediate in terms of their proximity and access to you, or even your access to them. I'm using the idea of immediate to mean present, existing, actual, urgent, and near you. Right around you are immediate opportunities to impact and open doors to serve the needs of others. They might be in your neighborhood or community, in your workplace or industry, or even within your family or your friends.

Impacting and serving others does not necessarily need to be a "go big or go home" sort of thing. In fact, it usually works best the other way around. Starting small and nearby is the best place to start, and when done well, it usually leads to big things. Think about "who" and "what" is right in front of you, waiting to be impacted, and needing to be served. I would classify and argue that those are the world's most immediate needs around you.

We have been talking about the intersection of stuck and lost throughout this journey together, but a new intersection is emerging right in front of us. I really do believe you will like this one better than the last. It has to do with your deepest burdens and the world's most immediate needs. Are you ready for it?

Your unique purpose exists at the intersection of where your deepest burdens align with the world's most immediate needs.

This intersection is so much better than the corner of stuck and lost, now isn't it? This intersection is the starting point for discovering your purpose, and it can become your new address—a place where you give your life away to others and experience immense fulfillment doing so. Yet, you can only get to this new intersection by taking the journey we have been on together.

The journey to this intersection starts with the truth of transformational breakthrough found in clarity that we talked about in the last chapter. That perspective and clarity continues as you discern the meaning and burdens deep within you.

As you are able to see where those burdens align and intersect with the opportunities and needs of those immediately around you, you will find yourself at an intersection so very few people reach. This new location is a place where you can truly begin to discover and live a life of purpose.

To continue your journey and to narrow in and locate this new intersection in your life, look for tools, assessments, resources, and guides that help you find meaning and evaluate opportunities in a healthy way. Find tools, resources, and people that will help you:

- Learn what drives you, motivates you, and compels you
- Unpack and articulate your passions, obsessions, desires, hopes, and dreams
- Recognize and identify where you find meaning, burden, impact, and purpose

- Identify the opportunities for impact
- Find open doors to serve those in need
- Truly discover and live life with not only a sense of purpose but a clarity of purpose
- Stay focused and humble as doors of opportunity to both be fulfilled and impact others continue to open

I have already said it a number of times, and I will say it again and again. You are created for a purpose—a unique purpose. Somewhere buried deep within the meaning you draw from these categories, lists, and truths is a unique purpose that is yours and yours alone.

Additionally, no one else has immediate access to the opportunities to impact and the open doors to serve those who are right in your community, industry, or family. As a result, no one else can fulfill your life purpose.

In fact, without you discovering and living out your life purpose, the world at large, especially the world immediately around you, is very much missing out on something very meaningful. The world is missing out on *you* and all of the blue skies and endless possibility of a life of impact and greatness you have to offer.

It is time you truly gave the effort to seek meaning in your life and begin to discern what is being evidenced: the purpose for which you were made.

You see, seeking meaning deeply inside and widely beyond us will reveal purpose in our lives. Purpose is something I know you long for, but there is even better news, my friend. Purpose leads to the creation of something you also need.

You were created for a purpose, and as a result, purpose also has a creative nature to it—more evidence of its transcendence. Purpose is like a fountain of youth for the soul, only instead of creating youth, it creates something else—something even more valuable than youth. Purpose naturally creates and perpetuates something you need to continue to soar into the blue sky: *courage*.

Check out "Part B" of the second simple truth of transformational breakthrough.

Simple Truth of Transformational Breakthrough #2

YOU NEED PURPOSE
because

(Part B)

PURPOSE CREATES COURAGE...

Courage is not something that can be bought. Nor is it something that can be borrowed. And truthfully, it can't be found in a bottle or a can either, despite what some might say. Yet, courage is something that can be possessed and even stored up in reserve.

At first glance, you might be thinking I'm not making a whole lot of sense. It sounds a bit like a riddle. What *can't* be bought, borrowed, but *can* be possessed and stored up? Or, said another way, what can be possessed and stored up, but not bought, borrowed?

Well, I'm not a huge fan of the cutsie, clever, manipulative riddles, but this isn't that kind of riddle, because I have already shared the answer with you—the answer is *courage*. So, why does courage answer this little riddle? Here's why:

Genuine courage is the naturally created result of purpose.

When purpose is discovered and clarified, courage is created and birthed within you. You can't get true, life-changing courage anywhere other than from within anyway.

You can't beg, borrow, or get it from someone or something. No one can hand you their courage. You either have it within or you don't, but my friend, when you discover your purpose, you will receive courage, created naturally within you. Additionally, when you have purpose, no one and no circumstance can take courage away from you.

Oh, they will try, but when you have purpose, they won't fully succeed. The reason is that even if courage is stolen momentarily, purpose will continue to create courage, welling up from within you like a spring.

Before I go further, let's look at what courage is not, so we can understand *what it is*. I'm not talking about blind stupidity and doing dumb things without thinking about the consequences. That's actually not courage. I am also not talking about needing to get attention or wanting to show off for someone or show someone up. That's not courage either.

I'm not talking about swagger, acting macho, or carrying an internal machismo either. Those aren't forms of courage, not in any genuine way. I'm not even talking about living with abandon and fearlessness. That is not courage. Courage is not fearlessness. *Wait a minute, what did you say?* You read it correctly.

Courage is not fearlessness.

Stay with me on this. Courage can be defined as the ability to exemplify strength or to take action *in the face of pain, grief, or fear*. Do you see what that means? Pain, grief, and/or fear *must be present* for an action to even be considered courageous.

True courage requires the presence of fear, or it isn't courage after all.

Doing dumb things, showing off, puffing up, and acting fearless are all forms of something (maybe pride, maybe insecurity) but they aren't forms of genuine courage. Courage then, when created by purpose, is powerful. Not only do you need purpose, but you need courage, because when you begin to live life with purpose, you are going to need to tap into courage to reach your potential.

A FRIEND OF MINE, NAMED KELLY, COINED A PHRASE ABOUT ME nearly 20 years ago. She is a veterinarian by trade, and a good one at that. But beyond her expertise in her profession, there are extra layers of depth within her, and part of her created purpose is to impact the world for good by seeing deep into the hearts of others. Because of this, when she speaks, I listen carefully.

One time, while she and her husband were over at our house with a number of other couples, she looked at me and said, "Jeff, you are a gem digger." My first reaction was uncertain and curious, because a similar phrase (gold-digger) has such negative connotations. I asked her to elaborate, not sure where she was going to take the conversation.

Kelly kindly unpacked what she had meant, saying something like, "Jeff, you see the nuggets and gemstones of greatness that are buried within people. And, more than just seeing them, you have an ability to unearth, identify, and bring to light the beauty of those gems. You're a gem-digger." I was blown away. It's true, and she saw it and called it out of me.

Years later when working through all of the clue categories in my LifePlan, I found all sorts of clues that evidenced both talent and meaning with regard to helping people in this way. There is no doubt I draw meaning from it, but more than that, I feel a unique weight of responsibility with it as well.

To have the ability to see into the hearts, souls, and spirits of the people and teams around me, to see their goodness, their potential, and their passions, and to do nothing about it would be to abdicate my role in their lives as well as neglect my own purpose.

I do truly feel a unique burden, a weight of responsibility and personal stewardship, if you will, to help individuals, couples, teams, and organizations find those gems within them. The clues in my categories all point toward it and so do my talents. As a result, I have discovered a huge part of my purpose in discovering and revealing those gems within others.

Looking deeply within helped reveal the meaning and fulfillment I find searching for and unearthing the gems I find within people. Not only did it identify the burdens within, but it gave me an ability to begin seeking meaning widely beyond me.

I was able to begin to easily see so many opportunities to impact and to also see open doors to serve the people who were closest to me. In fact, it was all around me. People everywhere find themselves stuck and lost, often so unaware of the gems within, let alone the potential bound up within them.

Kelly had observed me living out my purpose in the lives of those around me long before I had even truly discovered and articulated my purpose in my LifePlan. In many ways, I was well on the way to the intersection of where my deepest burdens aligned with the world's most immediate needs—my own unique life purpose.

That purpose, affirmed by the perspective and clarity of my life story and the process of the LifePlan itself, began to produce a natural wellspring of courage. If you remember back to Chapter 3, I shared my purpose with you. In case you don't remember, here it is:

<u>Jeff Rasor's Life Purpose—Why I Exist</u>
I exist to lead people and teams to breakthrough,
to guide them into their unique purpose, and
to inspire them to fulfill their potential.

As a reminder, when I entered into my LifePlan, I was bound to the corner of stuck and lost like I had never been before. I was more than four years into a severe vocational wilderness that had all but destroyed any sight toward a hopeful future for me.

The Clouds of Confusion were overwhelming, to say the least. The clarity that I discovered certainly produced confidence, and the purpose I had discovered in the process created a courage I had never known.

Within four months of the LifePlan, I had resigned from my job and started my own consulting business with no capital, no savings, no budget, no income, and no marketing and/or business plan. At the time, my wife, Janette, was a stay-at-home mom, and we had two children, ages six and a year and a half.

There was a substantial amount of risk involved in this decision to leave the unknown, to venture out and to offer myself to the marketplace in a new way. Even the very thought of it required courage, let alone taking the action to jump into an ocean of risk.

Not only did it require courage to get started, but it required courage to navigate the ongoing clouds of uncertainty. When I would have a setback or a lull in client work, it would have been easy to fall into despair. Yet, all I had to do was be reminded of my purpose statement again, and the wellspring of purpose would go to work within me, creating a seemingly endless supply of courage. Remember, purpose creates courage.

I had never done anything entrepreneurial like it before, so I had no experience to draw from. Yet the courage that was being created by purpose welled up within and propelled me toward my potential —it was beyond something I had ever experienced.

The courage that was being created (as a result of truly knowing my purpose) caused me to be internally postured in a way that not only attracted clients but allowed me to perform for them with an ease and a sense of success and fulfillment I had never experienced before.

You have probably heard a certain phrase from athletes when they are able to take huge risks and succeed at a high level—they call it being "in the zone." I began to readily experience that myself. Because my purpose was creating more and more courage, I often found myself able to take risks and succeed like I never had before.

Even though I wasn't on a field or a court, in so many ways, I was in the zone. Continuing to live in and from that intersection where purpose is found—the intersection of my deepest burdens aligned with the world's most immediate needs—my client list continued to grow in size and stature.

Ultimately, and in a very short amount of time, I found myself guiding many people and organizations to breakthrough, even guiding types of people and organizations I had up until then only admired from a distance.

That purpose-created courage gave me the power and strength to face my fears, take risks, be transformed in the process as I was learning to apply this second truth of transformational break-through. During that season and every endeavor since, my purpose has been creating within me a wellspring of courage I could never muster for myself or even borrow or buy from someone else.

There is no courage like the courage created
by discovering and living your unique life purpose.

We began this chapter and the second truth of transformational breakthrough by discussing fear, but we have yet to complete the thought. As I said before, fear must be present for courage to truly exist, for without the opposition of fear, courage isn't necessary. Not only does purpose create courage, but courage has a power over fear that we will need to discover and apply anytime fear rises up to oppose us.

This leads us to "Part C" of our second simple truth of transformational breakthrough.

Simple Truth of Transformational Breakthrough #2

YOU NEED PURPOSE
because
PURPOSE CREATES COURAGE
and

(Part C)

COURAGE SEVERS FEAR

COURAGE AND FEAR CAN AND OFTEN DO COEXIST. JUST BECAUSE YOU experience fear doesn't mean courage is absent. In fact, the inverse is more likely true. When you experience fear, it is time to bring out the truth of purpose that creates courage from within. Remember, you cannot truly act courageously *unless* you are facing pain, grief, or fear.

You can observe this correlation between purpose and courage, not just in my life, not just in the lives of the clients and people I have guided, but even throughout history. I will share one story in particular where I believe this truth played out, changing a nation and even the world forever.

My daughter, who is just about to turn 10 years old, has taken a liking to history, so when traveling, we often take time to stop and visit historically significant sites. A few years back, our family was traveling in Washington DC, and we were able to visit Ford's Theatre, the location where President Abraham Lincoln was shot in an assassination plot by John Wilkes Booth.

We were also able to visit the Petersen House, the boarding house across the street where the wounded president was taken for treatment and ultimately passed the next morning. It was a fascinating, yet saddening experience to be so close to such a devastating tragedy.

While these two buildings represent a monumental event in the history of the United States, they fall short in comparison to the monumental and courageous leadership Lincoln displayed in his presidency. His courage was a courage that welled up from within him, because he had a laser-like focus on his purpose. With his purpose as his guide and source of courage, he nearly single-handedly led the United States through one of its darkest and most trying seasons in its history.

His purpose created a natural courage within him to lead the nation to two very necessary outcomes: 1) to eliminate the evil of slavery and, at the same time, 2) relate to the opposing South in a way that maintained and reconstructed the unity of the nation post-civil war. Leading the North to victory, then in his very few remaining days, setting the tone and vision for a re-united United States of America required as much courage as any president before him or after him has ever had to display.

His life, so impactful then, and still to this day, that at the Ford's Theatre Centre for Education and Leadership, you will find a stacked tower of 6,800 of the more than 15,000 published books about him, his life, his presidency, his leadership, his character, and his impact. No, the museum doesn't carry that many titles on its shelves. In fact, the books aren't even for sale, nor are they books at all.

Instead, it is an art installation of mocked up books, stacked en masse all around a support column to a giant multi-level spiral staircase in the store. The tower of "books," at least 4 feet in diameter, reaches more than 30 feet high. With each year that passes, more books are still being authored as historians, authors, and students of people and leaders continue to explore the depth of purpose and impact that Lincoln's life has had.

If you haven't been there, and you can't make a visit soon, simply type "tower of Abraham Lincoln books" into your favorite search engine, click on images, and be amazed. Or, for a time lapse video of the art exhibit being installed, go to the blog section of Ford's Theatre's website.[2]

History tells us that Lincoln valued the depth of truth that all men are created equal as established before him by the founding fathers. We also learn that he walked in a quiet courage few have ever walked in life. Knowing his purpose gave him the courage as a president to first and foremost uphold the values of the founding fathers and their intended positive impact on all the citizens of the nation he led.

No doubt, his was a purpose that was centered on his deepest burdens and the world's most immediate needs. It created within him a wellspring of courage even right up to the end of the Civil War, which effectively ended only six days prior to his death, when General Robert E. Lee surrendered the Confederate Army to Ulysses S. Grant.[3]

His purpose gave him courage right to his dying breath. In fact, two days after Lee's surrender, and only four days prior to his assassination, Lincoln made his final public address from the White House. While many assumed he would address the nation with a celebratory tone due the victory the Union had over the Confederacy, Lincoln took a completely different approach.[4] While he did celebrate, he did not celebrate the victory as much as he celebrated the end of a war that had taken the lives hundreds of thousands of American soldiers on both sides.

More importantly than who won the war, Lincoln celebrated that the bloodshed and fighting was coming to an end. From there, he quickly moved the tone of his speech to more of a melancholy mood and described the great need of the nation to quickly mend itself.

He made the case that there was much work to be done in restoring unity across the nation and in making plans for the safety and provision of approximately three million slaves to find freedom. This approach drew criticism even from his allies, who expected more of a victory speech for their political side and certainly drew criticism from his critics who felt like the reconstruction of the nation was all but impossible.

Yet, Lincoln had the courage that the impossible was possible for a hurting nation. Instead of seeking to leverage the moment for his own popularity, he did something very sacrificially. In the face of pain, grief, and fear, Lincoln courageously disappointed them all, knowing his purpose was to cast a vision for the healing of a land ripped apart by deeply engrained political differences and devastating civil war.

Just four days later, John Wilkes Booth, who had been in the crowd at Lincoln's final address,[5] plotted to and assassinated the president, never allowing him to see the fruits of his sacrifice, his purpose, and his courage.

The deeper plot behind the assassination was to murder more than just a man, but to murder the man's dream, purpose, and life's work. Booth plotted to murder Lincoln, while Booth's accomplices were plotting and unsuccessfully attempting to assassinate Lincoln's Vice President and Secretary of State. The objective was to create political disarray and prevent the fragile nation from healing and unifying.[6]

Tragically, Booth succeeded. Fortunately, Booth's accomplices failed, and their deeper motive never materialized. The nation ultimately healed, reconstructing itself around the 13th Amendment, and the vision Abraham Lincoln, the Great Emancipator, set in motion.

In life and in death, Abraham Lincoln lived a life of purpose—a purpose that transcended political lines, the color of one's skin, and even transcended life and death itself. While his life was cut short,

Lincoln lived out his Blue Sky Potential to his dying breath. As such, his life reached the endless possibility of impacting literarily millions of people for good in his time, not to mention the hundreds of millions of people impacted since.

Through Lincoln, his purpose also created a courage in others that ultimately prevailed over and severed the tether of fear that had chained the nation to the bondage of slavery and war. In him and through him, good prevailed over evil, light over darkness, and truth of the equality of man prevailed over the lie and deception of slavery.

As Lincoln consistently applied the power of purpose to every situation around him, the nation was the benefactor of the power and transformational breakthrough that resulted. Here is one of many things I have observed and learned from studying courageous heroes from history and courageous heroes who have personally impacted my life.

Courage is best exhibited as you deemphasize
self-preservation and prioritize purpose.

That is where purpose and courage will take you, my friend. Courage will take you to a place where you are no longer worried about yourself but are instead more concerned about how your life will impact others for good.

True courage will take you to a place where you are no longer worried about your status, your success, or even your reputation, because you are more focused on living a life that benefits others. That is what true courage and true purpose genuinely look like. And that kind of courage absolutely severs the leash of fear every single time you wield it in fear's toothless face.

You and I may never lead a nation through civil war in order to end the evil of slavery, and we may never have 15,000 books written about us, but that is not the point. That was the purpose for which Lincoln was created. You and I could never fulfill his purpose because we weren't created to do that. Along those lines, here's another sobering truth you need to hear…

As great a man as Lincoln was,
he could never fulfill the purpose for which you were created.

Think about that for a moment. Go ahead, feel free to put the book down for a minute and let that sink in.

He didn't have your life experiences; he didn't have your story; and he didn't have your burdens, talents, and dreams. He didn't have your purpose, nor the courage created by your purpose.

You see, you are called to do great things, different things than he, and he could never do the things you are called to do. Your purpose is *that* unique. When you live out your purpose courageously, it is going to impact someone's life for good. While in many ways we are all impacted deeply by Lincoln's life, the people you impact directly by courageously living out your purpose will be impacted by you at a greater depth than Lincoln's life ever could.

That is my motive for writing this book and my desire for your life after you read it. I passionately want you to experience the power and transformational breakthrough found in purpose, and I want others to benefit and experience breakthrough in their lives as a result of *you* finding and living out your purpose.

Over and over again, on the journey through the Opportunity Zone and into your Blue Sky Potential, you are going to face the opposition of fear—even fears you thought you defeated multiple times before. Courage and fear are not necessarily equal adversaries on the field of battle within your heart, mind, and soul.

You have known fear for way too long, my friend, and it has too many victories and held too much power over you. Let me encourage you, however, that courage is more valiant than fear. Much like good is greater than evil, light is greater than darkness, and truth is greater than deception, courage will sever fear, battle after battle, when you learn how to wield it.

However, that courage is only as mighty as it is founded in purpose—because purpose is what creates genuine courage in the first place. This is why it is so important you begin to discover your purpose. Not out of ambition, but out of the clues when you search for meaning deep within, and as you observe the opportunities to impact and the open doors to serve others which align with those clues. Over and over again, I have seen this truth and its power in historical heroes, in the lives of those I have lead and served, in my clients, and so very often in my life too.

As I discovered and lived out my life purpose, a well of courage began to spring up from within. That courage has severed fear every time fear has tried to have its way with me. And, to be honest, sometimes it is a daily battle. That's not necessarily because I'm weak or prone to fear but because I spend the majority of every day pursuing my Blue Sky Potential and helping others do the same.

As my own life continues to elevate across my Opportunity Zone, my life continues to run up against new fears. Each time it does, I wield the simple truth of purpose and the courage it creates. In doing so, I experience the power of transformational breakthrough in the face of my fears.

The same can be true for you. And it begins with you searching for meaning deep within your heart, spirit, and soul. You have a whole bunch of gems inside of you, and it is time for you to begin to do a little gem-digging yourself. It's time for you to look deeply within to find, unearth, identify, and bring to light the beauty of meaning and burden buried within your heart.

Once you have done that, it will be time for you to look widely beyond yourself. When you do, you will quickly see opportunities to impact and as well as see open doors to serve the needs of others. And, while those might at first seem like small opportunities and narrow doors, the impact you will have on others for good will lead to larger opportunities and wider doors. It is time for you to discover and live out your purpose because I believe it is something the world needs to experience.

Remember, purpose is transcendent; it transcends your life and even your awareness of it. When you are able to discover and articulate your purpose, it will just happen wherever you go, often flowing from your life effortlessly. And, when fear raises its ugly head and attempts to tether you back to the ground, and try it will, purpose will create courage like a wellspring from within. When you wield the power of that courage, you will be able to sever the leash of fear and continue to elevate through the Opportunity Zone as you soar toward the blue sky of your potential.

It is time for you to become aware of your purpose. It is time for you to discover and define it. As you do this by seeking meaning, you will soar through the clouds with the courage your purpose creates. When you do, your life will experience another boost of power and transformational breakthrough, and you will never be the same.

As a final reminder, here is the second simple but profound truth of transformational breakthrough:

Simple Truth of Transformational Breakthrough #2

YOU NEED PURPOSE
because
PURPOSE CREATES COURAGE
and
COURAGE SEVERS FEAR

You Begin the Journey to Purpose by Seeking Meaning

CHAPTER 10

RHYTHM — MOMENTUM
GENERATES CONVICTION

---

*"There is music wherever there is rhythm,
as there is life wherever there beats a pulse."*

- IGOR STRAVINSKY

NOT ALL THAT LONG AGO, IF YOU HAD ASKED ME ABOUT transformation and breakthrough, I would have simply pointed you to the power of finding clarity and discovering purpose. I would have been and have since discovered that I was *completely wrong*.

Let me explain.

I would have made the argument that someone who truly possesses a genuine clarity in life and a deep understanding of their purpose would have all they need to experience breakthrough and transformation. It would have been easy to see that their clarity would help them regularly defeat doubt, and their purpose would give them the strength to consistently overcome fear. The assumption and truth I would have professed would have been that they had all the tools they needed to experience breakthrough and elevate into their Blue Sky Potential.

I would even have had all the personal experience and antidotal "before and after" stories to "prove it." What I mean by that is I had descriptive "before" stories of how stuck and lost my life was before my LifePlan, which brought heaps of clarity into my life, not to mention a focused and accurate understanding of my purpose. I would have also had plenty of "after" stories of how the clarity and purpose I possessed had opened the doors of many opportunities to impact and serve the needs of others.

As my client list began to grow, I would have also had "before and after" stories from my clients—individual after individual, couple after couple, and business after business that were somewhere near the corner of stuck and lost before inviting me to guide them, who all experienced the power of clarity and purpose during our time together.

I could easily observe and articulate the difference between the before and the after that an individual, couple, or business experienced. For so many years, I had a valid and market-proven justification that clarity and purpose were the pathways to breakthrough. For the longest time, I thought I had the answers, and based on evidence, I truly believed I was right.

However, the reality is *I was missing a vital piece of the puzzle.*

As I have shared a number of times, I am a keen observer of human behavior, and not just an observer, but also a learner. I'm able to learn from patterns and trends I see in my own life and those I see in the lives of others.

The idea that clarity and purpose are not enough to result in genuine transformational breakthrough was not something I learned in a book, nor in a training session, nor in some professional experience. No, it was something I could only begin to see and discover through personal experience and observation.

For the longest time, the reality of a third truth of breakthrough was hidden from me and, I believe, is still hidden from so many others. I found it hiding in the shadows of all of the glow and shine that clarity and purpose can produce in someone's life or business.

Let me tell you with excitement that there absolutely is a tremendous glow that happens within and around you when you arrive at clarity and discover your purpose. That glow can be blinding. It is blinding in a good way, mostly, because of the joy it brings. But, that glow is also blinding in a way that is problematic, in that it can hide from view the last truth of transformational breakthrough —a truth you absolutely need to discover and experience.

In fact, for me it was so hidden behind the glow of clarity and purpose that I didn't even perceive or imagine its very existence, let alone see what that truth was. That is, *until* I first stumbled on the leash it was associated with. It was the leash that led me to the truth, and I found the leash by first observing a pattern in my own life, confirmed by patterns I observed in others.

It was when I looked back at my own life, even the seasons and years that followed after the LifePlan, that I saw a clear pattern emerging. Although full of clarity and purpose, I noticed a lot of short periods of start and stop, trial and error, success and failure. This is sort of how life goes when you are attempting to reach your dreams.

Yet, along with that pattern, I noticed something else, something that was actually more concerning. I noticed those very typical and normal experiences of trial and error, start and stop, were separated by much longer periods of, well, "meh." And in case that is a new word for you, I'm using the word "meh" in the way all the kids are using it these days. *Meh* is a total lack of interest, inspiration, or enthusiasm.

My attempts to start and stop were all part of the process of moving toward blue skies. That's actually normal. Yet, the clear pattern also showed me there were painfully long periods of time when my interest, inspiration, and enthusiasm to keep reaching for higher levels of blue skies were at all-time lows.

Sometimes a cloud of doubt moved in, but when it did, I could sever its leash with the confidence produced by clarity. Sometimes fear would work its way back into my heart and mind, and again, I could wield the truth of my purpose which created courage and sever that leash too.

Yet still, in the strangest of ways, there were significant periods when I didn't have the fire to try harder, work harder, and leverage the clarity and purpose I had to truly reach my dreams. I noticed I had long and numerous periods of *meh* in my life.

Maybe you have felt that too. Maybe you have desired something so strongly that you pursued it with hope and expectation, only to be stopped in your tracks by doubt, by fear, and/or by circumstances that prevented that desire from being met. Maybe you have experienced that reality not just once but over and over again, each time you attempt to pursue that desire or dream in your life.

Maybe it was a desire to lose weight, maybe it was to advance your career, maybe it was to become more productive, maybe it was to find a spouse. It could be anything really. Assuming you have experienced this reality at some point in life around at least one desire, if not many points in life around many desires, you will understand what I'm about to describe.

When you experience the pursuit of a desire or a dream only to be stopped in your tracks over and over again by doubt, fear, and/or circumstances outside your control, a new leash begins to wrap itself around your life and your potential.

Here is the sequence of how I see it happen: start, *doubt*, fail, stop, meh… start again, *fear*, fail, stop, meh… start again, *doubt and fear*, fail, stop, meh…. Repeat this sequence even once and the result is a leash on your life that also begins to erode the original desire from your heart and mind, not to mention limit the height of your dreams.

Repeat this sequence a few times or more, and the erosion is more like a mudslide, taking with it the very desire and dreams so dearly held in your heart. Ultimately, it can become a cycle of *meh, meh, meh*… From there, as we talked about in Chapters 2 and 3, the dream goes dormant, and at times, we assume the dream has *died*.

When this erosion takes place in our lives, it can be tragic, because we begin to enter into a losing negotiation with ourselves. We can begin to convince ourselves that we should have never held that desire or dream in the first place. We convince ourselves in the opposite direction of our desire and begin to believe things that oppose our dreams.

We think and say things like, "my genetics are working against me, and I'll never lose weight," or "I'm not as smart as my colleagues, so I'll always be stuck in this job," or "I don't have enough focus in my life to become more productive and achieve my goals," or "my life has been a mess, and no one will ever want to marry me."

The danger with some of these self-inflicted limitations is that they are often founded in half-truths. Maybe your genetics *are* working against you, or maybe you *aren't* quite as smart as some of your co-workers, or maybe you *do* lack focus, or maybe, in fact, your life *has been* a bit messy. However, it doesn't mean your interpretation is accurate—remember back in Chapter 8, we covered the idea that we all often have an inability to make correct interpretations in our lives.

Just because there may be some small element of truth to those thoughts, it doesn't guarantee that you won't lose weight, get a promotion, become productive, or get married. It may just mean you have some leashes to sever and clouds to navigate and overcome on the way to fulfilling your potential and reaching your dreams.

By the way, have you ever met anyone who reached their dreams who didn't have to overcome some limitation in some way? Most likely, nope. Most of our favorite heroes in business, leadership, the arts, and in our personal lives are people who had limitations just like you and I have, but who found the ability to overcome those limitations in order to reach their dreams.

That's why I know it is possible for you. The blue sky is for those who are courageous enough to cast aside every limitation that holds them back. That is you, my friend. I know you want that. It's time to be fully set free.

Unfortunately, as we cooperate with leashes of doubt, fear, internal and external circumstances, and the Clouds of Confusion, we can be guilty of rehearsing significant amounts of negative self-talk. When this happens, we can completely lose interest in our very *own desires*.

We often lose inspiration and enthusiasm for that very good and noble dream we originally had. We then fall prey to a final leash that holds us down to the corner of stuck and lost, one that holds us down with greater bondage than the chains of doubt and fear combined. It can be the most difficult leash to sever, and I call it the hidden leash of *apathy*.

THE HIDDEN LEASH OF APATHY

As you are reading this, you might be having an immediate, maybe even visceral, reaction to the word and idea behind apathy. I know how that feels. When I first discovered this pattern of *meh* and realized I was tangled by huge amounts of hidden apathy, I too had a strong and immediate reaction of denial. *No, no, no,* I thought… *I don't struggle with apathy…* If you knew me personally and spent any time with me at all, you would agree—you would easily see I'm one of the last guys to look at life with a "meh" mentality.

In my mind, someone who struggles with apathy looks more like a person who is half-passed out on the sofa, wearing an old baggy T-shirt, stretched out sweatpants, hole-filled dirty socks, and is binge watching cartoons, surrounded by a floor filled with empty soda cans and empty family-sized bags of Cheetos.

If that's you, I'm not trying to pick on you. We have all done something like that before. But, when I discovered the leash of apathy chained around my potential and keeping me from my dreams, it was surprising. In fact, it was shocking, because my life looked nothing like that television/Cheetos binging example. And, I'm guessing your life doesn't look like that very often either. Which tells me the hidden leash of apathy may have already you chained down, and you don't even realize it yet.

Follow me a little further on this. On the outside, my life looked really great and I was having a pretty significant impact in the world. Yes, I could have used a few less pounds, and yes, I could have been more focused and productive. Yet, by and large, I had clarity and purpose in life, and I was using both to help others find the same—clarity and purpose in their lives and in their businesses.

The problem was that when I saw this pattern of significant periods of meh by looking closer, I realized my potential was being significantly limited by an internal apathy. Somewhere deep down inside, I knew there was more potential for my life; there were dreams unmet and unpursued.

What I observed was something like my teenage years, when I had my heart set on attending the Air Force Academy, and let that dream passively drift away. Now, even thought I had clarity and purpose, I still had bigger dreams for my life, but I was passively letting those dreams drift away (again). And, for all practical purposes, I didn't care. At least, I didn't care enough to do anything more about it.

> *That is the very heartbeat of apathy – not caring enough*
> *to do anything about it (whatever the "it" is in your life).*

I would have told you I did really care about my life, my dreams, and my potential—and may have even pointed out a client I just impacted or how I had just trained for and ran a marathon. I could have shared my client list with you and told you a bunch of before and after stories.

In doing so, I would have had myself and you convinced that apathy was the *last* thing I needed to worry about. To be honest, it *was* the last thing I was actually worried about. I realize now that it should have been the *first* thing I was worried about. And, so should you.

> *Apathy doesn't always come in the package we imagine in our heads.*

I wasn't indulging in binge-watching, sweatpants-wearing, Cheetos-induced naps. I was running marathons and serving others. The truth is that my life didn't look like the typical apathetic life in any way, shape, or form. The deeper truth is all of the "evidence" is that I was wrong. I was allowing the hidden leash of apathy to chain my potential to the ground (even if there were some areas of life that were thriving).

I was having very deep impact in the lives of the people I was guiding, coaching, consulting, and pastoring. I was playing a significant role in the lives of quite a few people, a role I found provided a great sense of contribution and personal fulfillment. I had reached a level of impact in the lives of those I was working with that I had never expected to reach.

Yet, deep down inside, I knew my life was intended to have wide and broad impact in the lives of so many more than I was impacting, not just the few I could sit with face to face. To be honest, I just wasn't all that interested in doing anything about reaching even more people. As you know by now, I just don't measure success by numbers or dollars. And, at the time, it felt noble, and "others focused," in the sense I was deeply focused on the limited numbers who asked me to guide them away from their corner of stuck and lost.

Looking back, I can say my apathy was possibly more self-centered than I could have imagined. My impact was mimicking the sensation of reaching my own Blue Sky Potential, yet it didn't measure up to the dreams deeply buried in my heart—dreams I had allowed to grow dormant.

As I said before, the apathy was hiding in shadows created by the glow of clarity and purpose. It was hiding in plain sight, and it took me years to discover it, let alone figure out the truth of transformational breakthrough to sever it. But I was comfortable and therefore stuck in my own Comfort Zone with my level of impact, and although I didn't know it, that safe, comfortable apathy was selfish.

There were so, so many others I could have been helping and serving, and yet, I was not willing to do so. Because it would make me uncomfortable. So selfish. I wasn't willing to do so because it would push me out of my Comfort Zone, which would mean I would need to go through another Opportunity Zone.

By the way, "ouch," to that darn Comfort Zone again, keeping me safe and cozy on the trajectory of my current, status-quo-accepting reality. I discovered that my desire to stay comfortable and the willingness to let my own dreams drift away was actually a very selfish act.

If our lives are supposed to reach the endless possibility of impacting others for good, and we are not willing to move away from our own Comfort Zone to pursue our dreams, we are actually acting selfishly.

> *When we allow the leash of apathy to keep us from our dreams we are effectively saying to the world, "My comfort is more important than the good I can do in your life. My safety is more important than the positive impact my purpose can make for you."*

Ouch. So painful.

One of the lies you are probably believing is that following your dreams is selfish. If your dreams are narcissistic and ego-driven, then maybe you are right. But, I don't think that is you. For you, I would argue the opposite is most likely the case.

You are dreaming about how your life can both be fulfilling for you *and* have significant positive impact in the lives of others. For you to neglect those dreams is actually selfish. For you to pursue your dreams, to leave your Comfort Zone, to cross the Opportunity Zone, it is actually not selfish, but *sacrificial.*

Now, if you knew my entire story, you would see a pattern of breaking through Comfort Zones like very few have ever seen before. Breaking through Comfort Zones is pretty much the story of my life, but I had not realized I had reached a new plateau on my journey and, therefore, a new Comfort Zone. I hadn't known it then, but because of that, my life was tangled with apathy.

Thus, my life and my dreams were chained down, leashed to the ground, keeping my true, though deeply dormant, dreams out of reach. Because of that leash of apathy, the opportunity to truly soar in my Blue Sky Potential and the endless possibility of touching many, many lives didn't cause me so much as to lift a finger to that end.

For nearly a decade, I had clearly known a wider and broader impact was the intended destiny and reach of my life, and sadly, for the most part, I was completely apathetic toward it. When having coffee with a trusted friend, I could easily cast a vision for what I knew my life was meant to accomplish, while at the same time doing nothing about it. I could talk the talk of potential of my life, but I wasn't walking the walk.

That large scale impact wasn't just something I "knew" or "felt" inside, but something others often pointed out. For years, mentors, leaders, colleagues, and even random visionaries who possessed a gift of "seeing things" would pull me aside and attempt to encourage me about the possibility my life could accomplish for good.

Often, they knew the great impact I was already having, but they would challenge me that it was just the tip of the iceberg. After telling me all the possibility they saw in me, they would often ask me things like, "So, when is your first book coming out?" Not only did that question imply authoring a book, but often the comment "first book" would imply they saw more than one book inside of me, as if one book was just the beginning of something, that *something* they saw within me.

Unconscious of my own motives, I would often react with the same attention deflecting, false humility I offered to others as a kid, as if I didn't know what they were talking about. I would downplay their encouragement, or even act dumb, like, "Who me? You really think so? I have heard that before, but I don't know if I could really write a book." Now, honestly, there were some doubts and fears fueling that response, but most of it was self-centered false humility, fueled by apathy.

When these same people would say things like, "What are you going to do with your speaking gift?" I would respond with, "Speaking? I'm just not sure that is really me; I mean I know my speaking impacts people, but I have never sought the spotlight. I'd rather be behind the scenes." That sounds really noble on the surface, but if it is a noble way to deflect my apathy, then I would actually call it cowardice, not apathy.

If you remember my story about first grade in Chapter 2, I had an ability to score the second or third highest grade in my class.

Even as far back as that first grade classroom, I knew that I had the ability to shine even more, but that would draw too much attention, pushing me into the spotlight. Not only in first grade, but even as recent as the the season that allowed me to discover my historical track record of apathy, I have always felt more *comfortable* playing a smaller role than the purpose of my life calls for.

The problem with these mentors, colleagues, and visionaries casting a vision for a bigger role for my life, which did actually resonate with the dreams buried deep in my heart, is that it was too uncomfortable, too risky. The good (and bad) news was that the role I was playing was seen by those I was impacting (and myself) as noble, generous, impactful, and significant.

Therefore, I was happy hiding behind all those compliments and the big visions that came with them. In the rearview mirror, I have realized I hid (as did my apathy) behind my impact simply so I didn't have to take the risk to truly rise to the level of blue sky I and others knew that was intended for my life.

Just like the half-truths you might be saying to yourself about your genetics working against you, or not being as smart as some of your co-workers, or that you lack focus, or that your life has been messy, I was doing the same thing. I was letting the half-truths in my life lead me to inaccurate interpretations. I was letting half-truths predefine the outcomes, and to create negative self-talk, disbelief, and ultimately apathy.

In my life, I had plenty of track record and repetition of my own version of *start, doubt, fail, stop, meh, start, fear, fail, stop, meh.* And, while I had a lot of people affirm the author, speaker, leader, and guide within me—one that leads people and teams to experience breakthrough and freedom, I didn't take ownership of those truths.

To be fair, I have received more than my fair share of criticism and abusive attacks on those very things as well. Add my own predisposition to avoiding the spotlight along with the belligerent and personally charged letters of criticism that would at times come my way, and it makes sense I wasn't going to navigate my life out of my Comfort Zone and into any brighter lights. But, I'm not looking for a pity party. Truth is, I was hiding behind excuses for too long.

HAVING DISCOVERED AND COME TO A PLACE OF ACCEPTANCE regarding apathy in my life, I knew a posture of surrender was going to be required (there's that word, *surrender*, again). As I let go of my denial and began to embrace the existence of a leash of apathy in my life, I wondered if it was maybe just me. So, I started to look around. To my surprise and at times sadness, I noticed that even people who I had guided to clarity and purpose also had patterns in their lives that were just like mine.

While it wasn't my place to call it apathy because it is difficult, if not impossible, to judge another's heart and struggles, I could observe similar patterns of delay nonetheless. I could see these patterns in individuals, couples, and even in businesses. I saw plenty of evidence that the clarity and purpose I had guided them to was not translating into a genuine pursuit of their dreams, let alone any semblance of soaring in *their* Blue Sky Potential.

Many of these people and businesses were those I had guided to clarity and purpose, with the assumed hope of reaching their potential on the other side of those truths. I had the before and after pictures in the short term, to be sure. But, in the long term, they had not achieved the potential that I had guided them to discover. I could have faulted them for their lack of implementation or their failure in execution of the discoveries I helped them find. I could have faulted myself for failing *them*.

Yet, there was no need to find fault. Many of them were giving their very best, so there was no fault in them to be sure. And, there wasn't a need for fault or blame in myself because I had faithfully guided them further toward their potential than they had ever been.

Many of them, even years later, are still at a loss for words in how to thank me for the positive, hope-filled impact I made on their lives. If I had even attempted to apologize for what I *didn't* give them, it would totally confuse them and make them question the confidence and courage they so enjoy in life as a result of our time together discovering clarity and purpose.

Looking for fault was not the right approach, but I still needed answers. Instead, I wanted to look for a cause. So, at that point, I decided to let the past be the past. However, I knew that once I discovered the new truth associated with defeating apathy, I could always reach out and introduce them to it. Yet, without having that truth in hand, there was no sense in disturbing their journey and joy of possessing significant clarity and purpose.

At the same time, I was completely unable to ignore that there must be one more truth of breakthrough—one I had yet to discover but that would help me overcome the seasons of apathy I found so prevalent in my own life. And, just maybe if I found it, I could test it, experience it, and offer it to others. During this transitional season, I took a step back. It was time to get a new clarity in my life, not all that much different than the clarity I have talked about before, but a new tier of clarity if you will.

Additionally, seeing so much hidden apathy in the rear-view mirror gave me great concern about my character. Was there some flaw inside me that was preventing me from elevating? Was there a shortcoming within that was keeping me from reaching my dreams?

Since I was known to be a person who would have predomi-nately been labeled as interested, invested, inspired, and enthusias-tic, and yet, I was so riddled with apathy, I felt the need to question and seek perspective in everything. You see, as life gets confusing, returning to a posture of seeking perspective to renew clarity is always healthy. As long as you aren't in a self-indulging spiral of seeking perspective all the time, it can be helpful to pause, to look at what was and what is to get clarity on *what can be.*

As I described in Chapter 8, seeking perspective requires you to make a choice to slow down. So, that is exactly what I did. I slowed down in a lot of areas, and I even paused pursuing and taking on new clients. I was concerned I would continue to help people get clarity and purpose but would leave them lacking a significant truth of breakthrough and thus preventing them a genuine opportunity to soar into their Blue Sky Potential.

By most accounts, it was a terrible business decision to pause in the pursuit of new clients, not to mention a terrible personal financial decision, but it is what I knew I had to do to gain the clarity I needed—for me, for them, and for *you*.

I have learned that if money is more important than reaching your potential, you aren't going to easily reach your potential. Sometimes the pursuit of money and potential actually work in tandem, and other times, they will work in opposing directions. The journey will often require risk, sacrifice, and self-denial, and at times, that puts the pursuit of income at distinct odds with the pursuit of potential, and the ability to reach your dreams.

The saying goes that if you wait until you are ready to have kids, you will never have kids, because you are never truly ready for that responsibility. The same can be true for reaching your dreams. If you wait to pursue your dreams until everything else aligns, especially until you "have enough money," you may find yourself with more money but often also with more apathy for your dreams.

For me personally, discovering this final truth of breakthrough was more important than any amount of money I could earn and more important than simply serving the next client, and the one after that. For me, discovering this final truth of breakthrough was worth risking everything financially.

I'd rather find freedom from apathy than have a consistent income and still be stuck and lost. Additionally, on the other side of my own transformational breakthrough, if I were going to reach and serve a wider and broader audience with greater levels of impact, I was going to need to discover this truth to share it with those I would guide in the future.

Along those same lines, I also knew another truth about life, leadership, and guiding people, a rule of great leaders, if you will. I cannot genuinely guide people to a place where I have not gone myself. To pretend otherwise would completely lack authenticity, even integrity. And, as a nugget of wisdom for you… when you select a guide in your life, for whatever reason—health, fitness, finances, reaching your potential—make sure they are willing to go and have been where they are taking you.

To that end, I knew if I was going to have the impact my life was intended to make in the lives of amazing people like you, then I was going to have to risk it all to discover this final truth of transformational breakthrough.

I will save the details of *how* I discovered the final truth of transformational breakthrough for another time, but it happened during this season of slowing down, when I intentionally changed my focus from growing my business to seeking deeper levels of clarity. It was a huge risk and massive leap of faith. But again, it was a risk I was willing to take for the sake of my own discovery as well as helping others truly experience transformational breakthrough themselves.

In the end, it took me well over a year to discover it and to test it. Eighteen months went by without new clients. A year and a half of risking everything financially, seeking and experiencing greater levels of clarity, purpose, breakthrough, and transformation in my own life.

I was going to need to wield a final truth to sever apathy, and I was willing to do whatever it took to discover it and unleash its power. My friend, it was so worth it, and I can't wait to tell you about it.

BECAUSE WE ARE DEALING WITH APATHY, YOU MAY FIND YOURSELF assuming the truth has to do with passion. As you will see, passion is part of it, but it isn't the answer. Once desire and passion have been eroded, you can't just muster it up out of the mudslide of apathy. Passion has a role, but let's not get ahead of ourselves just yet. Just as much as the leash of apathy was hard to see and discover, so too was the truth required to set me free.

If you do not have the clarity or the purpose I have been describing that you need, do not neglect this third truth. Even without clarity and purpose, apathy is still going to hold you back, maybe even from taking the steps to begin the journey to seek perspective and to seek meaning. The worst thing you could do after reading this book is *not* take the next steps.

There are so many great guides out there, and whether you use their tools and resources, or the tools and resources I will be offering, you just can't let apathy keep you from that journey. So please, don't write off this truth and let apathy win, just because you are still in the early stages of your journey. In fact, apathy might actually be the first leash you need to sever and if so, I can't wait to tell you how.

Likewise, just like I did, you may already have all the tools you need to overcome doubt with clarity and overcome fear with purpose. Maybe you are further along in your journey and have a sense you are in some level of blue sky that is higher than you have been before.

Even if that is the case, I'm assuming you are still dreaming of higher and more impactful blue skies, and if so, I'm guessing there is some hidden apathy somewhere holding you back. I was stuck there for a long time too, pretending to not be stuck, because I could see and justify the great impact I was having.

Wherever you are in the journey, if you do not sever this newly discovered leash of apathy, you will find yourself chained to the corner of stuck and lost nonetheless.

No matter how bleak the clouds of internal and external circumstances are, and no matter how clear and free from clouds the skies of your horizon are, apathy will be a constant hindrance and obstacle in the journey to reach your dreams. When you first see the truth, you may not believe it. So, I'm just going to give it to you now and explain it later.

To experience the fullest and most freeing form of transformational breakthrough, there exists one final truth you need to wield. To continue to unleash your Blue Sky Potential, you need to understand, value, and wield the unleashing force of *momentum*. Here is "Part A" of the third simple truth of transformational breakthrough.

Simple Truth of Transformational Breakthrough #3

(Part A)

YOU NEED MOMENTUM…

Think about it. At its most basic level, momentum has to do with movement, doesn't it? You see, clarity has helped you get a sense of where you have come from and where you are now. Purpose has helped you discover why you exist and therefore gives you a better sense of where you are headed.

As a result, you are quite a bit *less* lost, maybe even *found,* if you will. As I said in the Introduction, I know the way from the intersection of stuck and lost to the intersection of found and free. You may be found, but, you aren't free, *yet.*

We have made huge progress with the "lost becoming found" part, but you are still stuck because we have not completed the process to be set free. The apathy-induced mud pit at the bottom of the mudslide of the erosion of your desire and dreams is more like quicksand. It often traps you against your will, even if you have clarity and purpose, as I described above in my own story.

Momentum then, is the energy, motion, and inertia that ultimately allows you to break free. In total, clarity, purpose, and momentum will move you from stuck and lost to found *and* free. When you arrive at *that* new intersection, you will be able to truly reach for your dreams.

In Chapter 8, I shared that *clarity* is *paramount*, meaning it is the most important truth in terms of understanding. In Chapter 9, I shared that *purpose* is *transcendent*, in the sense that your purpose transcends your very existence from simply serving your own desires to impacting others in a significant way.

Likewise, momentum has an essence as well. Momentum is *dynamic*. That is, it contains within it a natural force and energy. Going back to physics, let me share a more technical definition of something that is dynamic.

When something is considered *dynamic*, it means that there exists a process or system relating to forces that generate motion, as characterized by constant action, activity, and progress. If you are tangled by apathy, you are going to need a process or system that generates the motion, activity, and progress that will set you free.

The concepts behind "dynamic" and "momentum" are nearly interchangeable. Yet, the difference is distinct, even if ever so slight.

Momentum can be defined as the *quantity* (measurable amount) of motion of a moving body, or the impetus (force) gained by a moving object.

Dynamic explains the *system* or *process* of the motion, and momentum explains the quantity of that motion. So, you need momentum (a huge quantity of measurable movement) that is also dynamic (built on a system or process that leads to that movement) so you can break free from the apathy that holds you back.

When you are chained to the corner of stuck and lost, it would not be hard for me to convince you that you have very little, if any, momentum. Remember, start, stop, fail, meh? Apathy leaves you in a state of zero momentum, with no dynamic system or process to generate the energy that leads to motion, and therefore, the quantity of forward and upward motion in your life is also zero.

Clarity and purpose are no doubt powerful, giving you the ability to sever doubt and fear with confidence and courage. And yet, in and of themselves, clarity and purpose do not provide lift, thrust, or momentum for you to elevate away from the Comfort Zone and through the Opportunity Zone. And again, it is in the Opportunity Zone where your essence is reshaped, as you elevate through and above the Clouds of Confusion into the endless possibility of your Blue Sky Potential.

Clarity helps you more clearly see the possibility of your life as well as the confidence that the possibility actually exists, but it does not move you. Purpose gives you a compass that directs you and gives you the courage to navigate through the clouds toward that possibility, but it doesn't actually move you either.

That is why you *need* momentum.

With clarity and purpose, I thought I was set free to reach my dreams, but as I have shared, I was completely wrong. In what was a year and a half that I searched for, found, and tested what could set me free from apathy, I found it was actually the truth of momentum that could finally set me free.

That momentum would be generated by creating and implementing a dynamic process and system that resulted in energy, motion, and progress upward. We will get to that later, so just tuck it away for a moment. Without momentum, you will not likely be able to truly elevate, and you will remain stuck in the trajectory of your current reality.

Unfortunately, when you have clarity and purpose, but no momentum, it can be more painful and more discouraging than it was before you had the clarity and purpose. I believe it is actually more frustrating and more painful to be stuck, but not lost, than it is to be completely stuck and lost. As it turns out, stuck not lost, is where I lived a significant portion of my life.

When you are completely stuck and lost, at least you are naïve and unaware of all the possibility of your life. But, to have discovered clarity and purpose for endless possibility—to be found, if you will—yet remain completely stuck can be excruciating. In addition to the frustration, being found but stuck is as apathy-inducing as any other scenario. It isn't a fork in the road of uncertainty in the journey, but rather feels like a dead end, which leaves you thinking, *"Great... now what?"*

Apathy in any form, coming from any source, acts not only like quicksand but like gravity. Imagine for a moment you are standing outside, anywhere in the world you want to imagine. Go ahead, pick a place and imagine being outside.

You are looking up at the canopy of blue sky, knowing that somewhere up there is the endless possibly of the greatness of your life. You so desire to soar up there in the bright blue skies that you can't help yourself, so you decide to jump absolutely as high into the air as you can. What happens?

Actually, better yet, instead of imagining it, go ahead and put the book down, go outside, and try it. Seriously, go try it. Jump absolutely as high as you can in an attempt to reach the blue skies (maybe warm up first, lest you pull a muscle).

You aren't going outside right now, are you? Rather, you are raising your eyebrows at me for even suggesting it, now aren't you? Why is that? Because you *know* that as strong, as determined, and as hopeful as you are to live your life in the blue skies, you will never be able to jump with enough force to overcome gravity. Not only because of your jumping ability (or even inability) but because of the force of gravity.

Even at a world-class level, any small amount of momentum is quickly swallowed up by gravity. Similarly, when you start, stop, fail, meh, it is similar to jumping. Start, stop, fail, meh is nothing more than an attempt to jump into the blue sky of your potential, only to be swallowed up by the gravity of apathy.

You already knew this, though. You proved it by not setting the book down, stepping outside, and attempting to leap into the canopy of blue sky. You most likely rolled your eyes and were ultimately unwilling to go outside and attempt to jump because you knew that without question, jumping will never launch you beyond the force of gravity.

Gravity is a constant force that needs to be consistently and powerfully combatted by an opposing force. So too is apathy. Just as you can't jump or leap your way out of gravity, you can't will, strengthen, or goal set your way out of apathy.

When a jet plane (or even a rocket) is successfully launched into the canopy of blue sky, it isn't a jumping or leaping force that launches it. Maybe that is true for a catapulted stone or an acrobat shot out of a cannon at the circus, but they come back down to earth not long after.

Rather, a jet plane or a rocket is set in motion with thrust, which is a propulsive force provided by a process or a system that continues to oppose gravity. Over and over again, second by second, a dynamic system creates enough momentum to carry the jet plane or rocket into the sky, not necessarily beyond the reach of gravity, but far enough that it can truly soar.

Like gravity, apathy is a force that has to be constantly combatted. A singular attempt to act out of desire or passion will create upward force like a jump or a leap in your life, but it will only get you so high for so long before apathy takes over and pulls you back down.

Ultimately, being set free to launch your life into the blue skies where you can reach your dreams will require thrust, a propulsive force, or momentum to break though the gravity of apathy. The reason the truth was hidden is that you almost have to be a *rocket scientist* to discover it. That was a bad joke, but you get the point.

This transformational truth of momentum was well out of my reach, even though I had spent a lifetime observing, studying, and practicing the subject of human behavior and human potential. The leash of apathy, however, led me to the careful search for the truth that could sever the leash, and that is the truth of momentum.

Again, going back to the definition, momentum is the measurable amount of motion or the force being gained by a moving object. And, momentum has a dynamic nature to it, meaning it is built on a system or process that leads to motion and progress.

Even if you have clarity and purpose, if your life is stuck, there is likely no movement and, therefore, no momentum. If you attempt to jump or leap into the blue sky of your potential, momentum and force will be minimal and short-lasted. So, the obvious question becomes, how do we begin to experience and leverage a continuous, dynamic propulsive force that generates power of momentum?

SEEKING RHYTHM

We experience the dynamic power of momentum by seeking *rhythm*. Now, that took an unexpected turn, didn't it? Rhythm? *Really?* You were gracious enough to follow me though the thought process of the leash of apathy and the truth of momentum. So, I'm asking you to continue to allow me to guide you to something that was as hidden to me as it is to you now.

Remember, I described momentum as dynamic. In other words, it is a system or process characterized by action, activity, and progress that generates motion. Rhythm, at its most basic level, is a strong, regular, repeated pattern of movement or sound. Rhythm forms a framework that results in momentum. Let me provide a few examples.

When most people think of rhythm, they think of music or dancing, both of which are *not* currently areas of my expertise. With regard to dance, I have *no* rhythm. While I can keep time and move with the beat of the music, I'm not so great at doing so in a way that isn't publicly embarrassing to my children. For the most part, with regard to dance, you either have rhythm (moves) or you don't.

With regard to music, well, that's a different story. I've got moves for days, or at least I used to. Somewhere in the middle of my elementary years, my brother and I somehow found ourselves hoodwinked by our parents to join a competitive accordion club.

Ouch. I can't believe I just admitted that. And, yes, those three words—competitive, accordion, and club—do actually belong together in the same sentence, as hard as it may be for you to believe. No, I did not spend my youth in Germany, or Wisconsin, and I have never worn lederhosen. (Well, other than for that one skit I performed with my boss and friend, Harold, during a staff Christmas party in my late-20s, but that is a long story. I digress…).

For some reason, my brother and I missed out on the huge swell of the early heavy metal music days which were saturated with cool, flashy men, their electric guitars, and their new uses of electronic keyboards and synthesizers, not to mention plenty of long hair, leather, neon outfits and bandannas to go with it.

I may have missed out on those trendy instruments, but at least I did rock an ozone-killing Aqua Net hair-sprayed mullet that perfectly blended the soccer-playing, rock-listening, Diamond Back BMX-riding, Powell Peralta skateboard-cruising look I was going for. That hairdo went perfectly with my middle-school braces and hot-pink Ocean Pacific dressy T-shirt (Ocean Pacific was the Hollister of our generation, in case you didn't grow up in the '80s).

Instead of the more glamorous garage band instruments, my brother and I rode the [small] wave of competitive accordion, both as soloists, partners in duets, as well as participating in larger competition bands. Yes, "competition" and "bands" also go together in the world of accordion players.

We were both talented, and the boxes of accordion trophies from our youth are still gathering dust in our parent's basement. Again, those two words—accordion and trophies—do actually belong together. And, we do literally still have boxes of them. At this point, I *almost* feel the need to apologize for dragging out these details, yet I won't. I really do feel the need to point them out, lest the beauty and humor of it goes unappreciated, and because it sets up my point on rhythm. It would be such a shame to expose my past in this way and not get the fullest impact out of it.

Back to the point of rhythm. With regard to the accordion, a variety of rhythms could be put to use. We could create the rhythm with our left/bass hand and then create the melody with our right/treble hand. We could create a rhythm that established the framework for a waltz. We could create rhythm that shaped the foundation for a polka. We could play a rhythm that created the basis for a ballad. The variety was nearly endless.

Because of the capability of the left hand, we didn't even need a drummer or bass player to establish and keep the time of the music. Once our left hand established the bass line, we could lay a melody that fit over the top of it. As I described above, rhythm is a strong, regular, repeated pattern of movement or sound, and that arrangement forms a framework that results in something greater. In this case, the rhythm shapes the movement of the music.

I shared a little bit about it earlier, but my absolute favorite traditional job was when I spent four years producing and directing large scale transformative events in sports arenas all across the nation. My accordion days were well in the distant past, as was any competency in music.

Yet, one of my responsibilities was overseeing the recorded music produced for our albums in addition to the live performed music at our events. I absolutely love music, in nearly all forms, because music and lyrics have such transformative and inspirational power. So, producing events that had significant investment in the power of music and lyrics was an overwhelming joy and privilege.

For our events, we hired and assembled a band and vocal team full of Nashville talent. This team was made up of musicians and vocalists who toured with A-list artists or were regularly hired for recording sessions on big name projects, and some of them were even successful recording artists in their own right.

Those were great times for sure, traveling the nation together, impacting hundreds of thousands of people for good. Despite the profound significance and responsibility in front of the audiences, some of the other times behind the scenes were just as memorable. Backstage and between events, we could simply hang out, enjoy some meals, and cut loose in a good-natured way.

From those times, I still remember a corny joke one of the guys shared, "How do you know a drummer is knocking at your door?" Puzzled, we wondered how he was going to roast the drummer who was sitting next to him. "Because the rhythm of the knock speeds up with time."

Everyone burst out laughing, throwing a bunch of paper cups and straws at the drummer, like a bunch of kids at the playground. If you are a musician, you are probably laughing right now (unless you're a drummer—sorry). If you aren't a musician, you may not be sure what to make of this joke. Let me help.

The critique of many drummers is that they can't keep a steady rhythm. Often, they start off fine and on tempo, but as they get excited drumming in a song, they lose themselves in the music, get pumped up, and without knowing it, begin to accelerate the tempo. The song naturally begins to speed up, which if the song calls for it, is just fine. But when the song is supposed to keep a steady pace, and the drummer lets the rhythm gather momentum and unintentionally speeds up the tempo, all the other musicians have to adjust. At times, it completely ruins the song along with its impact.

The point is that rhythm leads to momentum and rhythm is necessary for the movement and beauty of music. Without rhythm, there is no beat to keep time, no pulse to give life to the music. Without rhythm, music falls apart into unorchestrated notes, unarranged patterns, and while the instruments are still making musical sounds, the sounds don't come together to give life to the music.

In fact, notes and sounds not arranged and patterned to a rhythm aren't music at all; they are simply noise. There is a huge difference between music and noise, which had you heard me practicing accordion at times would have been obvious.

Life isn't much different.

Rhythm is necessary for the movement, momentum, and the beauty of life. Without rhythm, there is no beat to keep time, no pulse to give life to your activities. Without rhythm, life falls apart into unorchestrated actions, activities, and behaviors in unarranged patterns. While life is still "happening" all around you, your life is most likely full of the noise of activity, tasks, and overall around-the-clock busyness, but there isn't too much beauty or melody being made out of all that noise.

Like with music, rhythm in our activities and in our personal and family patterns gives us a beat we can use to mark time and create beauty. A rhythm in life establishes a healthy framework to make music in our arranged life patterns, resulting in the type of momentum that leads to forward progress.

I'll come back to this more in a little bit, but I wanted to establish a concept of rhythm with music before I took it too much deeper. At the same time, I'm going to shift from the value of rhythm in music to the concept of rhythm in sports. I only touched on how rhythm can impact the momentum, using a sub-par joke about drummers. I believe a few sports analogies will help us make an even better connection between rhythm and momentum.

Often when listening to athletes or coaches reflect on a game, rhythm will come up. You may hear a journalist ask something like, "Your team really seemed to have a lot success in the second half. What changed in the third quarter?"

An athlete or coach might respond, "Well, in the first half, we just weren't in sync as a team, but in the third quarter, our offense really found a rhythm. Because of that, we executed well on a few of those possessions and got the momentum moving in the right direction. Once we started moving the ball with rhythm and executing on our plays, we rode that momentum the rest of the game." Interestingly enough, this could be an interview of a coach or athlete from any number of sports: basketball, football, or soccer, just to name a few.

Rhythm and momentum are as applicable to individual sports as they are to team sports. A professional golfer gives great care to the rhythm of a swing, both backward and forward. It isn't just on shots off the tee or the fairway; great golfers work on the rhythm of the putting stroke too.

Sprinters are constantly working on their form, their stride, their turnover, all of which impact the rhythm of their running to generate the most amount of speed with the least amount of work. Hurdlers even practice the exact length and number of strides between hurdles to have a pre-defined rhythm that allows them to reach top speeds and clear the hurdle as if it weren't even there.

The number of sports where rhythm, cadence, and momentum are a significant part of the equation of success is lengthy, including speed skating, swimming, Nordic skiing, alpine skiing, and cycling, just to name a few others. In music, in sports, and I believe in life, rhythm and momentum play significant roles in success.

In Chapter 7, I described how we recently moved to Newport Beach, CA, and all the new experiences our family has been enjoying. Many of those experiences involve water, such as the opportunity take a stand-up paddle board out into the Newport Bay or Huntington Bay.

We love to cruise around, enjoying a self-guided tour of beautiful houses, boats (ok, a lot of them are yachts), and spend time as a family appreciating God's creation during a day out on the water. Sometimes we cheat, and instead of paddling on a stand-up paddle board, we rent a Duffy Boat, which is a small, electrically powered boat to take a leisurely cruise around the water. When we indulge in this more sedentary way of enjoying the water, we often bring a pot of homemade spaghetti or chili and enjoy a sunset cruise with family or friends.

While enjoying a variety of activities like these, I began to notice one sport in particular that revealed a genuine, tangible correlation between rhythm and momentum: team rowing. If you live anywhere near the coast or in an area with a lot of lakes or large rivers, you may have some familiarity with rowing and may be able to guess where I'm going with this.

I'm originally from Denver, and while there are beautiful lakes in Colorado, most of them are known for their cold-water fishing, allowing for only a short season of summer recreation. The rivers and streams in Colorado are better known for creating white water rapids for rafting and kayaking than they are for creating the flat, wide, straight, long stretches of water preferred for team rowing. If you grew up landlocked like me, team rowing might be a bit outside your experience.

Either way, being this close to team rowing was new for me, yet the truth of momentum, as established by the framework of rhythm, was in plain sight. There are a number of rowing clubs in the area, and at various times, I have witnessed them practicing and competing in a variety of areas.

At times, they will practice in the Newport's Back Bay, the inland portion of Newport Bay, an area with limited access and much less boating activity. They often practice in the main Newport Harbor and even at times row out to sea, taking their skills out into the Pacific Ocean. I have even had the opportunity to witness a genuine regatta, which is a fancy word for a boat race, as a couple dozen teams lined up just outside of Newport Beach's rock jetties to prepare to race from the tip of Balboa Peninsula to Catalina Island and back.

It is always such a regal and beautiful sight as these boats race by because they move with a stealthy silence across the open water, almost as if they are floating just above the surface. As much as I love the experience of watching it, I especially enjoy the process that takes place to create this serene, yet powerful imagery. What I love most is watching each of the rowers moving in absolute unison, committed to playing their role for the success of the team.

While, the image of team rowing often is displayed in office spaces as motivational work posters to inspire teamwork, those posters do not share the full story. The power of momentum is something you can only witness up close. From a distance, it is regal and serene, but up close, it is as intense and competitive as any other sport. Let me share and give some context.

Each of the boats usually contains 8 rowers, but there is a seat for another position, one that does absolutely zero rowing. You may wonder why there is an extra seat, especially for someone who doesn't row. Well, according to many, this position has the most important role on the boat. That position is known as a coxswain, or cox.

The cox is responsible for many things off and on the water. Off the water, the cox is responsible for implementing the training regimen for the team, as set forth by the head coach and even to step in to coach the crew when the coach isn't present. The cox also leads the crew to transport and store the boat safely and securely, among many other responsibilities.

On the water, the cox is the acting coach, providing feedback and instruction to the crew mid-race. The cox therefore needs to be a motivator and an encourager, knowing and understanding the capacity of the individuals and the team as a whole.

In addition to the athletic performance, the cox is responsible for the safety of the crew and the shell (the boat), steering and directing the vessel through and under bridges when on rivers, or across the wind and waves when in open water. In fact, the role on the water is so important that the cox is legitimately accountable under maritime law as the "Master of the vessel" if something should go wrong during the outing.

All those responsibilities are of significant importance, especially that of the safety of the crew and shell, but in the moment of competition, nothing is more important than the cox's ability to establish and command the rhythm of the stroke of the rowers. And, if you thought that is as simple as shouting "row" at the appropriate time like I did, then like me, you would be mistaken.

There are any number of commands the cox may shout during a regatta, with even beginner guides on "how to coxswain" having no less than a dozen basic mid-race commands. Each cox makes the role their own and adds their unique flair and flavor to commanding the rhythm of the rowers.

When I have observed it in person, I have noticed that when the rowing begins, often the vessel looks like it is barely moving. Even the pace of the strokes does not look rapid or chaotic. Instead, they are slow, intentional, and rhythmic, because again, the point is rhythm, not speed.

Yet, with each command of the cox, with each stroke of the oar, a rhythm is established. Combine the rhythm of each of the eight crew members, and the boat begins to accelerate ahead, gathering momentum with the power of each stroke added to the last.

When sensing an opportunity to strategically surge ahead, one of the basic commands a cox might give is a "power 10" or a "power 20." The cox will always give the crew a heads up that a command like this is coming, usually 2 strokes in advance, and would therefore call out, "in 2, power 10" which would clue the entire crew that in 2 strokes, we are going to increase the intensity and the power of the following 10 strokes, but we are going to do it in rhythm. Without rhythm, executing a "power 10" could simply become a chaotic slapping of a bunch of oars in the water, the lack of synchronization wasting the increased physical effort offered by the crew members.

However, with rhythm, a "power 10" can truly create a surge in momentum within the boat, helping a team move ahead, or even in a longer race simply to intimidate a competing team who can't add the same power with the same rhythmic consistency. The fascinating reality is that the rhythm of the stroke barely changes, if changes at all. But, when rhythmically executing a "power 10," or even a "power 20," a crew and its vessel can truly generate incredible momentum. Of course, the force is generated by the rowers, but the command is called, coached, and directed by the coxswain.

Without the rhythm, all of that strength, force, and effort would not result in momentum. At times, during lengthier races, the cox will even actually prioritize rhythm over power. When the cox can see that the rhythm is off, even slightly, and even when the power is high, the cox will command the team to take a certain number of strokes off in order to re-group and get back in the rhythm together.

Someone with a competitive, speed-driven mindset might think this is crazy—slowing down to speed up? Yet, rhythm is so important to momentum that the cox is willing to give up the speed to create the rhythm that will ultimately lead to greater power and momentum. Just as it is in rowing, so too it is in life.

When seeking rhythm in life,
you often must slow down in order to speed up.

We have been talking about slowing down a lot on this journey. Slowing down to seek perspective, slowing down to seek meaning, and now slowing down to seek rhythm. What so many people forget, deny, or ignore, is that while slowing down can be frustrating, require patience, and feel like the wrong strategy, it can actually lead to greater levels of momentum.

Like so many things, this is hard to see on your own. That's why a guide is so important. You need a trusted friend, a spouse, and many times a professional guide to help you observe these moments in your life, call out in you a need to slow down, establish rhythm, and allow that rhythm to create momentum in your life.

In many ways, the coxswain is that coach and guide in the life of the crew, guiding them on the water to generate rhythm and ultimately win the race. The role of the cox is so important that when a team wins a race, the tradition back at the dock is that the team of rowers will pick up, carry, and ultimately toss the cox into the water as a victory celebration. Usually the rowers are big, strong, lean, and muscular, and the cox is usually much more petite than the rest of the team, so if you just happened to walk by when this is happening, it looks like someone is getting bullied.

Yet, it's not bullying at all; it is gratitude and celebration of the cox, for the support, coaching, and rhythm that was set. It's not unlike when a football team pours Gatorade over the coach as the clock runs out on a sure victory. Type "coxswain throw" in your favorite search engine and check out the images and videos; it's wild.

If you find this a bit more interesting than you imagined, or if you feel the need to binge watch some videos with a bag of Cheetos on the sofa, I would encourage you to also search for, "coxswain recording" in your favorite search engine and click on videos. There are so many good videos that will give you a sense of how the cox commands a rhythm which leads to momentum.

I have watched a bunch of these lately, and I enjoy listening to and observing how both the male and female coxswains command a crew. One I enjoy in particular is titled, "MIT Men's Rowing V8+ Head of the Charles 2016." You may need to dig for that one, but all of them are pretty interesting.

RHYTHM—CAUTIONS

Before we get into the specific areas that I recommend you use to create rhythm in life, I want to offer a few simple cautions. As I begin to list and describe these areas I have found where rhythm leads to momentum, most people react one of two ways. Each way can lead to an inability to get the momentum you need to overcome the gravity of apathy.

The first reaction is one of disinterest. If this is you, you are likely to read through the next few sections and simply not believe these things can lead to dynamic rhythm in life. Or, you are going to look at these fairly simple areas to seek rhythm and think, "Well, I already do those, so tell me something I don't know." Either way, you react with a general "meh" and write them off as soft suggestions that don't have enough power to really help you.

I would caution against looking at these in that way. First, it is a sign of apathy still applying gravity to your potential and your dreams, and second, it is also a sign of arrogance. I know… that was blunt, but I am saying it to myself as much as I am saying it to you.

Before discerning the leash of apathy in my life, and before discovering the truth of breakthrough found in momentum, I would have never guessed that these little things can create the pulse and rhythm needed to generate momentum to fulfill my potential. To think you already have it figured out, especially in the areas where dynamic rhythm can lead to momentum, and then to look at your life and see a complete lack of momentum is a prideful posture to say the least. I know because I have been there.

An example of training in the small things that leads to success in the big things comes from the pop culture flick, *The Karate Kid*. The main character, Daniel (Danny) LaRusso (played by the 1980's heartthrob Ralph Macchio), falls victim to a group of bullies after he and his mother move across the U.S. from Newark, NJ, to the

San Fernando Valley, in the greater Los Angeles area, for his senior year of high school.

It turns out the bullies are a group of Karate students at the overly competitive local dojo, Cobra Kai.[1] In response, Danny wants to learn Karate to stand up for himself. He unexpectedly befriends the local repairman, Mr. Miyagi, played by Pat Morita, who just so happens to be a Karate Master from an equally powerful but more compassionate lineage of Karate.

One of the major friction points in the movie is that Mr. Miyagi started the training by teaching Danny things he didn't know how to do, or at least do well—things that didn't seem to be related to Karate in the least bit. Mr. Miyagi assigned Danny to train for Karate by doing various tasks around his own house—waxing the cars, sanding the floors, painting the fence and house.

None of these things in and of themselves were Karate-specific training, and it was very tiring and frustrating for Danny to keep asking for Karate training, and for Mr. Miyagi to continue to give him very physical chores.

Yet, in the end, Danny's hard work, his learned attention to detail, and his success in these assignments and tasks created the foundation which Mr. Miyagi could build upon within Danny. Unsuspecting at first, these skills built the framework to strengthen and deepen true Karate ability.

By the end of the training, Danny had become a local Karate champion himself, ultimately applying the more compassionate and holistic Karate approach to defeat the lead bully in the championship round of the local Karate tournament.

Just as displayed in this perhaps cheesy, yet profound story of overcoming and personal development, let the areas of rhythm I'm about to share become unassuming tools in your life. Let them be tools that create the foundation and framework to develop and strengthen the true abilities needed within you to reach your dreams.

THERE IS A SECOND TYPE OF REACTION AT THE OPPOSITE END OF THE spectrum I would also caution against. It is the reaction of lifting these tools to too lofty of a place of priority, to overemphasize them, or place them on a pedestal, if you will.

As I help and guide people to come up with a framework for rhythm, sometimes the list of activities and exercises becomes the greater agenda and starts to replace the dream. What I mean by this is that they become so supremely committed to the tasks themselves, the true dreams and the potential of reaching those dreams will go right out the window.

When you establish a rhythm and begin to have success in it, it is going to feel good, maybe even really, really good. For some, it is the first real sense of momentum they have experienced in years, which is exciting and also the goal. Yet, as success is experienced in the rhythm, it becomes easier and exciting to continue to build this momentum. As that happens, the temptation is to simply continue to get better and better at that rhythm, focusing more and more energy into it.

However, if you do not leverage the momentum to truly begin to elevate toward your dreams, and therefore move through the Opportunity Zone, it is unlikely you will even get near the endless possibility of your Blue Sky Potential. Using the *Karate Kid* theme, it would be as if you kept getting better and better at waxing cars, sanding floors, painting fences and houses, but never used it as a framework and foundation to actually learn Karate and face the bullies of doubt and fear.

I have fallen to this temptation as well, ending each day with a sense of major accomplishment because I had completed all the items that exist for the purpose of my rhythm but having made no progress on anything that moved me toward my dream.

Not only have I experienced the glorification of rhythm in my own life, but I have seen others do it as well. To this extent, be careful. The rhythm of a song is not the song itself, only the foundation, framework, and pattern upon which the beauty of the song is established.

The rhythm established by the coxswain's commands for team

rowing does not actually propel the boat. Rather, the rhythm of the commands generates the pulse, flow, and pattern through which the strength and power of the crew members are established. The combination is what creates the momentum. In other words, the rhythm is intended to serve you, not the other way around.

So, keep rhythm in its proper place. It is absolutely the foundation that leads to momentum. And yet, it is not the dream in and of itself. It will give you the beat, pulse, and foundation to build a life intended for greatness, but you won't likely reach greatness if the rhythm itself becomes the master.

With those cautions out of the way, it is time to guide you into the four key areas where you can and should begin to seek rhythm. I have found that when one or more of these areas is either lacking or is filled with busyness and chaos, rhythm is either nonexistent or is disrupted to the point that momentum is minimized.

Yet, I have found that seeking and creating a rhythm in these areas can and will lead to tangible momentum, a foundation you can trust and build upon as you begin to elevate your life toward the blue sky of your potential. Now, it is time to seek rhythm in *routine tasks and choices*, *refueling activities*, *life-giving relationships*, and *reflective exercises*.

SEEKING RHYTHM—ROUTINE TASKS & HEALTHY CHOICES

The first and easiest place to start is with small, everyday, *routine tasks*. Within this category of routine tasks, I would include *routine healthy choices*. For both, I'm talking small and simple. Small and simple tasks choices that take little time and investment act as a dynamo of sorts.

In this sense of the word, dynamo is the energy gained by small, consistent activities, which, over the course of time, begin to shift the direction toward momentum. You've heard it said of athletes, I'm sure. Maybe it was a bench player in basketball, not necessarily the star but someone who simply substituted off the bench and into the game, who hit the court with more consistent hustle and energy than anyone on the team had been displaying up to that point.

That player's hustle acted as a dynamo to ignite the hustle in the whole team. After a few offensive and defensive positions, this bench player's energy helped shift the entire momentum of the game. After the game, a player or coach being interviewed may be heard saying, "When he came off the bench and into the game, it got the whole team hustling because he's a dynamo. That's when the momentum began to shift in the game, and it carried us to the win." In the same way, small, routine, everyday tasks and choices done with consistency will act as a dynamo, creating a consistent pattern of behavior that over time swings the momentum.

For some, these involve tasks around the house. Simply making the bed, every single day, first thing when you get out of it, will add a sense of rhythm, momentum, and energy to the day. It could be checking, opening, and sorting the mail each day. It could be organizing and tidying your bedroom before leaving for the day.

For others, maybe the routine tasks more like healthy choices, as in taking supplements daily, which can provide a simple sense of accomplishment, investment in health, and a rhythm that leads to momentum. Maybe it is setting a minimum amount of water you want to drink each day, and doing it, without question every day. It could be taking that extra 10 minutes to do the stretching your physical therapist wants you to do on that shoulder or ankle, so you can avoid surgery.

Maybe you need some simple rhythm in the workday, and you start your day right by staying out of email and off social media. That's both a routine task *and* a healthy choice. Instead, you spend your first 15 minutes making a list of top priorities and important conversations you need to have that day, which will create a rhythm of staying focused.

For others who tend to schedule meetings up to and past the absolute time they need to leave the office, it would help to set aside 15 minutes at the end of each day to clean up, organize, and "reset" their desks before leaving the office, allowing them to arrive the next day to a neat and organized desk that subtly communicates order and structure.

I have tried and practiced any number of these simple routine tasks and healthy choices in various combinations. Some worked to add rhythm for me, and others didn't. I discovered there is no secret to which activities are the right ones for you. Simply start trying and testing some of these.

Sometimes, it is a matter of simply sticking to a few and committing to doing them every single day for a set amount of time. Many people have begun to talk about the power of habits and the power of having rituals. I believe the reason it has become so popular is that the rhythm established by these things really does lead to momentum. So, I encourage you to begin to establish a rhythm with simple routine tasks and healthy choices.

SEEKING RHYTHM—REFUELING ACTIVITIES

Beyond routine tasks and healthy choices, the next area I help my clients seek rhythm is by pursuing *refueling activities*, those activities that offer personal replenishment. Yes! You need to be regularly participating in activities that refuel you and bring *you* life. I'm giving you permission to take care of yourself! It's called self-care and it is vital.

So much of life actually depletes our energy tanks that it makes sense to invest some thought and time to find and participate in activities that refuel our energy reserves. In general, it is easiest to break these energy reserves into four major categories of energy tanks: physical, intellectual, emotional, and spiritual.

The refueling activities you identify need to work in combination to keep each one of these energy tanks as full as possible. When these tanks are full, you have a greater ability to operate with a significant amount of strength. Beyond that, when you create a rhythm in activities that are replenishing to you, the momentum that builds up can be significant.

The list of activities that people find refueling is as unique and as eccentric as each individual I have helped. I have seen everything from painting to exercising, from alone time with a novel to playing cards with friends, from puttering around the garage to gardening garlic. I'm not even kidding… "gardening garlic" hit the charts with one of my clients. The ability to garden home-grown garlic in the garlic-growing season was on the rhythm chart of this client's refueling activities. Who knew? Garlic season?

Again, like with routine tasks and healthy choices, there is no limit to the amount and the type of activities that may refuel you. Instead of focusing on the "what" and "which" activities, I want to focus on the why. The whole principle here is not unlike the announcement made aboard an airplane before departure. And, since our working metaphor is shaped around soaring the airplane of your life into blue sky, it is fitting too.

The flight attendant will give an announcement about the oxygen mask dropping from the ceiling when needed. Three things stand out in these announcements that I believe are worth pointing out, especially when considering the seeking and establishing of rhythm with refueling activities.

The first is that the flight attendant always says something like, "If you have a child traveling with you, please make sure you place the oxygen mask on yourself before assisting the child." This is counterintuitive for most parents, especially moms who intuitively nurture and protect their children before themselves.

The reason the flight attendant shares this order of priority is because if mom passes out while struggling to put the oxygen mask on the child, the end result is that neither the mom nor the child is safe. Yet, if the mom can quickly and safely put her oxygen mask on first, then she has the oxygen and strength necessary to help her child.

Just as it is good advice as you prepare to soar in the blue skies while traveling in that airplane, it is good advice I'm giving you as you prepare to soar in the blue skies of your potential. I am assuming that in some way or another you have a responsibility to take care of others, or at the very least impact others for good, whether that be a spouse, child, boss, or employees.

Therefore, it is important that you refuel your life, so you have the strength and stamina necessary to take care of the needs of others too. If you pass out, whether literally or figuratively, while trying to help someone else advance in life, then neither of you are able to safely get to your destination.

There is a second similarity between your life and the flight attendant's announcement about the oxygen masks. The pre-flight announcement usually includes the reminder of something that sounds like, "*If...* the air pressure changes, the oxygen masks will drop from the ceiling."

Fortunately, in the airline industry, the use of the word "if" is appropriate, because it is a rare experience to have the oxygen masks deployed on a flight. I have flown countless flights and countless miles and have never seen it happen. But the precaution is there for all of us, because it does in fact happen on occasion. Unfortunately, in life, there is no *if* the oxygen runs out. I don't have to tell you, but I will... it is more a matter of *when* the oxygen runs out in life.

What I mean by that is there is no question that we run out of energy, we hit the wall, and we deplete ourselves often to the point of exhaustion, whether it be physically, intellectually, emotionally, spiritually, or all of the above. I'm thankful that as much as I have traveled, I have never been on a flight where that "if" became a reality.

However, on a personal level, I have come to a place countless times when I was severely depleted and well past the point of needing to refuel. I'm sure you have experienced these seasons countless times as well. You need a system to refuel you, not *if* you run out of energy but that keeps you from running fully out for *when* the challenges of life suck out all the oxygen you have.

As a result, you most likely need to find ways to refuel daily. It is so much easier to keep the tank topped off than it is to go completely dry and then try to fill it back up. Even if you completed a major refueling activity with the rhythm once per week, it would be like eating as much as you can at a buffet and then fasting the rest of the week. Or, it would be like sleeping 24 hours in a row and then staying awake for the next 6 days straight. Participating in some form of refueling activity should be part of your daily rhythm.

Finally, the third similarity is based on what triggers the oxygen masks to drop from the ceiling. Usually, the flight attendant says something like, "The masks will *automatically* drop from the ceiling, and the oxygen will *automatically* begin to flow."

I hate to be so blunt, but when was the last time you had a system established in life to help you *automatically* seek to be replenished? That's what I thought. That's ok—you aren't alone. I have met very few people who had a system in place to tell them when they needed to replenish either, let alone a system to help them *actually* replenish.

The reason none of us have an automatic system is that there is no way to measure exactly when the time is right. And, what is worse is that we always assume we are okay, well, until we are already not okay. Over the years, I have created a system where I can both monitor my sense of replenishment, and make sure I'm automatically refueling. I help my clients create the same tools in their lives. These systems are vital to a successful journey toward your reaching dreams. Here's why:

Sometimes we hit unexpected turbulence. We get surprises in life that can hit us without warning, even if we thought we were in a fairly good place of replenishment.

We might feel strong, replenished, and refueled, and then one team meeting goes badly at work, one deal with a client goes sideways, or one really frustrating interaction with your teenager or toddler erupts (are teenagers or toddlers really that different?), and your tank is absolutely empty. There is no warning system that can automatically tell you when to refuel.

Even if the bells and whistles were to go off to tell you that you are on empty, you most likely are at such a low point that you would have no energy and/or are too apathetic to do any of the activities that would refuel you. That is why you need to establish a rhythm that *automatically* refuels you no matter how you feel, before you get depleted.

My friend, I probably don't have to tell you this, but my guess is that at the end of most days, you feel depleted. Now, to be fair, there is a good depleted, as in when you give your life to your dreams, have left it all on the field and are fulfilled in your depletion. But there is a bad-depleted too, and you probably know this all too well.

It happens when you have run around chaotically all day putting out fires at work and in the family, only to be totally discouraged and depleted at the end of the day. It doesn't have to be this way. There is another way to live.

In order to stop the madness, it will require you to prioritize your replenishment over many other things and even at times over the needs of others. I imagine there are people who depend on you in some way or another, and you probably spend much of your energy taking care of them first, and you second, if at all. We need to flip that. We need you to take care of yourself, so when you need to take care of them, you can do so from a place of strength, not from a place of emptiness.

The rhythm you need to establish is based on a regular, pre-determined sequence of activities that refuel and replenish you. You need to create a system that will lead to regular and *automatic* replenishment. When you are able to find the right combination of activities and frequencies, not only will you be replenished and refueled, but the rhythm created by these activities will create an unstoppable momentum.

Now, every time you hear this type of announcement on an airplane, you are going to think of the truth of seeking rhythm and momentum. My hope and prayer for you is that when you do, you smile because you have found and established a rhythm of activities that are regularly refueling you. As you ponder it while on that airplane, I also hope you are experiencing momentum created by that rhythm as you soar in the endless possibility of blue skies of your life.

SEEKING RHYTHM—LIFE-GIVING RELATIONSHIPS

By now, you are understanding the pattern of the metaphor. It is basically finding good things in your life, doing them regularly, consistently, and rhythmically to create the momentum your life needs to elevate your trajectory and reach your dreams. That's how it works. It is both simple and profound.

You will have to be intentional in this pursuit of rhythm, especially in this next area. Just as it is important to create rhythm around routine tasks, healthy choices, and refueling activities, it is important to create rhythm around the idea of *life-giving relationships*.

Not every relationship in your life is there by design. In fact, more often than not, it is likely the people you interact with most are in your life out of circumstance, not out of choice. As a result, your life is impacted, and your energy depleted by so many relationships that are not life-giving.

Can you even think of more than a handful of life-giving relationships that you have? So very few people I guide can name more than a few relationships in their lives that actually give them life. They can name a lot of friends, or a lot of co-workers or colleagues, or other moms they connect with at meetings at church, or other parents on that traveling youth sports team, but it is rare for people to quickly and easily have a list of people who bring life to the relationship.

What does that mean, practically speaking? Most, if not all of their relationships, therefore, are depleting in some form or fashion instead of strengthening and building up in nature. Maybe even some relationships in which you have an expectation to be life-giving aren't life-giving right now. Maybe interactions with your spouse have been full of friction lately. Maybe quality time with the kids doesn't feel so much like "quality" these days.

As you know, relationships are like a two-way street; they go both ways and there is always give and take. Yet, because humans are relational by nature (yes, even introverts like me—it just manifests differently), it is important to establish a rhythm in life around those relationships that are inspiring, encouraging, and life-giving. And, if there are committed relationships in life that you desire more from, whether it be a spouse, kids, siblings, parents, or even best friends, you owe it to yourself to pursue rhythm and life in that relationship.

Of all the areas of rhythm you need to establish, this may be the most difficult. Relationships can be challenging and ever-changing. Beyond that, busy schedules and the general rapid pace of life make it tough to establish a genuine rhythm.

My recommendation is to at least become more aware of who you are spending a lot of time with and whether or not those relationships give or deplete your life. In general, move toward life-giving relationships, but in a healthy, non-clingy, non-dependent, non-stalking sort of way.

And, if necessary, move away from relationships that lead to your depletion, but do this carefully, slowly, and in a non-judgmental, non-relationally destructive way. I'm not at all recommending that you ditch people, divorce people, or abandon people. I am simply saying to become wiser with the life-giving and life-depleting relationships and time you give to them.

More practically, with regard to improving life-giving relationships, consider these four simple steps:

1. Identify those relationships that are already life-giving or relationships that you desire to be life-giving
2. Intentionally find a way to call, visit, or meet with them and share with them how important the relationship is to you and how much it gives life, or how much you desire it to give life
3. If they feel the same, ask them to help you come up with ideas of how to work together to intentionally have more time together, and ideas that will help that time be more life-giving for both parties
4. Commit to the rhythm and type of quality time you have agreed to share with each other.

As you spend more time in life-giving relationships, that rhythm can only lead to an increased momentum in your life.

SEEKING RHYTHM—REFLECTIVE EXERCISES

Have I mentioned yet how important it is to slow down? I know, you are getting tired of hearing it, but as you slowdown in order to speed up, it can help you re-calibrate with the use of *reflective exercises*.

If we don't reflect on our journey at regular intervals, we are likely to become stuck and lost again. It is one thing to slow down in order to seek perspective to arrive at clarity, to seek meaning to arrive at purpose, and to seek rhythm to arrive at momentum, but it is wholly another thing to slow down to continue to "check your gauges," if you will.

One of the rhythms I have found most powerful in helping me establish a framework for momentum is the rhythm of regularly participating in reflective exercises. And, I'm not talking about yoga, meditation, or mindfulness, although I find power in those things too (for me, these would probably better fit in the *refueling activities* category).

I'm talking about actually taking time to reflect, to write things down, to evaluate what is working, what is not working, and what you are learning. I'm talking about finding a rhythm to reflect on gratitude, which by the way, is a focus in almost every reflective tool I have explored.

I'm also talking about reflecting on your routine tasks and healthy choices, your refueling activities, and the quality of your life-giving relationships. Yes, pausing to reflect and evaluate is a vital part of developing momentum.

Additionally, if you have come to a place where you have clearly developed purpose, vision, and strategy for your life, or even goals you have set for yourself, regular times to reflect on these times will help you stay the course and continue to elevate your trajectory.

As you reflect and write down what you are sensing and discovering, you will also be able to identify where you feel doubt, fear, or apathy creeping back in or even if you are experiencing areas of life where you feel stuck and lost again.

Regular times of reflection are going to give you the opportunity to create rhythm, which will likely increase your ability to navigate the Clouds of Confusion that you come across while you elevate through the Opportunity Zone and into the Possibility Zone. There is no right or wrong way to do this, as long as you are establishing a rhythm of reflective exercises that are leading to momentum.

If you don't maintain some rhythm to your reflection, you will most likely only turn to reflect in troubling times, which is a good posture to have when life gets hard, but if you had the rhythm and momentum already working for you, you may have been able to avoid that troubling time in the first place.

There are all sorts of tools, resources, and guides that can help you be reflective in life, so start looking into a few and begin to try them out.

SEEKING RHYTHM—NEXT STEPS

Wow! Take a deep breath! We have covered a tremendous amount of distance together on apathy, rhythm, and momentum. I believe it has been worth it, every single word. I have found that apathy is the single most destructive leash of the three, and without exposing it for what it is, you may never discern its gravity-inducing grasp on your dreams.

Additionally, momentum, found when you seek rhythm, is the most elusive truth of the three, but once discovered and established, it is the strongest available force to generate the thrust your life needs in order to truly to leave the gravity and the grasp of apathy behind.

I've taken much time and given much effort to describe how this truth can operate in your life because I believe it can truly help you be set free to reach your dreams. The rhythm your life must be dynamic.

Again, a dynamic rhythm is simply and profoundly a process or system of routine tasks and healthy choices, refueling activities, life-giving relationships, and reflective exercises that work together to create a framework and foundation for momentum.

I recommend that you look for tools, assessments, and resources that create rhythm in a wide array of areas. Find tools that help you:

- Develop and establish powerful habits out of daily, routine tasks
- Understand and set in motion the types of activities you find refueling
- Replenish and stay sharp physically, intellectually, emotionally, and spiritually
- Discover how to manage your energy instead of just managing your time
- Engage in healthy, life-giving relationships and how to establish and deepen them
- Create rhythm in life based on the above areas of focus, whether those rhythms be in the morning, evening, or throughout the day, week, month, or year

Put all these together in the right system, process, sequence, and framework, and it becomes dynamic. Dynamic rhythm turns activities and actions into progress and momentum. You need momentum, and you find it by seeking dynamic rhythm.

Not only did I discover that momentum is the third truth of transformational breakthrough, but I have discovered how it generates power within us to defeat apathy, which is a power I personally was completely lacking, despite all the huge amounts of clarity, purpose, and even impact I was having.

Yet, the benefits of rhythm go beyond momentum because momentum has a power in it too. Momentum generates something you need to reach your dreams: *conviction*. Check out "Part B" of the third simple truth of transformational breakthrough.

<u>Simple Truth of Transformational Breakthrough #3</u>

YOU NEED MOMENTUM
because

(Part B)

MOMENTUM GENERATES CONVICTION…

Yes, momentum generates conviction. I'll get to what conviction is and how it is generated by momentum in just a minute, but let me first share with you an internal wrestling match I had for this specific section of the book. As I was observing and living out these truths while developing the content for this book, everything within me wanted to say that "momentum generates passion." Passion is such a rich, popular, and easy to grasp concept. It would have sounded great.

And, yet something wouldn't let me use that word. I don't want to write things that simply *sound* great: I want to write things that actually *are* great. As a guide, I have been faithful to that commitment throughout this book, even when the great thing I need to tell you is going to be hard for you to hear. So, it makes no sense to change direction now.

I will give you this… in a sense, passion actually *is* great; it may just be overrated. In the end, I really had to relinquish "my passion" to tell you about how momentum and passion go together. Here is why I couldn't tell you that: passion and momentum are actually not correlated. It's true. There is no direct relationship between passion and momentum.

Think about it. You and I have met a lot of people with passion who had no momentum. You and I have met a lot of people with passion, yet they had no elevation in the trajectory of their lives. You and I have met a lot of people with passion, yet they were not at all set free and no closer to reaching their dreams as a result of the passion they possessed.

Not only have you and I met people with passion and no momentum, but at times, we probably *are* those people. Maybe you are there right now. A lot of passion, especially since we have stirred up and rekindled your dreams, but maybe you don't *have any* momentum.

I know I have lived in that painful reality myself. For most of my professional life, reaching my own potential by helping others reach their potential has been my "passion." As I have shared a number of times already, that specific passion opened a lot of great doors, especially when I combined it with clarity and purpose. And yet, it did little to defeat the leash of apathy, let alone provide the thrust to reach my dreams. Passion excited me, but it did not elevate me. Passion ignited me, but it did not empower me. Maybe the same is true for you. There is passion somewhere within, but something is still missing.

That is why I uncovered and ultimately had to tell you about conviction. I know… it isn't a word that is used very often. I don't believe we don't use it because it isn't a good word… that's a brain twister. Instead, I believe we do not use the word *conviction* very often because very few people truly exhibit a conviction about something or anything in life.

Too often, we are moved by the winds of the latest fads, the most recent socially correct posture, and simply the opinion of others, like peers, celebrities, or even the masses, whoever they are. With the significance of the role that social media plays in our collective and individual psyche, we can easily be swayed by an online post, an idea, or a concept that goes viral and collects followers.

A belief or behavior that is in vogue and popular one day can literally be out of tune and even seen as criminal the next. Listen, I am all about the transparency and exposure that social media has created and demanded of leaders, celebrities, and those in positions of unchecked power.

So to be clear, I'm not talking about those benefits that are reaped by society at large—those have been beneficial at exposing hatred, abuse, and deception on many levels. I'm talking about the moment by moment swaying of opinion and "personal passion," without any sense of conviction. So few people truly operate their lives out of a place of conviction, but before I go further, let me tell describe what conviction is.

Conviction is the quality of being firmly convinced what you believe is deeply true and demonstrating it in how you think, speak, act, and live.

This goes beyond how we live our lives in public. Conviction should also guide our private lives, especially how we see ourselves and how we feel about pursuing our dreams. In order to elevate through the clouds that you will face on the journey to living your dreams, it will require conviction.

Certainly, passion is inherent in conviction, but there too must be something else that goes deeper than passion. You see, even the most fiery forms of passion will ultimately fade, but conviction is steadfast. Desire fades too, but conviction is enduring. Passion is an external trait, but conviction is an internal quality. Passion can be an external volume of someone at the podium or on the stage, but conviction is an internal steadfastness that is quietly compelling.

The "something more" that is contained with conviction but is lacking within passion alone is the concept of commitment. Passion doesn't always imply a dedication to something, so commitment started to work into my testing and thought process around this truth. I even played with the idea that "momentum generates commitment," which possibly could have worked. But, it too only *sounded* great, without really *being* great—at least in terms of this truth. Commitment at its most basic level is the quality of being dedicated, which on the face of it, feels like it could help us combat apathy.

Yet commitment alone, in all of its stubbornness and grit, isn't enough either, because it can be diminished to a robot-like duty, which often lacks passion. I have met many committed people who completely lacked passion for the thing they were committed to, and that usually leads to a life of duty and often drudgery. They had commitment but didn't have conviction, because they didn't have passion. You need both passion and commitment, and that, my friend, is where conviction comes in. This lead us to another inter-section you are going to appreciate.

> *Conviction is the internal quality developed and experienced at the intersection of fiery passion and unwavering commitment.*

Talk about the opposite of apathy and the opposite of a life of "meh." Fiery passion *and* unwavering commitment—that's convic-tion! Conviction is formidable, a force to be reckoned with. Conviction moves you to and through the fire of transformation. This is why you need conviction, because if you don't have it, you will likely give in and possibly quit when things get hot in the Opportunity Zone. Just like you can't muster up confidence, nor can you buy or borrow courage, you are not going to be able to harvest conviction out of thin air.

However, there is hope. There is a way you can generate conviction within you. Yes, you alone have the power to generate it yourself. Just as clarity produces confidence and purpose creates courage…

Conviction is naturally generated by the power of momentum.

Like clarity and purpose, which are discovered by slowing down to evaluate and reflect, you must slow down to try and test a variety of rhythms. However, unlike with clarity and purpose, to begin to generate conviction, you can and must have an active role in developing momentum.

Seeking rhythm invites you to action, and as such, you can take action by establishing a rhythm, which leads to momentum. When you experience momentum, it will actually generate conviction. On this one, you can literally take action to generate the conviction you are looking for. It is a process which requires a dynamic system and it takes time, but you can do it nonetheless.

As you begin to seek rhythm in life, you are going to experience momentum, not only in the tasks, choices, activities, relationships, and reflection that all begin to become rhythmic, but that rhythm can create a momentum in life all around.

As you experience that momentum, it is going to generate a conviction within you. The more rhythm you create, the more momentum you will begin to experience. As you experience an increase in momentum in a wide variety of areas in life, it is going to generate a conviction—a passion and a commitment to stay the course, to be set free, and to reach your dreams.

The rhythm will likely lead to a momentum in areas of your life you once felt impossible in which to make progress. As you get rhythm in routine tasks, it will create a momentum in taking care of the small things, and as you take care of the small things, you are going to experience momentum in bigger areas. Let me share an example of how this can work.

IT IS POSSIBLE THAT THE RHYTHM OF KEEPING YOUR BEDROOM TIDY and keeping your desk organized daily may motivate you. As a result of experiencing a tidy bedroom, you may decide to clean out the closet on the weekend, and because you are organizing your desk, which is usually piled with receipts, you find yourself entering those expenses into a software and managing your budget a bit more closely.

The supplements you are taking and the water you drink throughout each day are unintentional reminders to manage your portion sizes and say "no" to second helpings and even desserts. When asked about dieting, you honestly respond and say, "No, I'm not dieting. I'm just taking a few supplements and making sure I drink water each day." But others are noticing you are also passing on the dessert even though that wasn't in your plan.

Then, because you also identified a few refueling activities, you are now taking 30-minute power walks on three days each week and taking 30 minutes each of the other four days to read that e-book on "lifestyle blogging as a side hustle." Because of these rhythms of activities that are refueling to you, you are getting replenished physically and intellectually.

Give it a few months, and then combine those new realities of momentum with the fact that your budget is looking a little better, and here is what might happen—you can invest in a "new" used camera for your blog, and you have lost 10 pounds because the supplements, water, portion sizes, and walks are all beginning to add up. It is a bit crazy because you didn't even set a goal to save money for a camera, or to lose 10 pounds, but you ended up doing both, albeit a bit unintentionally.

Let's keep going because this is how I have experienced and seen it work. You pursued and coordinated a once per month coffee with a friend who is very life-giving, and she has become a mentor and prayer-partner of sorts, offering wisdom to some of the marital friction you are feeling and parenting mistakes you have been making recently.

You are regularly reflecting in your journal about those conversations and how you catch yourself over-reacting to your spouse and even your kids. As a result of the reflection and writing down your desire to change and to be the joyous parent you never had, you came to the realization that, just maybe, you are as much a part of the friction as your spouse and kids are.

As a result of the life-giving friendship, mentoring, and reflective journaling, you now regularly catch yourself before you over-react. Funny, but the kids aren't as argumentative as they were back when you were overreacting more often.

Hmmm… Your spouse has noticed your improved attitude and how your reactions have changed too, not to mention noticed the tidied bedroom, desk, closet as well as the cute fashionista photos of you on your Instagram profile and the 10 pounds that have gone missing. Somehow, that has led to a few date nights even though you didn't schedule them, and even some marital intimacy that has been missing the last six months.

Take a deep breath for a second. That all sounds dreamy, doesn't it? You may think I'm exaggerating, but this is how it works. Not always specifically this way, but I have regularly observed and personally experienced how rhythm establishes a framework, a pulse, and a beat that builds a foundation and brings about the music and the beauty of life. It starts small, but when it is dynamic, the impact of rhythm multiplies quickly. As the areas of growing momentum overlap and cooperate with each other, the momentum surges forward in other areas of life too.

But, wait. Were we not talking about conviction? I've made the case for rhythm and momentum, but how does momentum generate conviction?

The rhythm and momentum experienced will lead to an increasingly larger sense of accomplishment, and that sense of accomplishment is going to reignite a passion within you for a lot of things, especially for those things that are most important to you— maybe even your dreams. What's more, as you experience this type of life-changing momentum, you aren't going to want to go back to an old way of life. You have found a commitment that you have never been able to muster by yourself.

The "who you are" now is so different than the "who you were" only a few short months ago. In fact, you have already become a better version of your true self, and you have even become truer to who you know you truly are. Because of that, you have more passion for things you used to ignore or neglect, and you are more committed to things that only a few short months ago, you had no commitment for. You have generated conviction.

In fact, many of those things, like taking a power walk, making your bed daily, or reflective journaling are all things you used to have a deep apathy for. Take a power walk? Today? Meh… that won't do much good, used to be the answer. Make the bed? Meh… I'm just going to get in it again tonight, right? Journal reflectively? Meh… mom always used to say if you have nothing good to say, don't say it at all…

Now that you have momentum, it has generated a conviction that you have rarely if ever had; it is a passion and commitment to do things that you tended to be regularly apathetic toward. The conviction causes you to leave a function early to make sure you get your power walk in for the day. It causes you to put down your phone, to leave social media behind, and to pick up that book. Conviction causes you to clean the desk, and while you are at it, log that receipt into the budgeting software.

It causes you to pick up your journal and begin to reflect even if it is already after midnight on a jam-packed day, because even if it means less sleep, you have noticed how much better you sleep after getting things off your chest and into the pages of your journal.

Not to mention, you have a conviction (passion and commitment) to journal even though you are tired because you have had some pretty big breakthroughs in your journaling, and you can easily point to the fruit of that daily effort. Your passion and commitment in the form of conviction was generated by that momentum, and as a result, you simply won't allow yourself to fall asleep without keeping the rhythm of reflection active and present in your life.

You are now seeing how this is all tied together. This is how your resolve is forged into conviction—a fire passion and unwavering commitment. Not because you made a New Year's Resolution or swore to yourself again to start that diet Monday morning, or because you spent a weekend writing down your quarterly goals. Your conviction is generated as you establish the framework of rhythm in a way that leads to momentum. Momentum will generate the conviction it will take to truly be set free from the leash of apathy.

This leads us to "Part C" of our third and final simple truth of transformational breakthrough.

Simple Truth of Transformational Breakthrough #3

YOU NEED MOMENTUM
because
MOMENTUM GENERATES CONVICTION
and

(Part C)

CONVICTION SEVERS APATHY

REMEMBER EARLIER IN THE CHAPTER, WE TALKED ABOUT HOW IT would be impossible for you to simply leap into the canopy of blue sky above? And, instead how you would need something that could consistently and powerful oppose the gravity of apathy.

Well, we have found it, my friend. Conviction which is generated by momentum severs the tether of apathy. That combination of fiery passion to stay the course and the unwavering commitment to not give up or give in is the exact type of gravity-opposing force it takes to be set free from the leash created by apathy.

Breakthrough happens when you leverage rhythm to establish momentum to generate conviction. That process can give you the thrust to exit the gravitational force of apathy.

In years past, I had assumed I had experienced breakthrough, simply because I had more clarity and deeper understanding of purpose than 99% of the people I met. Yet, I didn't have the full breakthrough, nor transformation necessary for me to truly be set free to reach my dreams. I only had clarity and purpose, which are very good things, but not sufficient in and of themselves. I was missing the final truth of transformational breakthrough, the truth found in the power of momentum.

As I discovered the leash of apathy impacting long stretches of my past, even stretches of time when I was having clear impact on people, I was frustrated. How is it possible that I have apathy in my life? But, once I was willing to accept it for what it was, I could begin to go to work on finding the truth that could set me free from that terrible leash of apathy that had a death-grip on my dreams.

As I saw rhythm begin to develop a momentum, I knew I was onto something. As the momentum truly began to change my life, I could feel a conviction being generated, a combination of passion and commitment I had never experienced before. I was both fiery passionate and unwaveringly committed to be set free and reach my dreams.

This very book is the first of many fruits of that conviction that was generated in my life. Now that I have elevated away from my Comfort Zone, through the Opportunity Zone, I am truly breaking the barrier into my Possibility Zone like I never have before.

We have not talked about the Wright Brothers in quite a while, but let me shed some light on how I see momentum playing a role in generating conviction in their pursuit of creating the first flying machine and ultimately soaring into the blue sky of their potential.

At the very beginning of Chapter 1, almost in passing, I mentioned how the first four flights the Wright Brothers piloted were in a face of a 27-mph headwind. It made flight very challenging to be sure, but they succeeded nonetheless. What I did not share before is that if you do the math of how far each flight traveled over the ground, combined with the amount of time each flight was in the air, you can calculate their groundspeed.

It turns out the average groundspeed for each of the flights was somewhere in the neighborhood of 6.8 mph. Pretty slow, especially for flying, isn't it? In fact, that is so slow, it wouldn't be all that difficult for a child to pedal one of the Wright Brothers' Von Cleve bicycles faster than they were flying their first airplane. By today's standards, you might not even consider that flying. Yet, they had broken the barrier into the Possibility Zone. They had done the impossible—piloted, controlled, heavier-than-air flight.

Here is what is even more interesting about their speed, though. When you combine the 6.8 mph of ground speed of the plane moving forward in the face of a 27-mph headwind pushing them backward, the net airspeed (the speed of an airplane relative to the air around it) is actually 34 mph, nearly triple the speed that would have been experienced relative to the ground.

Let me encourage you with this: As you begin to get rhythm and momentum, don't look for speed. Because at first, it won't feel like speed at all. Just like that 8-membered team rowing shell is barely moving when the rhythm begins.

Instead of looking for speed, simply seek dynamic rhythm and allow it to establish the foundation for forward progress and momentum, ultimately generating conviction. Don't focus on speed, because speed is relative. Any rhythm and momentum you get, no matter how small it feels, no matter if it is in the face of great headwinds, is forward momentum nonetheless. And, some rhythm and some momentum, no matter how small, is 100% more than the no rhythm and zero momentum you are most likely experiencing right now.

Finally, don't be discouraged when it looks like others are moving faster. Remember, the Wright Brothers' competitors were all very busy building more powerful engines. Yet, the Wright Brothers had all the conviction (the fiery passion *and* the unwavering commitment) that they were the ones taking the correct course toward building the control mechanisms that allowed them to pilot the flight, not just power it.

Additionally, unlike actually flying an airplane where the weather conditions are generally the same in the same airspace, your conditions are completely unlike anyone else's around you. The weather patterns and clouds you are facing are relative to your sky, your life, your potential, your dreams, and therefore *entirely* different than anyone else's. So, stop the comparison game of how fast, or how high your life is moving and simply begin to seek dynamic rhythm.

Trust that the rhythm will lead to momentum. And, as it does, enjoy the momentum as it begins to generate a deeper conviction within you. As that conviction forges into resolve, use the fiery passion and unwavering commitment to sever the leash of apathy holding you back as strongly and as staunchly as gravity is holding you to the ground. It is time to be set free and reach for your dreams, my friend.

As a final reminder, here is the third simple but profound truth of transformational breakthrough:

Simple Truth of Transformational Breakthrough #3

YOU NEED MOMENTUM
because
MOMENTUM GENERATES CONVICTION
and
CONVICTION SEVERS APATHY

You Begin the Journey to Momentum by Seeking Rhythm

CHAPTER 11

SET FREE — IT'S TIME TO SOAR

---

*"One cannot consent to creep
when one feels an impulse to soar."*

- HELEN KELLER

IT IS IN YOUR NATURE TO HAVE THE DESIRE TO SOAR. *THAT* IS A good thing. Not only is your desire to soar a good thing, it is well within your capacity to do so. The good news is that you are not going to have to transform to possess that desire. Yet, you are going to have to experience a transformational breakthrough to tap into it.

Just because it has felt so out of reach for so long does not mean it has to stay that way. It is very possible, my friend, even probable for you to experience that breakthrough, especially with the right tools, resources, and the right guide. I am here for you, and I want more than anything to see that happen for you.

Along those lines, as a guide, I'd like to point something out to you. During our journey from that corner of stuck and lost where we first met, all the way up to where we are now, something has changed. Something is different. Something is new. What is it?

You know *where breakthrough happens*.

Yes, you do.

If you have not put it together in the last few chapters, I will make it clear here.

Genuine, life-changing, transformational breakthrough happens within you.

Genuine breakthrough happens within. Transformational breakthrough always starts inside of us first. Sure, we often say we need a breakthrough in our marriage, or in our career, or in our parenting, or in our health, or in our finances. And yes, we often do need breakthrough in those areas, but at the end of the day, those external "breakthroughs" are often simply based on a desire to change our circumstances.

When circumstances change for the better, we tend to call it a "breakthrough." But, I don't think it is accurate or reflective of a genuine breakthrough. Why? Because circumstances can improve without any internal breakthrough or transformation occurring within us.

So, instead, we might say, "I need the circumstances to change." That statement would be more accurate based on what we are actually looking to see happen. However, we don't say that because we know circumstances rarely simply improve without reason. We realize that we often do need a breakthrough, and therefore, we say it that way. Unfortunately, we often look in the wrong place. We look for it in the circumstances around us, instead of beginning where we need to begin, which is *within*.

We need to begin where you and I began this journey together, which is by looking within. We need to tap into what has been supernaturally deposited there—your desire to soar in order to see your unique dreams become a reality. From that starting point and with a willingness to change, we can move toward the truths of clarity, purpose, and momentum in order to experience transformational breakthrough *within* us.

Often, when we experience that transformational breakthrough internally, it gives us the ability to navigate those external circumstances in a healthier way, which often creates breakthrough in those circumstances too. Yet, internal transformation doesn't necessarily guarantee external change of circumstances. That does not mean it is not worth pursuing. In fact, the opposite is true.

The beauty of seeking the transformational breakthrough within is that even if the circumstances don't change, we are so much better for it, so much stronger, so much surer of ourselves. You see, success isn't necessarily best measured in how our circumstances turn out. No, true success is measured another way. I said it in the very beginning of this journey, in my Introduction (and invitation to you). But, I will say it again, with a little more emphasis.

> Just maybe, you will discover that your transformation *and breakthrough* into the best version of yourself is the greatest definition of success you could ever know.

It means we have learned to put less emphasis on our circumstances and more value on the better version of who we have become. We have more confidence, courage, and conviction, even if the circumstances aren't in our favor quite yet. That type of breakthrough is the type of genuine, deep, authentic transformation we are truly looking for. Because it is lasting… it is transformative. It gives us a new nature, a new ethos, and a new essence.

As vitally important as it is to discover where breakthrough happens, you have also discovered *how* it happens. How breakthrough happens is by severing the leashes of doubt, fear, and apathy as you begin to be set free from the Comfort Zone and elevate into the Opportunity Zone. It continues to happen by navigating the Clouds of Confusion and uncertainty—both internal and external—as you lift through, past, around, and above those clouds that have historically stood in your way.

Finally, as you near the upper limits of that Opportunity Zone, your life will begin to press up against the barrier of the Possibility Zone. Most likely, there will be some final test, or a return of the clouds, in greater form than you have ever faced, which will all work together to attempt to keep you from breaking through this barrier.

As you press through the final test, elevating higher into the blue skies, attempting to break through, there is no need to experience despair, because you have all the tools you need to burst through this final barrier. The final breakthrough happens by harnessing and wielding the power of clarity, purpose, and momentum to push into the Possibility Zone, experiencing a genuine transformation in the process.

It is then that you will be truly set free to reach your dreams and soar in an endless possibility of a life of greatness that makes an impact on others for good. When you get there, the confidence, courage, and conviction you will possess will strengthen you in a way that makes the upward trajectory of your life nearly unstoppable.

Earlier in the journey, we paused at a scenic overlook to evaluate how far we had come. When we paused, we looked out over the expanse of what it would look like to see your dreams rediscovered, rekindled, and restored. We looked out toward the canopy of blue sky, the Possibility Zone, where your life *could* exist. It was beautiful, to be sure, and it likely created a bit of nerves or even an over-whelmed feeling at the beauty and enormity of it all.

It is possible that tension was created in part by a few powerful tethers, leashes, and chains that were still tugging on you, but now... now is *not* the time to feel overwhelmed. Because, my friend, we have arrived at a new scenic overlook together. By finishing this book, you have reached the summit on this first leg of the journey.

Now... is the time to feel hopeful. Now... is the time to feel prepared. Now... is the time to feel inspired because there is a new freedom and a new power within you. Now... you possess the three simple truths of transformational breakthrough you need to sever those leashes, to be set free, and to reach your dreams.

You have come further and higher—maybe even further and higher than you thought possible. This is another scenic overlook, not all that unlike the first scenic overlook in Chapter 4. Consider this new scenic overlook, not just an overlook, but instead a first summit, in what can become a journey of reaching higher summits with your life. I am going to give this summit a name.

I'm going to call it *hope*. That's right.

You have arrived at a summit called hope.

I said it much earlier in the journey, but it is worth the reminder. When you are held down, tethered too long at the intersection of stuck and lost, hope usually evaporates.

Well, hope has returned, my friend.

As much as hope has evaporated out of your soul before, drink it up now and allow your soul to be drenched with hope again. You deserve hope, and the journey ahead will continue to require it. So, for now, let's enjoy reflecting on this summit, what has brought us here, and let's soak up hope like skin soaks up fresh rays of sunshine cutting through the blue sky on a warm summer's day.

What a journey it has been through these pages together, and what a summit it is. Wow, right?

Take a deep breath and a good look around again. Inhale. Exhale.

This summit is not only beautiful, but it is majestic. It is awe-inspiring. It is jaw-dropping. It is such for so many reasons, but mostly because you have a hope that reaching your dreams *is possible*, maybe for the first time in a long time, if not the first time *ever*.

That hope is founded on the reality that you know *where* breakthrough happens, and you know *how* breakthrough happens.

As a result, you now possess the pathway, the map, the flight plan needed to experience that transformational breakthrough you have been longing for.

Consider this summit to be a perch of sorts for you, not unlike an eagle, sitting high upon the ledge of a rock face, far above the ground. The earth, valleys, meadows, and wilderness are all below. Yet, as you allow your gaze to rise, to look up, you see there is an expanse of blue sky above, and your heart is filled with hope.

High on this perch, you are already higher into the blue sky than you were when we began. And, yet, there is *so much more* for you.

As you look out over the majesty of all you can see, you realize that you have already begun to gain a new *perspective*, to see life through a new lens of *meaning*, and have a newfound appreciation for the power of *rhythm*.

As a result, you also realize the *clarity*, *purpose*, and *momentum* you have been missing in life are truly available to you. That is a hopeful thought, isn't it?

As majestic as this view is, you recognize that just above, there is still an Opportunity Zone you need to navigate. Yet, what continues to fuel your hope is a new belief. You believe that elevating your life is possible, even with some confusing and uncertainty-inducing clouds sure to arise at some point.

You also believe that as you continue to elevate through, around, and above the Clouds of Confusion, you can develop and possess the *confidence*, the *courage*, and the *conviction* needed to soar—a confidence, courage, and conviction you have rarely, if ever, possessed. That hope and that belief is going to fuel your journey.

I believe something too, which I have believed in from the very beginning.

I believe in *you*. I *always* have.

If I didn't believe in you, I wouldn't have hung around so long waiting for you at the intersection of stuck and lost. If I didn't believe in you, I wouldn't have risked 18-months of no new clients to discover where breakthrough happens. And, if you thought I did that for myself, you'd be mistaken.

Remember, I exist to lead people like you to experience breakthrough, to guide you to discover your unique purpose, and to inspire you to fulfill your potential. My life has always been about you, and I walked out my entire journey of transformational breakthrough with you in mind. I had to go myself, where I knew that I was supposed to take you. To that end, I wrote every word in this book with you in mind.

I believe in you. I always have. And, I do now, more than ever. I believe you have what it takes to wield the truths offered to you and to be set free to reach your dreams. Now, it is your turn to experience that same type of transformational breakthrough, and when you do, you will never be the same.

As you wield these three simple and profound truths, you will possess the power you will need to sever the doubt, fear, and apathy that will be fighting to hold you back. The intersection of found and free is your destination, and it is nothing like the intersection of stuck and lost.

As you are gazing over how far you have come, contemplating how high you an truly soar, you need to know this. There is no leash holding you to that ledge that you cannot successfully sever and overcome. You have all you need—not only to be set free, no longer held down by your current limitations, but to remain free, never to be held down by limitations again.

You have a genuine opportunity to reach your dreams and spend a lifetime soaring in the Possibility Zone, living a life of greatness.

Even if others still try to tell you otherwise.

ON JANUARY 13, 1920, THE *NEW YORK TIMES* PUBLISHED AN editorial in which a journalist called into question the validity of the claim made by rocket pioneer Professor Robert H. Goddard. Goddard claimed it was scientifically possible for a rocket to be launched in such a way that it could successfully overcome gravity, leave the earth's atmosphere, and even successfully maneuver in the vacuum of space.

The editorial journalist, clearly frustrated and bothered by such a claim, laid out a case in the *New York Times* as to why Goddard was wrong, and how his theory was naïve and "scientifically" impossible.

Even though Goddard served as the chair of the physics department at Clark College (now Clark University) and was backed by funding from the Smithsonian Institution,[1] the editorialist fired away at Goddard, even seeming to make a personal dig, questioning the science professor's basic knowledge of high school level science.

The journalist publicly wrote that Goddard "does not know the relation of action to reaction, and the need to have something better than a vacuum against which to react—to say that would be absurd. Of course, he [Goddard] only seems to lack the knowledge ladled out daily in high schools."[2]

Interestingly enough, on July 17, 1969, nearly 50 years later, the *New York Times* offered a retraction. On this day, after the Apollo 11 rocket had left the power of earth's gravity (not the first rocket to do so, mind you) and was soaring through the vacuum of space, en route to successfully deliver the first human beings to the moon, the *Times* printed a tongue-in-cheek retraction of their original editorial.

The retraction read, "Further investigation and experimentation have confirmed the findings of Isaac Newton in the 17th century, and it is now definitely established that a rocket can function in a vacuum as well as in an atmosphere. *The Times* regrets the error."[3]

Goddard did not live long enough to appreciate the paper's long overdue humility. Yet, in opposition of the naysaying journalist, and probably many others, Goddard would continue to pioneer in science and physics.

His work contains the complete theory of and mathematical formulation of rocket design and space flight. Professor Robert Hutchings Goddard is now known as "The Father of Modern Rocketry," and the journalist is, well… long forgotten, neither identified in the editorial nor in the retraction.

While that unknown journalist confidently declared it as *impossible*, Goddard confidently pursued, studied, and pioneered what would later be proven as in fact, *possible*.

Oh, the nerve of *that* journalist. Now that's an old phrase. It sounds like something my late grandmother, the one who helped our family discover our relation to John Alden, the barrel maker on the Mayflower, would say. But that's ok, it is a fitting phrase, so I will use it again.

Oh, the nerve of *your* critics. Those critics, every last one of them, *know not* the potential you have stored up within you. They have no idea what is possible in and through your life.

So, let me encourage you with this. No matter what your critics say about you, your story, your failures, your shortcomings, your abilities, your environment, your circumstances, your reality, your future, your anything… *they are wrong.*

While what they have confidently (and maybe even publicly) declared and deemed impossible in your life may seem impossible, don't believe them.

You now have a pathway and flight plan to pursue the impossible in your life. Like Goddard's, your critics won't be remembered. No, they will be forgotten—you will forget their names, words, and deeds.

You will soar so high that their criticism will grow so small in relation to your altitude, you won't see it or hear it any longer. Much like attempting to identify a single human being from 30,000 feet in the air, they will be in the distant past, minimized in proportion to the height of your elevation.

If, for some reason, their words and deeds reserve a small place in your memory, it will ultimately shrink to the size of a speck of dust. That dust-sized memory particle originally filled with pain and disbelief may even be replaced with a memory of gratitude—gratitude for where you have come from and gratitude toward them for providing a source of motivation you may have needed to take the risk and finally soar.

Yes, when you take flight and soar above the clouds, your critics and their words will be *forgettable.*

Yet… Y*our legacy*, marked by your life of impacting others for good as you soar in the endless possibly of your Blue Sky Potential will be *unforgettable.*

You *can* do this. You *are* doing this.

Because…

You now have hope, belief, and a flight plan.

Maybe you didn't realize it, but we have been building a flight plan throughout this journey. The three simple truths of transformational breakthrough, when displayed in relation to each other, create a flight plan.

This flight plan takes the form of a matrix, which will serve you both now and in the future as your journey continues, as you begin to elevate your life into the blue sky of your potential. Here is the the flight plan to your Blue Sky Potential:

The 3 Simple Truths of Transformational Breakthrough

Truth #1	Truth #2	Truth #3
You Need CLARITY	You Need PURPOSE	You Need MOMENTUM
because	because	because
Clarity Produces CONFIDENCE	Purpose Creates COURAGE	Momentum Generates CONVICTION
and	and	and
Confidence Severs Doubt	Courage Severs Fear	Conviction Severs Apathy
Begin the Journey by Seeking PERSPECTIVE	Begin the Journey by Seeking MEANING	Begin the Journey By Seeking RHYTHM

This flight plan or matrix works a couple of ways. You can evaluate this flight plan matrix vertically or horizontally.

If you want to evaluate it vertically, start on the left side with the first truth, and move through that truth top to bottom.

When you finish the first truth, move to the right and work the 2nd truth top to bottom, and repeat for the 3rd truth, much like I unpacked the content in Chapters 8, 9, and 10.

In doing so, the flight plan would look like this:

Simple Truth of Transformational Breakthrough # 1
You Need Clarity because
Clarity Produces Confidence
and Confidence Severs Doubt
(You Begin the Journey to Clarity by Seeking Perspective)

Simple Truth of Transformational Breakthrough #2
You Need Purpose because
Purpose Creates Courage
and Courage Severs Fear
(You Begin the Journey to Purpose by Seeking Meaning)

Simple Truth of Transformational Breakthrough # 3
You Need Momentum because
Momentum Generates Conviction
and Conviction Severs Apathy
(You Begin the Journey to Momentum by Seeking Rhythm)

As you continue to elevate, the process of discovering clarity, purpose, and momentum will act in a way like stairs.

Let me explain with a story, especially for those who appreciate the land/trail vision of journeying and elevating toward your Blue Sky Potential.

A number of years ago, I competed in several adventure races with one of my very best friends, Todd. These races are often advertised with the number of hours expected to complete the race listed in the title, like the 12-hour Vail Adventure Race, or the 8-hour Breckenridge Adventure Race.

These lengthy adventure races usually consist of four distinct disciplines—trail running/hiking, mountain biking, kayaking, and orienteering (map/compass skills) to various checkpoints in the challenging and high-elevation terrain of the Colorado backcountry wilderness.

To prepare for such an endurance event, Todd and I would often train on a well-known local hiking trail in Boulder, CO. The trail is known as the Royal Arch Trail, one of many gems in Chautauqua Park in the internationally known Flatiron Peaks at the edge of the Rocky Mountains.

Out the door and often on the trail before 4 am, with headlamps as our only source of light, Todd and I would often hit the trail for the out and back journey before the sun was rising. At the summit, we would pause for a minute, simply to take in a bit of water and calories and to watch the sun crest over the horizon for a beautiful Colorado sunrise.

The momentary pause was all the inspiration and motivation we needed to turn our headlamps back on to race back through the densely forested terrain and back to the trailhead well before most people were awake.

When we really wanted to push our training for an upcoming race, we would "double up" and do the entire out and back course, from the trailhead to the summit, two times. Yes, twice, running up and down, only to turn around and do it all over again.

The trail is only 3.5 miles out and back, which would equate to 7 total miles on our "doubles" day. Yet, it has 1,400 feet of elevation gain in that short length. This equates to 2,800 of elevation gain in a 7-mile "doubled up" trail run/hike.

It is an arduous and challenging hike, let alone run, but it is an amazing race preparation trail. On this particular trail, there is a significant section of the course that has a significant length of trail made up of boulders.

These boulders create large "step-like" features and are fairly steep, so running/speed-hiking these sections was always grueling on the quadriceps. The beauty of these sections, however, was the step-like nature of the boulders were such that you could go into "autopilot" mentally for a while.

Make a misstep, and the consequences were going to be painful, but get a sequence and rhythm going, and you could really ascend quickly without having to think too much, climbing your way to the summit, running and elevating up the trail one step at a time.

Here's a diagram of how the three simple truths of transformational breakthrough can work in a step-like nature in a similar way:

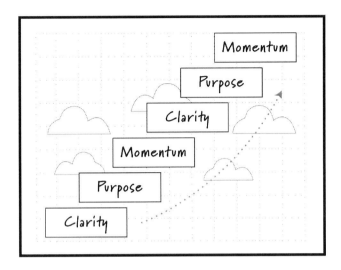

When you approach the flight plan of breakthrough like this, you can simply keep putting one step in front of the other as you get clarity, purpose, and momentum. It is definitely going to take effort, focus, and working the process along the way, but you now have a flight plan to help you ascend into blue sky.

Just as you can move through the matrix vertically, top to bottom, you can evaluate and harness the truths by moving horizontally through the matrix as well. Starting in the upper left, simply move across left to right, and then drop down to the next row, and move again left to right. That way, your flight plan looks like this:

<u>You Need</u>
Clarity, Purpose, and Momentum

<u>Because They Result In</u>
Confidence, Courage, and Conviction

<u>Which Provide An Unleashing Force to Sever the Chains of</u>
Doubt, Fear, and Apathy

<u>You Begin the Journey to Transformational Breakthrough</u>
By Seeking Perspective, Meaning, and Rhythm

As you progress through the flight plan this way, it won't be as linear or as stair-stepped as the version I described above, but that's ok. We all see and experience the world a bit differently. Instead, you might find it to be a bit more cyclical. A diagram displaying this process may look something like this:

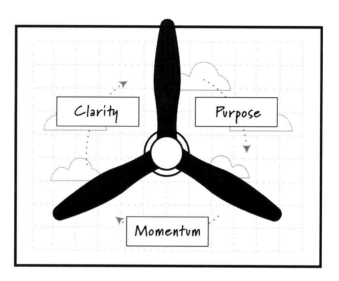

It looks like a propeller, now, doesn't it? On a number of occasions, I have shared that Wilbur and Orville Wright pioneered the 3-axis control system to stabilize, balance, and control the flight of the craft.

What I have yet to share is that in the process that led to those first successful flights at Kitty Hawk, they pioneered propeller technology as well. In fact, they were shocked to learn that in all the years the US Navy had been employing the use of propellers on ships, there was no scientific or mathematical theory, nor any documented research that described and/or defined the performance of various shapes of propellers.[4]

Early in the journey, the Wright Brothers created their own wind tunnel to perform this research and made a striking discovery. It may not sound so striking now, as we have the benefit of learning from history, but it was a striking discovery in their day. They realized a propeller was simply a wing traveling or revolving in a spiral course. In doing so, like a wing that produces lift upward, the propeller acted as a wing that produces lift forward, known as thrust.

You see, if you can begin to spin clarity, purpose, and momentum at an equal rate around your life, and if you can begin to seek perspective, meaning, and rhythm so that confidence, courage, and conviction revolve around your life too, you will have the thrust you need to move forward and the lift necessary to move upward.

As you move forward and upward, you will begin to soar away from the Comfort Zone, through the Opportunity Zone, and into the Possibility Zone.

WHEN TRAINING FOR THE ADVENTURE RACES WITH TODD, THE ONLY thing that was going to keep us from the summit of the Royal Arch Trail was not taking the next step.

When the Wright Brothers towed their not-yet-a-flying machine out to that beach in the face of the blistering winds, the only thing stopping them from those first four historical flights would have been a reluctance to take the next step—to crank the engine, spin the propeller, and get in the cockpit.

No matter which way you prefer to put this flight plan to use, let me encourage you with this…

It is time for you to take the next step.

At this point, *not* taking the next step is the only thing that can stop you from embracing the journey to discover how the power of clarity, purpose, and momentum will set you free to reach your dreams. Not taking the next step is the only thing keeping your life from becoming a great adventure.

As I said before, please do not forget that you are not alone in this journey. I believe in *you*. It is time for you to *believe in yourself*.

If you can't quite get there yet, it is time for you to at least believe in the process and the flight plan I have laid out for you.

Whether you believe in yourself or not, it would be my privilege to continue on with you on your journey and guide you with each step you need to take. So, what is that exact next step? It's easy. It is time for you to begin to look for the tools and resources that will help you seek perspective, meaning, and rhythm. From there, you simply need to trust the process, trust the flight plan, and go for it.

At the beginning of our journey together, we met at the corner of the intersection of stuck and lost. I did not promise this book would solve all of your problems. Instead of making cheap claims and inflated promises, I told you this book is simply (and profoundly) intended to do four things: 1) guide you to discover where breakthrough happens, 2) demonstrate the power of clarity, purpose, and momentum, 3) provide you with a flight plan to help you reach your dreams, and 4) inspire you to begin to soar toward your Blue Sky Potential.

We have come a long way together on that very journey already, so let's not stop here. You now know where breakthrough happens —within. You know how breakthrough happens—through discovering and wielding the power of clarity, purpose, and momentum to set you free to reach your dreams. And, you are now inspired to live a life of endless possibility in the blue sky of your potential.

It is time to take the next step, and I can help you. And just as much as I have guided you from the intersection of stuck and lost to the summit of hope at the end of the first leg of your journey, I can guide you further, higher, and closer to your dreams than you ever imagined possible.

I'm not asking you to follow me, necessarily, because the exact endpoint of my destination is uniquely my own. Instead of you following me, let me join in with you, walking alongside you on your unique journey. Let me be your personal guide, encouraging you, inspiring you, and guiding you to the destination that is uniquely yours.

Let me guide you to higher levels of clarity, purpose, and momentum, so you can reach higher levels of confidence, courage, and conviction. It is the purpose and mission of my life to help you truly be set free, to reach your dreams, and soar in the blue sky of your potential.

To continue this adventure together, you can find me at www.jeffrasor.com, on Facebook, LinkedIn, or on Instagram with the handle @jeffrasor, or even follow this book through its own personalized Instagram handle @wherebreakthroughhappens.

I will be offering encouragement, inspiration, and motivation as well as tools, resources, courses, and experiences that will align exactly with the three truths I have described in this book.

What's more, through my website and social media, you will have the opportunity to join in with a community of dreamers, just like you and me, who want to shake off their limitations and see their lives account for greatness.

So, it's time. It is time for you to take the next step—to truly begin to seek perspective, to truly begin to seek meaning, and to truly begin to seek rhythm.

You now have a personal 3-axis control system by which you can power and pilot your life with control and intention. This book is only the first of many tools and resources I am creating to help you truly be set free, to help you truly reach your dreams. Oh, it is an endless possibility to be sure.

Your story isn't over yet. The journey has just begun, and the great adventure still awaits. It is time to experience the transformational breakthrough it will require to be truly unleashed from all that holds you back.

It is time to be set free, so you can reach your dreams.

It is time for your life to take flight. It is time for you to soar in the blue sky of your potential. It is time that your life counted for greatness in the endless canopy of blue sky and the endless possibility of impacting others for good.

You are worth it. *Your future* is worth it.

The world needs you to experience it and is waiting for you to take your place and play your role.

It is not time to be passive.
It is time to be powered and piloted.
It is time for you to soar, my friend.

Soaring in the blue skies is one of the best feelings you will ever feel. Flight is magical. Doing the impossible is magical. Living in the blue sky of your potential is magical. I have been there, and yet, I am still headed there.

I'm still elevating into my own Blue Sky Potential, the endless possibility of impacting others for greatness, and I pray I always will be. I want the same for your life, for the remainder of your entire life. Now, I'm not just aiming for the blue sky, but I'm shooting for the stars too. And so should you.

I hear the universe is filled with endless possibility that is well-beyond the blue sky. I imagine the journey is going to be pretty grand. In fact, your life is going to be one of those great adventures that becomes one of those legendary stories. I imagine it will require more willingness to change, more transformation, and more navigating challenging situations, but I know it will be worth it.

Transformational breakthrough is always worth it, even if, and especially because it takes us beyond what we already know.

You now have a new definition of what is possible in life, what is possible for *your* life, and it is going to be a magical ride along the way.

Your life has only just begun to take flight. So, let's keep you moving forward and upward. Let's create the thrust and lift you need to leave the Comfort Zone, to power and pilot yourself through the Opportunity Zone, and to soar into the Possibility Zone.

Your dreams are up there, in that bright blue canopy of blue sky and all of its endless possibility. And, they still exist. They are not dead. Most likely, they are simply dormant, or latent, waiting for the right time, when everything has come together in the right conditions and the right circumstances, waiting for something magical to happen.

Now, is that time. So, remember…

A rekindled dream is the beginning of restoration,
a life you only imagined possible.

Something impossible has happened, something magical—your dreams are awakened, you have a flight plan, and you have the hope and inspiration you need to begin the journey toward your Blue Sky Potential.

You have discovered *Where Breakthrough Happens*.

I believe in you. Now, *believe in yourself*.

It is now time for you to experience a genuine transformational breakthrough within you, so that you can take flight and reach your dreams.

Your breakthrough is coming. It is time to be set free.

It's time to soar!

NOTES

1. IMPOSSIBILITY — REACHING FOR THE SKY

1. Wright Brothers National Memorial North Carolina, National Park Service, "1903 – The First Flight,"https://www.nps.gov/wrbr/learn/historyculture/thefirstflight.htm.
2. Gillispie, C. C., "The Montgolfier Brothers and the Invention of Aviation – 1783-1784," p. 21.
3. Gillispie, C. C., "The Montgolfier Brothers and the Invention of Aviation – 1783-1784," p. 92-3.
4. Smithsonian National Air and Space Museum, "The Wright Brothers – Inventing a Flying Machine: Patenting," https://airandspace.si.edu/exhibitions/wright-brothers/online/fly/1903/patenting.cfm.
5. Rumerman, Judy, US Centennial of Flight Commission, "Sir George Cayley – Making Aviation Practical," http://www.centennialofflight.net/essay/Prehistory/Cayley/PH2.htm.

6. FUEL — THE POWER OF TRANSFORMATION

1. Smithsonian National Air and Space Museum, "The Wright Brothers – Who Were Wilbur & Orville: The Wright's Bicycle Shop," https://airandspace.si.edu/exhibitions/wright-brothers/online/who/1893/shop.cfm.
2. Smithsonian National Air and Space Museum, "The Wright Brothers – Who Were Wilbur & Orville: The Wright Bicycles," https://airandspace.si.edu/exhibitions/wright-brothers/online/who/1895/index.cfm.
3. Smithsonian National Air and Space Museum, "The Wright Brothers – Who Were Wilbur & Orville: The Wright Bicycles," https://airandspace.si.edu/exhibitions/wright-brothers/online/who/1895/index.cfm.
4. Smithsonian National Air and Space Museum, "The Wright Brothers – Who Were Wilbur & Orville: Cycle Production & Sales," https://airandspace.si.edu/exhibitions/wright-brothers/online/who/1895/production.cfm.
5. Smithsonian National Air and Space Museum, "The Wright Brothers – Who Were Wilbur & Orville: The Wright's Bicycle Shop," https://airandspace.si.edu/exhibitions/wright-brothers/online/who/1893/shop.cfm.

7. BREAKTHROUGH — LIVE ABOVE THE CLOUDS

1. Johnson, Caleb H., "The Mayflower and Her Passengers," p. 33.

8. PERSPECTIVE — CLARITY PRODUCES CONFIDENCE

1. Smithsonian National Air and Space Museum, "The Wright Brothers – Who Were Wilbur & Orville: The Wright Cycle Co.," https://airandspace.si.edu/ exhibitions/wright-brothers/online/who/1893/index.cfm.

9. MEANING — PURPOSE CREATES COURAGE

1. Got Questions, "What Does It Mean That Everything Is Meaningless?," https://www.gotquestions.org/everything-is-meaningless.html.
2. Ford's Theatre, "A 34ft Tribute: The Lincoln Book Tower," https://www.fords .org/blog/post/a-34ft-tribute-the-lincoln-book-tower.
3. The History Channel, "What Lincoln Said in His Final Speech," https:// www.history.com/news/what-lincoln-said-in-his-final-speech.
4. The History Channel, "What Lincoln Said in His Final Speech," https:// www.history.com/news/what-lincoln-said-in-his-final-speech.
5. The History Channel, "What Lincoln Said in His Final Speech," https:// www.history.com/news/what-lincoln-said-in-his-final-speech.
6. The History Channel, "Abraham Lincoln's Assassination," https:// www.history.-com/topics/american-civil-war/abraham-lincoln-assassination.

10. RHYTHM — MOMENTUM GENERATES CONVICTION

1. IMDb, "The Karate Kid: Plot Summaries," https://www.imdb.com/title/ tt0087538/plotsummary?ref_=tt_ql_stry_2.

11. SET FREE — IT'S TIME TO SOAR

1. Clark University, "The Robert H. Goddard Special Collection: FAQs," https://www2.clarku.edu/research/archives/goddard/faq.cfm#nyt.
2. New York Times, "150th Anniversary: 1851-2001; The Facts That Got Away," https://www.nytimes.com/2001/11/14/news/150th-anniversary-1851-2001-the-facts-that-got-away.html.
3. New York Times, "150th Anniversary: 1851-2001; The Facts That Got Away," https://www.nytimes.com/2001/11/14/news/150th-anniversary-1851-2001-the-facts-that-got-away.html.
4. McDaniel, Joe W., Wright Brothers Aeroplane Company, "1903 Wright Propellers," http://www.wright-brothers.org/Information_Desk/Just_the_Facts/ Engines_&_Props/1903_Props.htm.

ACKNOWLEDGMENTS

"Aviation is proof, that given
the will, we can do the impossible."

- EDDIE RICKENBACKER

I opened this book with a quote from Walt Disney about the fun of doing the impossible, and I close with a quote from World War I American Flying Ace and Medal of Honor recipient Eddie Rickenbacker about the same thing—doing the *impossible*.

For more reasons than I can even begin to list here, for me, writing this book was an impossibility. Note the operative word of that last statement, *was*.

It *was* an impossibility that, by God's grace, I was able to defy and turn into possibility. In doing so, I have done the *impossible* in my life. Impossible, you ask? Maybe not for you, but for me, yes.

I have described it already in Chapter 1 of this book, but my childhood personality of running away at the first glimpse of spotlight was so extreme, it has been nearly impossible to shake. Add to it the amount of hurt, pains, criticism, and heart-targeted soul-stopping arrows of harsh things that have been spoken as lies over me as a communicator, and I was at risk of never being willing to be vulnerable to an audience ever again.

With justification and maybe some false humility, I could have easily hidden behind my genuine, servant-hearted leadership approach to stay behind the scenes and make others shine. Combine all of that together and there was more than enough doubt, fear, and apathy to leash me to the ground for more than a few lifetimes and never pursue writing this book.

However, when I took the risk, the words came easily as the content and concepts flowed from my heart, to my mind, to my fingers, and to the keyboard without trouble. The extreme challenge and impossibility was not the words, but instead the continual, nearly unending battle to sever fear, doubt, and apathy about putting my name on the cover of a book and risk putting myself in front of an audience.

Yet, the truths that I have shared with you in this book are undeniable. As I discovered them and implemented them in my own life, there was no stopping the power they offered. As much as I pushed back against it, these truths freed me to do the impossible, what I otherwise would not have done on my own. Without the undeniable power of these truths, I would have never been able to actually write a book to share those very same truths with you.

The very truths I aimed to tell you about continued to set me free from my Comfort Zone, even as I typed them out, one word at a time. These truths helped me elevate through yet another trip through my own Opportunity Zone. These truths ultimately empowered me to break through into the endless possibility of the Possibility Zone to impact others for good with this book.

If I had quit at any moment, if I had quit leveraging and wielding those truths to sever all that was holding me back, then this book would have easily remained an unfinished document buried in the files on my computer. Yet, in all the personal effort, wrestling, sacrifice, and surrender this book has required of me, I have not made it here alone.

There has been a tremendous amount of love, support, and sacrifice made by so many others who prepared me for this journey or championed me in the midst of it.

For me, this book, let alone soaring in the blue sky of my potential, would have been truly impossible without the sacrifice, investment, belief, and support from those around me. Significant thanks and gratitude are owed to so many, but it is worth taking time to make some highlights, beginning with my family.

FIRST AND ABOVE ALL, TO MY WIFE, JANETTE. You are my very best friend, my absolute love, and the greatest single gift God has ever given me. You rescued me from my own disbelief more than 25 years ago, and you have not stopped rescuing me since.

You patiently and graciously walk through the valleys and the shadows within me that most will never know exist. All at the same time, you see more of the God-given greatness inside of me than I could ever imagine for myself.

Your gift of faith, as evidenced by your unwavering belief in seeing the impossible become possible, has always and will always inspire me. Thank you for your sacrifice, your voice, your warmth, and your unconditional love. I'll never know why I ever deserved someone like you by my side, but I am so very grateful. I love you with all of my being.

NEXT, TO MY CHILDREN, DAVID AND SEVILLA. You are my pride and joy, and my joy and pride. You are the greatest gifts God has ever given your mom and I together. Each of your lives is a legitimate miracle in the face of impossibility.

As such, you carry within you the DNA of the gift of faith, an ability to envision the impossible as if it were already reality. Walk in it, grow in it, and offer it to others. While my role in your life will change through the passing years and seasons of life, there exists no greater responsibility or higher calling in my life than the privilege of being your father.

No amount of opportunity, fame, or fortune will ever distract me from doing whatever it takes to steward your lives and the greatness God has deposited within each of you. While I will fail often, I will not relent in offering all of myself to you. Along with your mom, you are all my first and most important ministry. I love you both with my whole heart.

To my parents, Bruce & Rhonda, and to my brother, Kevin. Thank you, Dad and Mom, for the years of sacrifice, love, and support. You both have worked multiple jobs through most of your lives to provide, create experiences, and make a bunch of unforgettable memories.

I have seen, felt, and benefited from your love, dedication, and work ethic since my earliest memories and still reap those benefits to this day. And, for all those unseen sacrifices you made that I will never know, thank you.

Kevin, thank you for being my childhood best friend, for years of mini-bat baseball, catch with the football, video games galore, and for the enjoyment of a round of golf. Unfortunately, I didn't understand enough about life to offer you much brotherly guidance in our earlier years, but I hope I can continue to make it up to you the rest of the way.

Thank you, Dad, Mom, and Kevin, for supporting and loving me even when I didn't know how to love back or didn't love myself enough to know how to love back well. I love you all.

To my in-laws, Mickey & Darlene, and to Jason & Sheryl. Thank you, Mickey and Darlene, for seeing potential and promise in a shy, quiet 17-year old boy, who could hardly lift his eyes from under the brim of his ball cap to say hi. Thank you for not ushering me out the door based on that lackluster first impression.

Thank you for raising your daughter in a way that inspired her to put the Lord and His ways before all things—I am the man I am today because of the woman you raised. Thank you for your unending support, love, prayers, and encouragement on a journey of faith that is far more adventurous than I would have naturally signed up for. Thank you too for your unceasing prayers for me and my family. I love you both.

Jason and Sheryl, thank you for welcoming us on a trip of a lifetime to visit you in London and for the deep relationships our children cherish as friends and cousins—a lifetime of memories already, and yet still to come for these world changers. Sheryl, thank you for marathon memories that I'll never forget. Thank you both for taking up the mantle and carrying the torch for the future of FBC.

And, to my four grandmothers—Marie, Anna, Elma, and Imogene—for grandmotherly laughter, warmth, love, prayer, and the legacy of faith.

To a number of men who are both close friends and mentors in my life. Men who have stood with me, or even held me up when I otherwise would have fallen down along the way.

To Todd Gentry, a Brother and fellow Son of Thunder. While others work on the lightning shine, we work on the thunder. I've never had a friend like you who wanted so much to see the thunder within—in yourself and in me—shake the earth for good. Thank you for despising the status quo.

Thank you for being a true brother from another mother and for being a best friend. Never stop maximizing the greatness of your life. I'm still asking God to align our paths to do some thunderous stuff together, but until then, we will keep running the trail marked ahead for each of us.

To Ben Cort, a Brother of Inspiration. You have modeled and inspired what it means to endure, to suffer, and to overcome against all odds. Walking with you as a friend all these years, I can honestly say I have never seen anyone walk through hotter fires of tumult, pain, and suffering—period. And at the end of the day, you have done so within the context of a living, active, and genuine faith.

Thank you for your love, support, and belief in me. Your self-lessness, generosity, and unyielding hope offered to me, to your family, and to the world around you are, in a word, supernatural. Thank you for your integrity, authentic walk, and your unrelenting passion for people.

To MATT COFFMAN, A BROTHER OF ENCOURAGEMENT. When the guy who helps people figure out *their* life, is stuck and lost himself, you know it is bad. That was me not all that long ago. Thank you for your patient posture and guidance in helping me move away from that corner, even if ever so slowly.

Thank you for helping me see up from down and for walking alongside me during my most recent ascent through yet another Opportunity Zone. Of course, thank you too for your artistic and creative brilliance, most of which the world has yet to experience. And, thank you for letting a little bit of that splash onto the cover and interior artwork of this book.

To THE JAM BROTHERS: RANDY PHILIPS, PETE RICHARDSON, STAN SINCLAIR, AND HAROLD VELASQUEZ. Thank you for your leadership, friendship, mentorship, love, and investment in me through our men's group, which was formative in my leadership and ministry journey.

Throughout my vocational wilderness season, individually and collectively, you offered a cup of fresh, cool water to a thirsty soul every time we met for breakfast, coffee, or connected in Pete's office. There are so many treasured memories from our years together and I am forever grateful. By the way, when is the reunion?

To PETE AGAIN, AND TO TOM PATERSON. Thank you, Pete, for my LifePlan and for opening my life to the brilliance, mastery, and heritage of Tom Paterson and the early days of the Paterson Center. I am thankful too for your sacrifice and willingness to invest in me and how that lit a fire in me so early in my life and career journey.

I am thankful for the pioneering work Tom offered to the world —a work of meaning that transcended corporate success, making it about impacting real, everyday people. Your life, Pete, lived with humble greatness and generosity, has resulted not only in transforming my life, but has truly impacted millions of others for good. Truly, thank you for the legacy you personally imparted into my life.

To Harold again, and to Chantel Hinkle. Thank you, Harold, for pouring your life, wisdom, leadership, and gifts into my life so sacrificially. Thank you for being the first living example of what I had only theorized to that point—that servant-hearted leadership is the most Biblical and most effective form of leadership that exists. Your model of leadership forged my leadership beliefs into convictions that shape me still to this day.

Thank you both, Harold and Chantell, for taking a chance on me and for depositing in me a passion for the heart of men. Not to mention a relentless pursuit of excellence centered on developing transformative messaging as well as producing and directing experiences that result in a transformed heart. Thank you both for some of the very best years of my life and for showing me how to righteously pound the table for what is right, no matter the cost.

To Stan again. Thank you for your friendship, guidance, and for your listening ear and encouraging voice in my early days of church leadership. The wisdom and experience you offer through the filter of your own portfolio career provides affirmation and confirmation in my journey still to this day. Thank you too for your generosity and creative talent in design and web development. Finally, thank you for the belief, the open arms, wisdom, and perspective on our journey to SoCal. We would not be here without your sage counsel.

To Randy again. Thank you again for your friendship in my life and leadership in the kingdom. While I never had the privilege of formally working with you at Promise Keepers, my entire life has been enriched and set free because of your sacrifice and the impact of your work—spiritually and professionally.

To a number of couples who have played a significant role in our marriage, our parenting, the lives of our children, and who have supremely enriched our spiritual journey. There is not room enough to express our sincere appreciation, but I will try nonetheless.

To Craig & Rhoda Schultz, and to your entire tribe. Thank you for more steak, homemade pizza, fried dough, along with more laughter, tears, and friendship than we could ever account for. Thank you, Craig, for your professional generosity, wisdom, and for modeling what it means to be a sacrificial and indefatigable leader in your home.

Thank you, Rhoda, even for roller-blade/backpack-delivered spaghetti meals to our family, at the risk of your "near-death" experience on our front lawn. Thank you for being like a big sister to me, and thank you too for your love for my wife and for our children as if they were your own.

To Don & Betty, and Scott & Jeslin Jones. Thank you, Don and Betty, for opening your doors and hearts to our family and for your practical generosity and hospitality over a decade of family vacations. And, not to mention responding to our "emergency" with the Huntington Beach police while you were traveling in China. Thank you too for sharing your wisdom and encouragement to lift us up while in many of our valley seasons.

Thank you, Scott and Jeslin, for your friendship, laughter, support, and for always standing with us, even with our many imperfections. We are thankful that we have stood with each other through the valleys, the mountaintops, and everywhere in between. Thank you too for living a way of life that believes the impossible is possible, and then walking out that experience in faith.

To Gregg & Julie Peterson. Thank you for what feels like a lifetime of friendship, support, and encouragement. Thank you for opening your doors and your hearts to our family and for being there for us every step of the way. We are grateful that you have always welcomed us and now call us family.

Thank you too for delicately playing your role in helping us respond to the invitation to Southern California. And, more importantly, in those key moments, in those challenging seasons, thank you for your faithfulness in having the exact word from the Lord in response to our prayers.

To JOSH & DAINELE MENDENHALL. Thank you for the friendship, support, and practical generosity to me and to our family. Thank you, Josh, for the inspiration and doors you have opened for David.

Thank you, Dainele, for your encouragement, belief, and vision for me, not to mention creative input on everything from content to cover design. Keep soaring toward your dreams, my friends!

To MARC & KIM ANEED. Thank you for an unexpected friendship founded on "Hmmm…" and "Amen." It's a friendship built on shared values, complimentary gifts, and a life surrendered to a complete walk of faith. We are grateful to have met co-transplants in SoCal. Both of you, your encouragement, and family have been a significant part of the new soil that has enriched our lives.

Thank you too, Marc, for calling out a better bumper sticker in titling this book. Not only did your candid feedback alter the title, but it enriched the direction of the content within. Looking forward to a future of spurring each other along as we seek to reach the dreams God has planted in our hearts.

To DR. ROBERT & GAYLE BUCKNAM. We cannot thank you enough for the impact and influence you have made on our marriage, our family culture, our children, and our approach to parenting. Thank you for giving us the tools, the funnel, the fabric, and the ethos of what healthy and intentional parenting truly looks like.

Thank you for shaping our world-view and our decision making framework about education, sports, leadership, and everything that goes into developing and preparing our children for success in the world today. Of course, thank you Dr. Bob for your generosity, flexibility, and availability in our office visits, whether in person or virtual. Your entire family is an inspiration, and we are so grateful.

To my two pastors and three influential authors, speakers, and leaders—all who have each supremely shaped my life, both up close and from a distance…

To WES SWANSON. Thank you for your passion for God's Word and for His Bride, the Body of Christ. As I sat in the pews each week as an extremely shy youth and young adult, you opened my eyes and heart to the idea that the local church could and should be a launching pad for people to find their purpose and calling. You demonstrated truth and grace in every message, using the power of communication to call out the best in people. Thank you for deeply impacting my calling by being faithful and fruitful in your calling.

To GEORGE MORRISON. Thank you for the opportunities and open doors that you provided to me. A significant majority of my spiritual growth can be directly tied back to your leadership, pastoring, love, and investment in my life. I am grateful.

To JOHN ELDREDGE. Thank you for opening my eyes to the wild heart within and for the invitation to the epic story of my life, thereby catalyzing my soul into freedom.

To ERWIN MCMANUS. Thank you for inspiring a barbarian, crash-like pursuit of God's voice and path on my journey of faith, and for cultivating the beauty and truth that exists within culture that others too often overlook and dismiss.

To BILL HYBELS. Thank you for modeling that a strategic, business, organizational leadership mind could align with a gospel-centric, love for others heart in a way that expands the kingdom and trans-forms lives.

There are hundreds more that I could list here, but I would like to give special thanks to a number of individuals who have at one time or another made a deep, lasting deposit into my life.

To MIKE McCALL. Thank you for being a dear friend, an ideal client, and for trusting my guidance on your most recent journey through your own Opportunity Zone. You are an inspiration to me, not to mention a perfect case study, model, and example of how clarity, purpose, and momentum can truly send someone soaring into their blue skies.

The endless possibility of living a life of greatness that impacts millions of lives is already a reality for you, and yet, it truly has only just begun. Your potential is so very high, so keep soaring, my friend!

To VINCE HODGES. Thank you for encouraging me to leave behind a land of *Familiar* and voyage into the *Unknown*. Thank you, too, for helping me see the need to *sever* in the journey to *persevere*, and for the observation and affirmation of my ability to rise to the occasion in the face of great challenge. We both run the race of endurance set before us, but thank you for modeling what it looks like to run in such a way to win the prize.

To DR. GAVIN GRANT. Thank you for your timely and edifying words of encouragement. You have encouraged and strengthened us with every visit. You and your family's ministry to our physical and spiritual needs has made an indescribable impact in our lives, in this season and for seasons to come. We are so very grateful.

To KARY MILLER. Thank you for being an encourager and champion during my very first steps through a significant life gate years ago. Although our time walking together was short, it was deep and transformative. You helped me first see that the burden I carried was not weight, but wings. I miss our time together and I am forever grateful.

To Zach Malito. Thank you for standing with me as a friend, protégé, and encourager for more than a decade. Thank you for your unwavering integrity and always keeping your word. There is much blue sky ahead, my friend. Let's soar!

To Brannon Mooney. Thank you for your friendship, support, and encouragement through some very challenging seasons. Thank you for seeing the greatness within me, for praying to see it become a reality, and for the steadfast belief in my destiny.

To Tyler Hannan. Thank you for your understanding, empathy, healthy perspective, sage advice, and friendship in the right doses in the right moments during the dry seasons. Time with you is always fruitful and I am so grateful for you, my friend.

To Brenda Rossi. Thank you for the prayer, intercession, revelation, and encouragement. Thank you for being a faithful friend, full of strength and wisdom—to me and to so many others.

To Kelly Knoll. Thank you for gem-digging the gem-digger within me and for cheering me on from the very beginning.

To Larry Magnuson. Thank you for peering inside my heart and calling out the larger role for me to play. Thank you too for always dreaming about the possibility of "What if?" and for encouraging me to do the same.

To Sue Mosebar. Thank you for your tireless editorial elbow grease and for offering your expertise to me on this writing journey. Thank you too for your patience, graciousness, and encouragement in my ups and downs throughout the process.

To Mrs. Eklund. Thank you for graciously and lovingly holding me in from recess to get my work done in 1st grade, even though I overreacted and stopped dreaming. No doubt, God has used it for good.

To Mrs. Stinson. Thank you for inviting me into Advanced Placement English in 9th grade when I didn't know the difference between a verb and a noun and was still trying to read Hardy Boys books for book reports.

Your invitation whispered a belief in my heart for writing that I never had, nor believed I would ever have. That ember of a dream you deposited, remained warm enough within me to finally ignite nearly 30 years later into a flame that will now never be put out.

To Rock Harbor Church and the Rock Harbor leadership and ministry teams. Thank you for creating a church through which God's Spirit moved to renew, refresh, and restore us. Thank you too for leading a church that we believed only to be possible in our wildest dreams, only to find that the church of our dreams already existed, and in Orange County, no less.

Thank you too, Rock Harbor, for your open arms, surrendered hands, and for your courageous, authentic leadership—all of which has allowed our family to find a deep, genuine sense of belonging.

And, finally, thank you to Christ, my savior, king, and most intimate friend. Thank you for being the one who paid it all so that I might live, and not only that, but live life to the fullest. Thank you too for paying for the sins of those who lied about and hurt the rest of us. I'm not more or less loved by you than they are.

Your forgiveness, love, mercy, and grace in my life is unmerited, and I am exceedingly grateful for it. For only through the power of your forgiveness offered on the cross of Calvary, I can seek the forgiveness of those I have hurt and offer forgiveness to those who have hurt me.

Ultimately, thank you too, exceedingly, for the power of your resurrection and ascension, for through it, I can soar fully in the blue sky of my potential. Humbly, I thank you for the unforced rhythms of grace and the burden of my unique calling, a calling which you have fit me perfectly for and you have fit perfectly for me.

YOU MAY HAVE NOTICED THAT THIS BOOK WAS DEDICATED TO THOSE WHO HAVE BEEN TOLD: *"you cannot, you will not, and you are not enough."* This leads me to one last acknowledgment. I would like to thank those who whispered, uttered, spoke, and shouted those lies.

Thank you for setting a high ceiling of impossibility over our lives. For without it, we may have never aimed so high or been so motivated to break that ceiling and do the impossible. Through your disbelief, thank you for giving us a reason to never stop believing, to never give up, and to never stop transforming.

If only for the silver lining of motivation, thank you for the lies. May God's goodness and sovereignty reverse the poison that drips from each lie by transforming it into sweet redemption and restoration.

At last, thank you so much to each listed here and to so many others who through supportive efforts, encouraging words, or prayer provided strength and belief when I had none.

For those of you, who like me, have waited a long time to experience what it feels like to soar in the blue sky of your potential…

May we continue to find a hope that renews our strength,
may we continue to walk and not faint,
and may we continue to run and not grow weary
until that day we rise up and soar on wings like eagles.

With extreme gratitude and to a future of endless blue skies,

Jeff Rasor

ABOUT THE AUTHOR

JEFF RASOR EXISTS TO LEAD PEOPLE AND TEAMS TO EXPERIENCE BREAKTHROUGH, to guide them into their unique purpose, and to inspire them to fulfill their potential. He goes about it by using his unique gifts and talents to encourage, inspire, and unleash the unique gifts and talents of those around him.

The depth and breadth of Jeff's 20+ year vocational journey in executive level leadership spans across a multitude of sectors. He has worked and lead in a dynamic range of environments—corporate, quasi-government, and nonprofit—as well as an entrepreneur, consultant, and even as a teaching and executive pastor in a large non-denominational church.

As a result, Jeff has the unique ability to work with all types of organizations as well as with individuals, couples, leaders, executives, dreamers, and visionaries from all walks of life. He excels in any number of leadership roles—from keynote speaking and corporate seminars, to guiding leadership teams on strategic retreats, to facilitating strategic plans and shaping marketing/branding narrative, to offering powerful online coaching programs for personal, career, and business breakthrough.

He has been described as a "ninja" for his ability to read the room, see around corners, and guide people and teams to breakthrough without telling them what they should think, believe or know. Instead, he patiently and deftly pulls out truth from the participants in a way that leads to self-discovery, personal ownership, and transformational breakthrough.

In his work with teams and organizations, he has been privileged to come alongside to help some of the best and brightest. From the talented and charismatic Dave Ramsey with his Executive Board as well as his Financial Peace University and EntreLeadership teams, to the gifted and passionate leadership team at K-LOVE/Air1 Radio, all the way to small/nimble organizations like TellAsia, who with a 3-team staff are bringing practical hope and transformation to millions of impoverished, precious women and children in North-Eastern India.

With individuals and couples, leaders and dreamers, Jeff has helped anyone from multi-million-dollar entrepreneurs and business owners to redefine success and reorient their lives around what truly matters to them, to guiding song-writing, gold-record-producing creatives transition into the 2nd tier of their career, to a local fireman who suffered a career-ending injury and needed to re-invent himself in the marketplace in order to provide for his wife and four young children.

Jeff's behind the scenes work in developing inspirational content and in designing strategic pathways that create transformation and breakthrough has impacted, quite literally, hundreds of thousands of lives. And now with this book, all of that wisdom, experience, leadership and guidance is available to you.

Jeff and his wife, Janette, and their two children, David and Sevilla, are originally natives of Colorado. Together, they recently heard and responded to an invitational whisper in their hearts and said, "yes" to transplant their family in Newport Beach, California.

To find out how Jeff can help you experience breakthrough and transformation in your life, career, and business, you can find him at www.jeffrasor.com, or follow him on social media.

facebook.com/jeffrasor.bluesky

instagram.com/jeffrasor